Audible States

Audible States

SOCIALIST POLITICS AND POPULAR
MUSIC IN ALBANIA

NICHOLAS TOCHKA

OXFORD
UNIVERSITY PRESS

OXFORD
UNIVERSITY PRESS

Oxford University Press is a department of the University of Oxford. It furthers
the University's objective of excellence in research, scholarship, and education
by publishing worldwide. Oxford is a registered trade mark of Oxford University
Press in the UK and certain other countries.

Published in the United States of America by Oxford University Press
198 Madison Avenue, New York, NY 10016, United States of America.

Library of Congress Cataloging-in-Publication Data
Names: Tochka, Nicholas, author.
Title: Audible states : socialist politics and popular music in Albania / Nicholas Tochka.
Description: New York : Oxford University Press, [2016] | Includes bibliographical references and index.
Identifiers: LCCN 2016014875 | ISBN 9780190467814 (hardcover : alk. paper) |
ISBN 9780190467821 (pbk. : alk. paper) | ISBN 9780190467845 (oxford scholarly online)
Subjects: LCSH: Popular music—Political aspects—Albania. | Music and state. |
Popular music—Albania—History and criticism.
Classification: LCC ML3917.A6 T63 2016 | DDC 781.64094965—dc23
LC record available at https://lccn.loc.gov/2016014875

This volume is published with the generous support of the AMS 75 PAYS Endowment of the American
Musicological Society, funded in part by the National Endowment for the Humanities and the
Andrew W. Mellon Foundation.

9 8 7 6 5 4 3 2 1

Paperback printed by Webcom, Inc., Canada
Hardback printed by Bridgeport National Bindery, Inc., United States of America

For B.

Contents

Illustrations

Tables

Acknowledgments

I first heard light music during a trip to Tirana, Albania, supported by a Fulbright IIE grant in 2004–2005. A second visit in 2007, funded by an International Research and Exchanges Board Short-Term Research Grant, enabled me to begin exploring several themes that later moved to the foreground of the project presented here. I conducted the majority of this book's research in 2009–2010 with the support of an American Council of Learned Societies Dissertation Fellowship in East European Studies. I gratefully acknowledge these sources for their financial and logistical support.

In Tirana, I benefited from the assistance of a number of people and institutions. The staff at the Albanian National Archives granted me access to materials concerning the Radio-Television and its day-to-day operations. The librarians at the Academy of the Arts and the National Library also helpfully located sources. At the Radio-Television, Enkelejda Pazari graciously allowed me access to the audio archive. The Radio-Television's two archivists, Suzana Gazheli and Meliha Leka, took time from their regular duties to find materials, cue them up, and then help me make sense of what I was hearing. I am especially grateful for their good humor and advice. The late Selim Ishmaku kindly welcomed me into the Radio-Television editorial offices, inviting me to observe events and introducing me to his colleagues. And without the many musicians and listeners who took time out of their busy schedules to talk about light music with me, this project would not have gotten off the ground. A full list of their names can be found in the Appendix.

Since we met in early 2005, Klodjan Rama has been my sounding board in the field and a constant source of help during research trips to Albania. I especially thank him and the Rama family for their hospitality and kindness over the past decade.

At Tufts University, Northern Arizona University, and the University of Maryland, my academic homes since 2013, I am grateful to Joe Auner, Julie and Steve Brown, Bob Gibson, Olga Haldey, Barbara Haggh-Huglo, Richard King, Jim Leve, David Locke, Rob Provine, Bruce Reiprich, Rebecca Rinsema, Fernando Rios, Tim Smith, Todd Sullivan, Pat Warfield, and Larry Witzleben. Thanks especially to Bob and Pat for generously finding funds to pay for the book's indexing. I am also thankful to my Northern Arizona students, who suffered me to work out some of my ideas and writing strategies during our classes and seminars. At Oxford University Press, I am grateful to Suzanne Ryan for all her help throughout the entire process from prospectus to publication. The two anonymous reviewers who commented on the book greatly improved its organization and tone. In its earliest incarnation as a dissertation at Stony Brook University, this project received careful readings by my committee, including Sarah Fuller, Frederick Moehn, Jane C. Sugarman, and Katherine Verdery. I especially thank Katherine Verdery for her suggestions for revision, notes that helped me rethink my material for a wider audience. And I am particularly grateful to my graduate adviser, Jane C. Sugarman, who has given freely of her time and expertise while not only training me in the discipline, but also opening her home to me and my family since 2005. Her example has deeply imprinted my research and teaching.

I am grateful to Helen Tochka for preparing this book's figures; she also let me and my family live rent-free in her attic while I wrote my dissertation. At various points between 2008 and 2015, the state governments of New York, Massachusetts, and Arizona allowed me to write and teach by munificently subsidizing our health care and groceries. Sadie Behr, Dave Blake, Sarah Feltham, Aaron Hayes, Huck Katz, Miki Kaneda, Aurelian Smith, Jr., Mack Taylor, and Matthew Toth have been intellectual companions, in one way or another, during different phases of this project. Gerard Coletta, a New York–based poet, kept my writing on track at an especially critical point. David S. Blake and Ben Dumbauld helpfully commented on early chapter drafts.

And Keri-Ann Tochka, as usual, read the entire thing. Her contributions—wrangling children, commenting on drafts, providing tech support, finding misplaced sources, overseeing multiple cross-country moves, and much, much more—are too many to list. Thank you. My youngest child's due date in October 2015 firmed up the deadline for finishing this manuscript, while my middle child brought a lot of laughs to the process of writing and revising. My oldest child arrived way back when I was applying for fieldwork grants to fund this project in 2008. Now an author in his own write, he too likes to make stories. This book is for him.

Audible States

Introduction

The two young singers, Redina Tili and Artur Dhamo, approached the stage of the Palace of Congresses in Tirana, Albania, from an elevated platform at its center. They unclasped hands, and Tili descended slowly down brightly lit stairs adorned with flowers, stopping before a large prop reading *KENGA 90*—Song, 1990. Fans at home watched the performance on television sets bearing the *Iliria* mark of the People's Socialist Republic of Albania. They saw the Radio-Television Symphony Orchestra seated stage right, instruments by their sides, as the small *kompleksi ritmik,* or rhythm group, composed of synthesizer, saxophone, electric guitar, bass, and drum kit, began playing stage left. They followed Tili as the camera panned right and faded into a tight shot of the saxophonist. And then Tili, eyes cast down, began the measured, almost mournful verse.

This performance straddled two major periods of modern Albanian history. Over the next eighteen months, some four decades of state-socialist government gave way under reforms that formally decentralized political power and opened the closed borders of Tirana's planned economy to outside competition. In December 1990, viewers anticipated neither the nature nor the extent of these coming changes. Yet much of the wistful performance, beamed down by Radio-Television Albania to even the most inaccessible mountain hamlets in the small communist country, must have seemed relatively innovative. From Tili's stylish clothing, sparkling jewelry, and glossy lipstick, to Dhamo's sideburns and shaggy hair, from the relatively lavish stagecraft to the performers' choreography, KENGA 90 represented a shift in state media presentations. Even the event's name had been changed for this, its twenty-ninth edition. The annual *Festivali i Këngës,* the Festival of Song—colloquially called the December Festival and, as my consultants often said, a "veritable institution" as Albania's most eminent popular music concert—had provided the fulcrum around which composers, singers, lyricists, and media elites convened in competition for the distinction meted out by critical reviews, audience applause, and juried prizes since 1962.[1]

Fans tuned in to hear their favorite stars present the latest *këngë të muzikës së lehtë*, light music songs, composed by Albania's leading artists. And Party officials closely followed these concerts as the bellwether of a media policy charged with creating and disseminating the politically correct, subjectivity-forming sounds of the state.

So what to make of Dhamo and Tili's performance of this song, titled "Lule e Vetmuar," "A Solitary Flower?" Composed by Spartak Tili, the singer's uncle and a professional composer employed by Radio-Television Albania's music editorial office, on a lyric by the young poet Elvana Hysaj, the work seemingly resisted easy interpretation.

"A flower—a flower once bloomed. There once bloomed a flower," whispered Redina Tili, hesitatingly, *sotto voce*, repeating, even tripping over the words against the spare backdrop of the rhythm group. Exposed to no sun, no rain—the solitary flower blooms no more. Is this a song about unrequited love? The work seems to refuse any pretense to narrative, as under the oblique text and Tili's purposefully lifeless interpretation plods a mindless electric bass line. And just as the duet seemed to reach its climax, its volume dropped, the instruments faded out, and Tili with Dhamo reascended the stairs to exit. The song garnered Tili and Hysaj accolades from their peers, but no prize from the festival jury.

The singers almost did not reach the stage for KENGA 90. "A Solitary Flower" had been subjected to an exacting selection procedure dictated by the administrators of late socialist Albania's music economy. Centrally located institutions in Tirana like the Radio-Television and the State Conservatory provided the engines that drove this economy. Strong policy closely policed its boundaries, criminalizing the consumption of foreign media and popular culture as expressions of *shfaqje të huaja*, or foreign manifestations. Tirana's planned economies of symbolic production depended on expunging from its producers' works politically incorrect subjects, and on ensuring that the aesthetic resources state-subsidized artists worked and reworked in their musical pieces, novels, poetry, and films conformed to domestic models deemed appropriate for the moral and aesthetic cultivation of ordinary Albanians' tastes.

But conformity and control cannot by themselves explain the positive logic of state-directed projects to develop and reshape listeners' tastes, nor can an understanding of the negative exercise of state power over artists fully explain what my consultants called *krijimtaria*, their creative work. Control certainly figured in, especially at conspicuous presentations. "The more people that were watching and paying attention to an event," one former Radio-Television employee told me, "the higher the level of attention would be paid by people *nga lart*, from above," meaning Party officials. Yet "A Solitary Flower" employed a pop arrangement that would not have been out of place in an Italian disco. The performers paced the stage in Western-style clothing and jewelry, murmuring their words, comportment that just a few years earlier had been forbidden to stock-still singers interpreting in the declamatory *bel canto* style typical of light music performances over the previous two decades. The camera focuses in on the saxophone, an instrument that, at various points since 1962, had been excluded from broadcasts and, as a symbol of the decadent West, even for a time concealed behind curtains. The text's primary image, a solitary flower, invites speculation. It prompts questions, unlike the more clear-cut meanings of most political symbols—the national eagle, the red dawn of a new day, the blooming spring of the Albanian workers' paradise—that comprised the subject matter of so many socialist-era songs.

For these reasons the song was, initially, rejected.

"The Festivals were becoming freer, right?" the composer, Spartak Tili, explained to me in a café in Tirana in early 2010. "Well even so, the Radio-Television's general director calls me into his office, and he says, 'What is this? This solitary flower?' He was concerned—you understand?"

"Right."

"But he was an advanced person, someone with whom you could speak freely, right?"

"Got it."

"So I said, 'You know, Comrade Marash, the flower is a symbol, a metaphor. But it can be changed if need be.' Right? But like I said, he was an advanced person and, as it were, he turned a blind eye to the song. And it went through to the concert, no problem."

"Comrade Marash"—Marash Hajati, a high-ranking Party official in the Politburo and a 1950s journalism graduate from Moscow, had been appointed to direct the Radio-Television in the early 1980s. By 1990, he had succeeded in advancing tentative reforms intended to liberalize the content of its airwaves. Among state media employees, he held a reputation as a thoughtful man, someone with whom who you could discuss potentially problematic issues that might contravene media policies, official or implicit—like the peculiar image of "the solitary flower" and its strange music.

"This was like a play on words, it was something we intellectuals used to talk about," Tili explained to me. "The flower was Albania. Intellectuals would talk about how it seemed as if Albania had, out of all the eastern bloc countries, been allowed to become some sort of radical experiment in socialism. Cut off from everyone and everything. Right? So this is the solitary flower. A flower that has bloomed—but then rots."

This book examines the relationship between music and the state through a diachronic case study of Tili's "solitary flower," Albania, between the 1920s and the 2010s. Subsidies for the arts, public radio-television stations, protectionist broadcast policies, national performing ensembles, and massive investments in media infrastructure and technologies—over the past century, music-making has become progressively entangled with functions and practices of contemporary statecraft. But why has music become a concern for modern political orders? How do different orders manage their domestic music economies, and toward what ends? And what has the intensification of governmental concerns about sound meant for musicians and listeners?

In addressing these questions, I explore the conditions of possibility in which works like "A Solitary Flower" have been created under state-socialist and post-socialist regimes of government in Albania. As such, I approach the political-economy of music-making across three levels of analysis: at the level of national policy, where governmental projects to shape and reshape life through official statements about culture emerge; the intersubjective level of the broader cultural field, where negotiations among artists and bureaucrats occur; and the level of the individual, where musicians engage in personal, seemingly nonpolitical creative processes of self-making through the aesthetic labor of creativity. Examined at each level, minor texts like popular songs provide entry points toward understanding how power operates in the modern world. What cultural policies do state officials adopt to govern sound, and for what reasons? How do individuals—like Hajati or Tili—maneuver in implementing these policies, and from what dynamic processes of negotiation and interpretation does cultural governance emerge in practice? And finally, what kinds of artistic and political subjectivities emerge at the intersection between the policies, practices, and positions-taking that give rise to the economies in which people produce and consume music?

In examining the constitution of the Tirana-based economy and its transformation over time, my narrative traces the emergence of light music as an object of governmental management in post–World War II Albania. Throughout Eastern Europe, listeners enthusiastically tuned in to state-sponsored, mass-mediated popular music, variously called light, *estrada*, dance, or entertainment music.[2] Under state socialism, the musicians who composed and performed light music songs participated in government projects to organize a modern, cultured body politic. Today, popular musicians participate in postsocialist projects to shape capitalist, European subjects. The time span under consideration stretches back nearly a century, with an emphasis on the music economy's relationship to Tirana-based elites' ever-evolving projects to govern Albanian society under both state-socialism, from 1945 to 1991, and capitalism, since 1992.

By examining the political economy of popular music-making in postwar Albania, this book engages two broad conversations in the humanities and social sciences. On the one hand, I analyze in ethnographic and archival detail the political and economic structures in which musicians and listeners make and enjoy popular music.[3] I begin from the premise that the interactions between individuals and the social orders in which they find themselves must be characterized as comprising a two-way street, a dialectic in which the practices of music-makers cannot be reduced to the shaping effects of the state—and vice versa. On the other hand, I situate Albania's symbolic economy within the broader field of political power under both socialism and postsocialism. In the contemporary world in general and in Eastern Europe in particular, symbols articulate to processes of political legitimation in complex, unpredictable ways through the forging of popular consent.[4] The production of musical works thus cannot be disarticulated from the broader problem of social belonging in modern political-economic orders. And so here, I proceed from the assumption that there exists no space "outside" such orders, and that the diverse practices of creating and consuming popular music necessarily are enmeshed with larger problems of social and political organization.

Different forms of organization govern politically and aesthetically meaningful orders of sound in audibly distinguishable ways. But the models we adopt to understand the practice of government, and to more broadly make sense of the world and our place within it, matter deeply. We do not lack for evocative metaphors to describe modern political-economic orders. Hobbes had his modern Leviathan, and Weber, his iron cage. Postwar socialisms have been described as gulags writ large, or as "velvet prisons." Gorbachev and others have personified the socialist state as "voracious," while Havel arraigned it posthumously as a "monstrously huge, noisy, and stinking machine."[5] Certainly, models matter to the social architects who craft and seek to implement solutions according to their perceptions of society's problems. But models also matter to analysts who, though we lack the power to mold reality in ways we might deem necessary, come to hold particular biases and blind spots, cognitive schema that prompt ready answers to questions less posed than taken for granted.

And if models matter, so too do our metaphors for apprehending and explaining the social realities we encounter through our research. Metaphors of vision have dominated the humanities and social sciences, and for good reason. The principal sense of modernity, sight—as David Levin specifies, "an ocularcentric paradigm, a vision-generated, vision-centered interpretation of knowledge, truth, and reality"—has long grounded the dominant conceptual frameworks with which we interpret our worlds.[6] James C. Scott famously foregrounded the centrality of vision to diverse projects to manage and reform societies in the title of his seminal work, *Seeing Like a State*. Twentieth-century critics like de Certeau have decried "the cancerous growth of vision, measuring everything by its ability to show or be shown," while the dystopian futures authors of fiction imagine for us are populated by vacuous, screen-addicted university students majoring in Images, and the pasts, by totalitarian monsters bearing an all-seeing eye "rimmed with fire."[7] But might this overwhelming emphasis on vision blind us to other potential perspectives? As Emily Thompson quips, "[s]cholars who assume that consideration of the visual and textual is sufficient for understanding modernity seem, well, short-sighted to say the least."[8]

This book claims that modern orders render social life not only visible, but also audible. And in making social life audible, political-economic orders render reality governable in significant, albeit unpredictable, ways. I stress metaphors of audibility and audiation in order to reexamine the cultural projects intellectuals have pursued in making and remaking Albanian society over time. At the core of my narrative is the point where national policy, musical creativity, and the working lives of musicians intersect. I explore a diversity of strategies by which orders of audibility have come to be fashioned and refashioned over time, as musicians, listeners, and the sounds they produce and consume emerge as audible domains for not only control and censorship, but also reform and improvement. In sum, the following chapters parse the audible states to which human beings and their creativity have been addressed as objects for government in its many modern guises.

The Solitary Flower

As a metaphor for Albania, a solitary flower may seem at first glance a peculiar image with which to begin a case study on the audible dimensions of government. Yet it serves a useful heuristic purpose in suggesting the tectonic shift in political culture that gave rise to those forms of organization so characteristic of the modern world. The defining transformation can be found in the emergence of groups' potentials for collectively imagining their future forms—and then coordinating the action necessary to attain them. Ernest Gellner writes that for preliterate, spontaneous "wild cultures," the problem of implementing plans on a grand scale militated against complexity.[9] But over time, these wild cultures gave way to "garden cultures." Ordered, but also infinitely malleable, garden cultures generated novel problems regarding their care and cultivation. And more significant, garden cultures required the appearance of a new actor on the stage of history: the gardener who would oversee their cultivation.[10]

Alongside the emergence of a conception of social life as potentially cultivable and the role of the gardener to coordinate its cultivation came a host of distinctly modern problems. How should we best oversee our own lives and the lives of others? By what authority should the few govern the many? How must society be organized in order to function properly? And what constitutes a "properly" functioning society? These questions have to do with what Michel Foucault called government. Government, or the ways in which individuals and groups attempt to shape their own conduct and the conduct of others, comprises a phenomenon ubiquitous in modern societies.[11] Government is everywhere, but at the same time it can be reduced neither to the naked exercise of something called the State over its subjects nor its classic mechanisms of surveillance and violence. Politicians, economists, urban planners, and social scientists raise questions about government and pose solutions. But so, too, do painters, novelists, and musicians. They are gardeners, to greater or lesser extents, all of them.

In this light reconsider Tili's song. As an intellectual trope in late 1980s Tirana, the solitary flower powerfully suggested a local understanding of Albania as cultivable. Given the correct forms of concern, Albanian society might blossom; denied these forms, it would wither, alone, on the vine. By 1990, the state was indeed alone. A protectorate of Mussolini's Italy in the 1930s and a de facto republic of Tito's Yugoslavia following World War II, Albania aligned with the Soviet Union in 1948. But following Stalin's death in 1953, Soviet-Albanian relations deteriorated until, denouncing the Soviets as revisionists, the Albanian Party traded Moscow's patronage for Beijing's in the early 1960s. Following Mao's death in 1976, Albanian leaders forged an even more self-contained path, resulting in major economic problems and political isolation by the 1980s. But Tili's musical setting of the text—that is, his audible rendering of the trope—suggests more than mere words might. Wistful, inconclusive, monotone, the setting raises potential interpretations: that better forms of social engineering could have been imagined, or that the projects of the past were not wholly negative; that moving forward, society would need to be remolded, but that the form this process might take could not be foreseen—and might not necessarily be a cause for uncritical celebration.

But this is no vision for society, but rather its sonification, a kind of social audiation. And in raising questions about the state of society and its futures through their creativity, Tili and his colleagues acted as intellectuals. The term "intellectual," rendered *intelektual* by my consultants, has been a contested keyword in studies of Eastern Europe. Following works by Katherine Verdery, I understand intellectuals as the "sometime occupants of a site that is privileged in forming and transmitting discourses, in constituting thereby the means through which society is 'thought' by its members, and in forming human subjectivities."[12] I find this phrasing useful insofar as this "structural definition" emphasizes "intellectual *activity* over the social attributes of the persons who carry it out."[13] For a study on musicians, it seems not only possible but also necessary to expand this definition's focus on discourse and language to include musical style and sound. Language, as other commentators have theorized, played a key role in legitimating Eastern European regimes.[14] But how did other symbolic domains also contribute to this process?[15] The close examination of intellectuals working in nonlinguistic domains enables us to raise alternative questions—and suggest different answers—about the operation of power in the region and beyond.

The structural definition, too, is apt in that it parallels emic understandings I encountered in Tirana during eleven months of ethnographic and archival fieldwork between 2009 and 2010. At the midpoint of my research, one lyricist crystallized this for me after an interview. Grasping my shoulder, he said, "We have been talking together as intellectuals now, you understand?" I understood him to mean that we had not simply been engaged in chitchat, what my consultants called *llafa*, but rather had entered a more self-conscious mode of reflection and analysis where we addressed not only the cultural topic at hand, but its broader relationship to social values and their real-world effects. This is the governmental language of what sociologists George Konrád and Iván Szelényi have termed intellectual knowledge, "concerned with values that a society deems pertinent for orienting and regulating the behavior of its members": "What is good? What is bad? How are we to act?"[16] If I am correct in reading my colleague's statement, acting "as intellectuals" was and continues to be in large part a social position one can take vis-à-vis both other intellectuals in Tirana and the body politic itself. Moreover, occupants of this social position have not only concerned themselves with discursive values but also, as composers, singers, and broadcasters, with aural values.

In foregrounding the metaphor of the cultivable flower and by defining intellectuals in this way, I begin from two points. First, I am concerned with the positive social effects of music and the arts in shaping the lives of musicians and listeners. By positive, I mean constitutive, as in able to either establish life anew or render it systematized and organized in novel ways. But positive effects also contrast with negative ones, meaning effects that work by taking away from or disordering meaningful social realities.[17] Second, my approach broadly follows work that, as Begoña Aretxaga has summarized, foregoes an understanding of "the state as a unity center of power" for one that foregrounds "an array of practices and discourses aimed at the ordering and control of bodies and populations."[18] I approach the modern state's forms as existing only "in a continuous construction, and this construction," in the phrasing of Hansen and Stepputat, "takes place through invocation of a bundle of widespread and globalized registers of governance and authority, or . . . 'languages of stateness.'" This entails, the authors continue, a double move on the part of the analyst demanding that one ask "how the state tries to make itself real and tangible through symbols, texts, and iconography, but also that one move beyond the state's own prose, categories, and perspective and study how the state appears in everyday and localized forms."[19] The chapters that follow represent my attempt to extend this decidedly linguistic- and image-centered perspective to the domain of the aural, as well as to sound's enmeshment with the domain of language.

In proceeding from these two points, I do not claim that music, and maybe especially popular music, cannot sometimes provide important vehicles by which musicians and listeners might find meaningful new forms of identification in ways that can powerfully challenge existing power structures, whether under state-socialist or capitalist orders. But I do remain somewhat circumspect about this power. "Music is not going to move governments," as Cuban singer-songwriter Carlos Varela puts it. "But it might move people. And people can move governments."[20] Yet we must also recognize that English-language perspectives on popular music themselves circulate within a broader knowledge economy, a specifically First World economy where knowledge "produced either outside of, or in retrospect to, socialism, in contexts dominated by anti-socialist, nonsocialist, or postsocialist political, moral, and cultural agendas and truths" travel widely and remain closely held.[21] As I researched and refined my approach to this project, I came to feel that simply noting this caveat in passing would not be enough. The study that follows, then, also represents my efforts to find a conceptual language with which to address the wider epistemological stakes I discerned at play in the study of music-making and power in state orders like Albania.

Light Music and the Arts of Government

Popular music songs broadcast at Radio-Television Albania's Festival of Song provide an apt entry point for examining the aural dimensions of state-socialist and capitalist projects to shape society. In practical terms, Albania itself presents an instructive site for understanding how cultural policy worked at a level of archival and ethnographic depth unmanageable in a geographically or demographically larger state. "Tirana," one of my consultants liked exaggerating, "is like a high school"—that is, everyone knows and has worked with everyone else, and so for me the capital could function as a self-contained unit for analysis.

More significant, the creative work of Albanian musicians in general and at Festivals of Song in particular has been especially subject to critical reflection and calls for reform. Since 1962, the Festival of Song has been the highest profile event for *muzikë e lehtë*—literally, "light music." The term "light" distinguished the genre from Western-style "serious music" (*muzikë e rëndë* or *muzikë klasike*) of the formal concert hall and Soviet-style "folk music" (*muzika popullore*) arranged for national ensembles and mass spectacles. This genre was analogous to state-administered popular genres of *estrada* in the Soviet Union and elsewhere in the eastern bloc, genres that with few exceptions have garnered considerably less critical attention than non-state-administered genres like Western-style rock music. More simply put, light music songs and singers have been—and continue to be—immensely popular. For millions of viewers, the Festival has affirmed the nation's golden hits and stars. And a significant portion of the cultural field has, now for several generations, participated in the event, whether as composers, arrangers, poets, performers, critics, jury members, or organizers.

As the socialist period's premiere event, the Festival of Song generated debate and impelled the creation of a broad range of policies, especially on the correct role that media, symbols, and symbol-producers should play in a Marxist-Leninist society. Albania harbored no non-state, gray music economy as has been detailed in the wider literature on popular culture elsewhere in the region.[22] Media policy forbade non-state-subsidized popular or rock genres, and this lack of competition exponentially elevated light music's importance. Since 1992, the postsocialist Festival has been the only socialist-era event to retain almost full state subsidization, casting into sharp relief the ways in which the penetration of capital into Albania transformed the formerly noncapitalist symbolic economy as well as the lives of working musicians. At the same time, the very existence of "light music" has itself been called into question. When I first began conceptualizing the project that resulted in this book, I asked a number of people for their definitions of the term. One young woman working in a CD shop listed foreign artists like Whitney Houston and Céline Dion when I asked for contemporary examples of "light music singers." "In Albania," she claimed, "light music no longer exists."

Despite my focus on light music, this book is not a genre study in any strict sense. I am not primarily concerned with analyzing "what the songs mean." And I do not name and explain exemplary works and artists or trace the stylistic evolution of Albanian popular music, unlike the primary concern of the handful of Albanian-language works on this topic.[23] Instead, I examine particular moments, compositions, and performances in order to illuminate—or maybe better, given the broader aims of the study, audiate or "sound out"—the conditions in which light music, musicians, and listeners have been addressed as legitimate domains for governmental oversight. How has music production and consumption worked under actually existing socialist and postsocialist economies? Toward what ends have officials assumed their roles in shaping Albania's domestic music economy? How did "light music" emerge as a coherent, administrable genre in the first place? And why might its very existence be doubted today? In short, how and in what ways have light music songs—and their creators, interpreters, and fans—been made subject to government under and between different political-economic orders?

GOVERNING *KULTURË DHE ARTE*

By raising these questions, I address a longer historical context across which the would-be governors of Albanians have sought to govern *kulturë*, or culture. To elites, a domain termed *kulturë dhe arte*, or culture and the arts, has presented continuing problems related to widely circulating constructions of Albania and its populations as backward. The last of "Europe's nations" to attain national self-determination, from Ottoman Turkish rule in 1912, an Albanian-speaking People, or *populli* (cf. *narod* or *Volk*) historically figured prominently as the continent's primitive Other. Into the 1930s observers called the Albanians "civilization-proof," eliding their lack of "culture" with an inability to manage their own affairs. "The Albanian has no art, no literature, no national politics, no 'Albanian cause,' no individuality as an Albanian in contradistinction to neighboring races," an Englishman wrote in 1912, while elsewhere in Western Europe diplomats haggled over installing a continental prince as the new state's regent.[24] Following three decades of political instability, Albanian citizens then experienced relative stability under state-socialist (1945–1991) and postsocialist (beginning in 1992) orders. Novel among the eastern bloc's popular democracies, Albania's small band of communists founded their "dictatorship of the proletariat" without direct Soviet aid or a working class. Having consolidated political power by 1948, Party of Labor First Secretary Enver Hoxha tasked his administration with modernizing a people even his Soviet benefactor Josef Stalin had termed "rather backward and primitive."[25] Since 1992, Albanian officials have viewed their country to be engaged in a transition back into the European family, a transition characterized by periods of violence and widespread corruption, as well as the re-emergence, heavily documented in the Western popular and academic press, of "barbaric" or non-modern customs.[26]

To elites governing the Albanians in these varying states, representations of Albania and its population as culturally backward, non-European, or uncivilized have encouraged experimentation with political projects that might be termed modern. With the term *modern*, I emphasize a hallmark of modernity common to state-socialist and postsocialist orders: the adoption of teleological doctrines that, grounded by global forms of knowledge about the malleability of social bodies, have aimed to transform society's material conditions in order to produce new kinds of citizens. Just as utopian socialism sought to forge a new person by transforming individuals' consciousness, postsocialism's "return to Europe" depends on molding free capitalist subjects. Intimately bound to modernity's quintessential form of organization, the nation-state, the cultural projects through which elites have sought to instill in their subjects a modern personhood have figured prominently in postwar strategies for overseeing society.

State projects have shared in common a concern for *kulturë*, which to my consultants in Tirana and their forebears evoked a range of meanings across different contexts. One may "speak in a cultured way," or a lunch for guests may even be "set with culture." Some individuals may be characterized by an inherent quality of cultured-ness—*njeriu i kulturuar*, the cultured person—though in this usage, the term is also a rough synonym for "educated" or "learned," *i/e shkolluar* or *i/e edukuar*. One can "have" culture—or not. You can describe someone as *një njëri me kulturë*, literally "a person with culture," or denigrate him by saying *ai s'ka kulturë*, "he hasn't culture." Not simply reducible to an immanent quality, culture has to do with your bearing, training, tastes, and education, as well as your manner of relating to oneself and others. In these senses, behaving or simply existing *me kulturë* compares to the Russian notion of *kulturnost'*. As a noun, *kultura* also refers to artistic products, especially of high culture, such as novels, operas, sculptures, plays, and so on, which are also habitually rendered *arte*, the arts.

To disentangle the relations between culture, culturedness, and government as defined in the preceding paragraphs, I employ terms culled from what Nikolas Rose has usefully called the "analytical toolbox" of governmentality studies.[27] In its elemental forms, governmentality involves simply "some sort of attempt to deliberate on and to direct *human* conduct."[28] But government is more than the sum of any one group's worldview and their efforts to impose this worldview on others, whether through something we might call the State or other institutional edifices and apparatuses. Government depends not on "the expansion of the State machinery of control," but rather on "a diversity of forces and groups that in different ways had long tried to shape and administer the lives of individuals in pursuit of various goals."[29] As a "support for technologies"—or even "an effect of governmental strategies"—the State in its monolithic, all-powerful guise vanishes as an object for analysis.[30] Irreducible to the spheres of politics and economics, government in the above senses consequently raises questions of value, meaning, and aesthetics. And by aiming to shape socially and cultural meaningful lives for human beings, government necessarily operates through domains that include the media, music, and the arts.

I find this approach apt in that its breadth potentially includes institutions, social groups, and individuals, as well as objects, practices, and discourses. Not a grand unified theory about authority, this perspective comprises more a collection of strategies for approaching questions that link *potentially* discrete domains of social life that, in reality, overlap and intermesh with one another in often unpredictable ways. The language of governmentality eschews a vocabulary of control or domination for one of regulation, organization, administration, or reform, but also cultivation and improvement. The objects of governmental processes, as Mitchell Dean writes, may be quite diverse: "economies, populations, industries, souls, domestic architecture, bathrooms, exhaust emissions, etc.— but only in so far as the government of these things involves the attempt to shape rationally human conduct."[31] In this book, I focus primarily on three objects: the management of the domestic music economy; the habitus of professionalized musicians or, in local parlance, their internal sense of *individualiteti*, individuality; and "light music" itself as a coherent genre. I also examine policies targeting four different kinds of social bodies proposed by political and cultural authorities to comprise the State's population—*Populli*, the People; *Masat*, the Masses; *Kombi*, the Nation; and *Rinia*, the Youth.[32]

For expediency's sake, social reality is often divided into discrete categories, so that we talk about "the political sphere," "economics," or "culture and the arts." A governmentality perspective cuts across these artificial divides. It demands that the analyst first demonstrate how these domains came into being in the first place, before then reintegrating them through an analytics of the arts of government. For the reader's part, this perspective requires particular assumptions about how social reality works. But while several of Foucault's keywords have become commonplace in music studies, the terminology of governmentality in general still merits explanation.[33] In introducing these keywords now, I also present the following chapters' primary lines of inquiry and organization.

ORGANIZATION OF THE BOOK

The following chapters use the flexible conceptual language of programs, problematizations, knowledges, and practice. Programs comprise relatively coherent discourses that mold reality into the forms in which we can both apprehend and act on it. "Our world does not follow a program," Colin Gordon writes, "but we live in a world of programs, that is to say in a world traversed by the effects of discourses whose object (in both senses of the word) is the rendering rationalizable, transparent, and programmable of the real."[34] In Albania, and across Eastern Europe more generally, elites have shaped social life through three successive agendas: modernist-nationalist, state-socialist, and postsocialist/neoliberal programs. The chronologically ordered chapters to follow focus on the influence of the modernist-nationalist program on the development of Albanian socialism in Chapter 1, before examining the adoption, implementation, and subsequent dismissal of the state-socialist program in Chapters 2–4, and then finally concluding by considering postsocialist elites' mixed endorsements of a postsocialist program in Chapter 5.

For novel programs to emerge, the taken-for-granted ways of conducting our lives that so deeply structure reality must come to be understood as problems. Problematizations occur when an aspect of reality is in some way called into question, when an aspect of social life is identified as necessitating reform, improvement, obliteration, and so on. These occurrences—when Lenin asked in 1902 "what is to be done" about the revolutionary struggle, or an Albanian editorialist asked in 1924 "what is Albania doing about music today" (and implying, "not enough")—are rare. But they give rise to debate, and potential solutions, about social order, identity, and culture that involve intellectuals, artists, and musicians no less than politicians or economists. In Eastern Europe, culture has been understood by intellectuals to pose recurring problems. This has to do with the status of "culture and the arts" as a governmental domain vis-à-vis postwar politics. Here my thinking follows Katherine Verdery's theorization of state-socialist modes of control. Postwar states in the eastern bloc, Verdery has proposed, managed their populations through coercive, remunerative, and normative strategies.[35] Coercive strategies, which depended on an extensive domestic security apparatus, acted directly on individuals, but proved too costly and potentially alienating over time. Elites more often pursued remunerative strategies, especially market reforms enabling certain social groups to access material incentives, as well as normative or "symbolic-ideological" strategies, which comprised "value-laden exhortations, or attempts to saturate consciousness with certain symbols and ideological premises to which subsequent exhortations can be addressed."[36] Different states crafted distinct mixtures of these strategies.[37] And despite the swift dissolution of the institutional edifices of local socialisms, these symbols and values they produced—the "symbolic means that form subjectivities," as Verdery has elsewhere phrased it—have not disappeared under postsocialism, but remain embedded in forms of cultural knowledge and practice.[38]

In their implementation, programs and problematizations thus depend on and give rise to particular, organized ways of both apprehending how the world works and then acting on it. This book examines the appearance and subsequent mutation of different kinds of knowledge about society and creativity in order to parse how intellectuals and political elites have apprehended each as domains necessitating action. In doing this I highlight the flexibility of knowledge in general, and knowledge about music in particular. But over time, political disjunctures do not mechanically introduce new forms of knowledge. The three broad political programs sketched above each shared a dominant form of intellectual knowledge about the nature of individual and collective bodies, as well as their relationship to musical products. To presocialist, socialist, and postsocialist elites, modern social bodies have been understood to be malleable, able to be shaped or molded by culture and the arts toward particular teleological ends. Chapters 1 and 2 demonstrate how certain groups of musicians came to monopolize knowledge about creativity and its social functions within the domestic music economy; Chapters 3–5 show how these same musicians and their students then used their expertise to first disarticulate themselves from socialist-era politics, and subsequently question the postsocialist status quo.

Knowledges give rise to practice, including the execution of field-specific knowledges that might better be described as know-how. I understand practice to be organized into intermeshing, but analytically distinct regimes. Foucault famously focused on punishing and curing in his early works. In the chapters that follow, I focus on regimes of practice related to making, evaluating, and administering music. These regimes of practice link institutions and people, such as the Radio-Television, State Conservatory, composers, and singers, into seemingly concrete domains for action, such as "the music economy," but they also remain fluid, cutting across and between even seemingly distant social fields. Chapters 1 and 2 examine the practical constitution of a music field centered on Tirana and based on a hierarchy of creative practices having to do with identifying, administering, and elevating local musical resources between the 1950s and 1970s. This strictly hierarchical field came to stiffen, to permit little movement for composers and singers by the 1980s, a process described in Chapter 3, before the transition to market practices fragmented and deterritorialized the field, a process described in Chapters 4 and 5.[39] But while particular regimes of practice contribute to the shape of particular fields, each field remains a site for contestation and negotiation in which "the right way" of doing things can evolve or be modified over time. And through these potentially "residual" or "emergent" practices, agents may chart novel political and artistic ground.[40]

Finally, the discourses of government propose what kinds of human beings we should be, while its practices and knowledges then provide the means to shape ourselves and others into particular kinds of subjects. In this way, government operates through particular kinds of individual and collective identities. Yet modern governmental orders do not "determine" our senses of self, but rather "elicit, promote, facilitate, foster, and attribute various capacities, qualities and statuses to particular agents."[41] I focus on two kinds of personhood. Individual qualities and capacities, and especially ones concerned with being *modern* or *i/e kulturuar*, modern or cultured, comprise one focus. Social collectives that intellectuals have imagined into existence, including the People, the Masses, the Nation, and the Youth, comprise the other. In eschewing the term "identity" for "personhood," I mean to signal my emphasis not on "nominalist" identity categories, for instance, being "an Albanian," but rather on the ethical and moral dimensions of being audibly capacitated as a particular kind of person, social group, or population.[42]

The play between programs, the knowledges that these plans presuppose and on which they depend, and their implementation through routinized practices, produce apparently real objects, things like "madness," or "the nation," or "the individual." But if "'governmentality' is eternally optimistic," as Rose and Miller write, "'government' is a congenitally failing operation."[43] That is, while the majority inhabits a world constituted by the plans, desires, and dreams of a minority, in being implemented, the projects of these would-be governors rarely work out as planned. "To say that society and history are products of human action is true, but only in a certain ironic sense," Sherry Ortner writes. "They are rarely the products the actors themselves set out to make."[44] As a nonverbal, non-discursive domain, musical practice provides a key vantage point for examining the space between programs and their implementation, or what Colin Gordon has called the program and the programmed, that "ineluctable discrepancy between discourse and actuality."[45] A musical analysis of government, in short, sounds out those discrepancies between programs aimed at "the governed" and actual programmed reality, while at the same time accounting for how musicians themselves may become imbricated in projects to govern.

Within the territory between the program and the programmed may be found potentials for agency. Here, perhaps, stands a governmentality approach's most productive, and radical, assumption.[46] All objects exist in relation to practices— "the relation determines the object, and only what is determined exists."[47] And so we begin to approach the utopian ends of government, whether in its modernist, state-socialist, or postsocialist guises: as a *telos* that imagines, and seeks to shape and reshape, social domains, at the level of the individual as well as the collective body politic. The states to which this *telos* has been directed can be discerned not simply as reflected in language or image, but also constituted in and through sound. These audible states form a narrative thread for the chapters to follow.

History, Ethnography, and Truth in Albania

Programs and problematizations, practices, knowledges, and personhoods: these areas of inquiry overlap and intersect as I parse the sonic politics of government by examining the composition and performance of light music under actually existing socialist and postsocialist orders in Tirana.[48] My path toward adopting this approach began with problems I encountered with my initial research questions.

I arrived in Tirana in August 2009 wanting to understand how musicians' work allowed them, as I then put it, "to position themselves vis-à-vis one another and the State." But I increasingly found it difficult to make the sharp distinction between my consultants, their work, and the State on which my project seemed to depend. Moreover, I often failed to reconcile my archival work on media policy with what I heard screeching out from the degraded magnetic tape played by sixty-year-old, Czechoslovakia-made equipment in the basement archives of the Radio-Television building. And most troubling, at least for my project, interviewees overwhelmingly disclosed a lack of concern about having positioned themselves *against* the State.

The terms presented in the preceding section helped me to express questions about the intersections between policy, musical practice, and personhood. But I also found these terms useful in avoiding the problems inherent in research models dependent on binary categories like official versus unofficial music, or models of artistic subjectivity dependent on complicity versus resistance to political-economic orders. My consultants simply did not recognize these models or categories. And when interviewees did frame their interpretations in terms of resistance or complicity, I soon began to understand this stance as a dominant form of *postsocialist* political speech. In short, I came to understand the commonsense act of really hearing my consultants' voices on their own terms as the core ethical issue animating this study. In the pages that follow, I have endeavored to reproduce as much of the local categories of talk and analysis about musical sound as possible, to offer my interlocutors' interpretations and discussions of sound where possible through dialogue, while nevertheless interpreting this material through the conceptual framework of government.

But in this sense, the methodological, ethical, and theoretical goals of this study may present a potential contradiction. While I came to understand government as the best scheme through which to make sense of musicians' experiences and voices in a way they would recognize as accurate or truthful, its terms are not recognized categories in Tirana. My consultants never used words like *qeveri* or *qeverisja*, government or governance, to describe their work and worlds, though they did invoke *shteti*, the state, across a range of different contexts. Nevertheless, an analytics of government and its associated terminology do have the benefit of enabling me to elude a greater evil, what I have come to understand as the key epistemological difficulty facing North American researchers in examining music-making in Eastern Europe in particular and under nonliberal orders in general. The problem is a particular positionality, forged through the politics of the Cold War and sharpened by the institutional contexts in which research about Second World "others" has been possible over the last half century.

That ethnographers and historians must self-reflexively examine their positions in relation to the groups with whom they work has become a disciplinary given in the social sciences and humanities. My position as male certainly colored my research, giving me access to the kinds of information able to be accrued through the kinds of male bonding that take place in Tirana over strong coffee and cheap cigarettes. I also have "Albanian blood." Before World War II, my paternal grandparents emigrated to the United States from the southeastern city of Korça, *një vatër e kulturës*, or a hearth for culture, and became part of a vibrant Albanian-American community in Massachusetts. My consultants often assumed I came from a "cultured" family; moreover, many intellectuals with whom I worked came either from Korça and its surrounding towns or Shkodra, its sister city in the north.

But my Americanness also colored my work in ways that I was slower to realize. For its inhabitants, Americanness can function like an empty category, a default and unmarked position. But a First World Americanness constituted prime ground against which a Second Worldness came to be constructed during the bipolar era of the Cold War. I was an infant when Ronald Reagan made his "evil empire" speech, and still in grade school when the Berlin Wall fell. Yet my work has been made possible in part by vestigial Cold War programs to understand Eastern European and non-Western Others. My initial trip to Tirana, in 2004–2005, was funded by the Fulbright program, and my initial language training in Albanian, by government grants to train Americans in "critical languages." Pre-dissertation research in 2007 was funded by a grant from the International Research and Exchanges Board, an organization founded specifically to generate knowledge about the eastern bloc. All these programs derived from a broader postwar logic, a Cold War will to knowledge about non-American others at the heart of the enterprise of my home discipline, ethnomusicology, as well as area studies as practiced in the United States and the ethnographic disciplines more generally.

Yet I remained largely oblivious to my position as an American, even as I sometimes strategized in using my background to wrangle meetings with my largely pro-American consultants. This obliviousness remained even as I worked in my apartment off Bulevardi Xhorxh Bush, George Bush Boulevard, renamed amid much fanfare following the American president's visit in 2007. But one potential interviewee drove home the stakes of my project over a coffee toward the end of my time in Tirana. I had met this person, a former Party member and elite member of the Politburo during the 1970s and 1980s, through an acquaintance at Radio-Television Albania. We first talked in early March and agreed that, pending his approval of a list of interview questions, we would complete a formal interview two months later. So in late May we met, ordered coffee, and he began slowly reading through my prepared interview sheet, pausing every now and then to sip from his small espresso, prepared *të ëmbël*, sweet, with three sugars. Clearing his throat, he began lecturing me.[49]

"You have to understand that no matter what anyone says, no one was ever forced to write songs or create works of art. This is absolutely primary. It just never happened. Composers, they were the ones that chose their themes. The Party never looked at texts, listened to music, assigned themes to people—it simply did not happen," he began. "There was no formal commission that obligated composers to create songs for the Party or Enver. It was the composers themselves that chose these themes! So-and-so would choose himself! I think that they believed. . . ."

He trailed off, I think, because it looked like I was going to speak. But I did not have anything to say. At our initial meeting he had intimated these things to me, and I had been cautious (so I thought) not to include questions that assumed either that artists had somehow existed outside of political power, or that political power under socialism had existed as an essentially repressive force, and under capitalism, as a force of liberation. I thought I had, as an American doctoral student being trained in the humanities, by that point come to fully "eschew the model of the Leviathan in the study of power."[50] When I remained silent, he continued.

"Today, when all these singers or others say they were persecuted. . . . Look, it simply is not true. There were not wide-scale purges!"

Stopping, he began again, changing tracks.

"We have to understand something, together, though." And here he started talking about wages, and himself personally. "You are attached to an institution. You are the representative of an American institution."

"Well, I am a student—I represent myself," I said. "But yes, I am at a university."

"Okay, agreed. But you will return to America and will write, taking my answers to these questions"—tapping the interview sheet—"and putting them together into a narrative. I have been trained at a major university in the Soviet Union, I have held a number of major positions in government and the state media. This is who I am. This is where I am speaking from. Do you understand? Does your institution recognize this? Will this be acknowledged in your writings?"

I surmised these were not questions he expected me to answer, so I remained silent.

"What is my word worth? Will American readers realize what my word is worth? This is the crux of the issue. You will forgive me, because I know you are American, but what will my word be worth there? I, like everyone else, have written, worked, taught as a volunteer here during the socialist period, but now I no longer do this. My work and my time is not given away voluntarily. Do you understand me? Work must be compensated financially in the capitalist world, and America is part of that world."

We argued, going back and forth as to the value of his words, whether my funding enabled me to pay consultants the rate he felt was appropriate, how academic work in general should be compensated, and whether a Second World intellectual's words could be put into a First World researcher's narrative without necessarily undergoing major distortions of meaning. We ultimately agreed to disagree. He laughed, took my card, and stuck me with the bill. This experience forced me to evaluate my research process in important ways. Words, especially about the socialist past, are important commodities in postsocialist Albania. Singers and composers receive invitations for interviews not necessarily for their nuanced takes on the complicated politics of noncapitalist symbolic production, but for sound bites, newspaper ledes, headlines. Under capitalism, ideas and interpretations have value. And it was stupid of me to argue that the academic knowledge economy in which I am a player, however minor, functions differently. Certain perspectives or stances have currency. They generate academic distinction that translates into jobs and scholarly reputations. That music scholars can brand themselves, whether by adopting particular theoretical stances on resistance, or conflict and mediation, or simply the power of music in general, is no secret. As Marina Frolova-Walker tellingly suggested of music scholarship about Eastern Europe, terms like "totalitarianism" or "dictatorship" have in the past been "more often used as a marketing tool than as serious meaningful concepts."[51]

Researchers today rarely invoke the totalitarian paradigm. Yet a deeper epistemological issue remains. Many of the analytical categories and assumptions that music scholars employ have been constructed in contexts shaped, at least in part, by the Cold War itself. First World ideas—about the individual composer and artistic agency, the kinds of effects political-economic systems can have on musicians, or even the very potential for an anti-hegemonic politics of music in "singing" truth to power—provide common epistemological ground. These ideas bear key assumptions that we hold about musicians, their creativity, and their capacities for political action. To recast the issue in plainer terms, as Izaly Zemtsovsky has done, "real individuals worked within the system, and did what they could in various ways."[52] What do we mean by "real individuals," what kinds of musical work do we recognize in our research, and what precisely constituted "the system?" Post–Cold War music research should respond to these questions, integrating the responses we arrive at into our methodologies for researching and representing musicians.

My consultants in Tirana raised these questions with me in various ways. At the midpoint of my research, I sat smoking a cigarette and chatting with an employee at Radio-Television Albania. The electricity had gone out in her office, which was not attached to the backup generator, and she had nothing to do. She had worked at the Radio-Television since the late 1980s. Before that, she had been assigned to teach music in a small village after graduating with a degree in musicology from the state Conservatory in the mid-1970s. Educated in state music schools, and subsequently charged with educating the next generation of musicians, she had also seen and helped to implement broadcast policy under late socialism and now postsocialism. In short, she had an exceptionally detailed grasp of music policies both in theory and in practice across an impressive range of institutionalized contexts. Frustrated, and having difficulties reconciling what I was finding in the archives with my interviews, I began complaining. She listened sympathetically, before offering this advice:

Nga të thënë në të bërë, ka një det i tërë. "Between what is said and what is done," she suggested, "there lies an entire sea."

What follows cannot parse that "entire sea." But it aims to stake out some of its key features, albeit through the partial truths inherent in the ethnographic enterprise.[53]

1

Administering Music

In early October 1949, Tikhon Khrennikov arrived in Tirana.[1] Khrennikov, just recently appointed Secretary to the Union of Soviet Composers, swept through the music institutions of the People's Republic of Albania during a quick three-day tour. Albanian administrators escorted his delegation to the state radio, which broadcast the majority of its content, including a nightly Albanian-language program linkup with Moscow, from the Soviet Union. The group then visited Tirana's Artistic Lyceum "Jordan Misja," the performing arts high school where a handful of eastern bloc pedagogues were assigned. They concluded with meetings at the Palace of Culture, a centrally located cultural institution that, along with dozens of smaller Culture Houses and Red Corners, the Albanian state had constructed after the Soviet model.

At each stop, the Russians lectured local officials and artists on the state's role in planning culture and the arts. The delegation's visit culminated in a wide-ranging discussion on "impressions and proposals regarding the labor of culture and art." Held at Tirana's Committee for the Arts and Culture, the meeting opened with short reports from the Albanians, painter Foto Stamo and musician Baki Kongoli. Each reported on the country's current *niveli kulturor*, or cultural level. Comrade Tikhon then spoke. A secretary assiduously recorded his remarks, which first explained the practical aspects of the Soviet Union's planned cultural economy, and then proposed recommendations on installing "more correct forms of organization" in Albania. The discussion ranged widely. From how best to oversee bureaucratic committees, to the division of labor within the Composers Union, to creating a pay scale for performances, to the number of concerts the state should organize, Khrennikov explained in exacting detail the mundane inner workings of the Soviet Union's robust music economy.

In these notes Khrennikov emerges as a crack bureaucrat. State oversight, he admonished at one point, need not prove daunting to the administrators working in the capital. "If you have telephone lines you can know what goes on in each area," the composer advised, "and from the center you can send artistic groups to various regional centers."

The Soviet delegation found an audience eager for advice. The intellectual fore-bears of men like Stamo and Kongoli had for some twenty-five years deemed their country's apparent backwardness to be its fatal defect, the primary stumbling block on the country's path to modernity. Many educated Albanians viewed the Soviet example as a model for overcoming this defect by systematically targeting and, in intellectuals' parlance, "raising the cultural level" of the population. Following Albanian communists' seizure of power in 1944, these men and women assumed powerful government positions and, for the first time, began erecting the cultural infrastructure they and their predecessors had been envisioning as a means to administer culture and the arts since the 1920s. This chapter describes that process, tracing the presocialist roots of early Albanian administrators' desire to rationalize the music economy and examining the consequences of their efforts between 1945 and the early 1960s.

"Hitherto, philosophers have sought to understand the world," Karl Marx famously wrote, "the point, however, is to change it." For intellectuals in Tirana, Marxism provided a radical stimulus for apprehending the nature of social reality and, in apprehending this nature, subsequently acting on it—that is, it provided a potentially powerful program of government. But Marx theorized the inherent mutability of social reality in a particular way, as occurring through radical struggle and revolution by which changes to the material conditions of a society would initiate changes to culture, art, and ways of thinking. For the inheritors of Marx's perspectives, the seizure of the control of consciousness itself, or how ordinary people apprehended reality, became a key site for real-world applications. But it was Lenin's insight that proved decisive for Marxism's practical implementation as a governmental program. No matter how many revolutionary pamphlets, speeches, or opportunities for discussion revolutionaries provided to ordinary people, Lenin observed, these people failed to attain true consciousness, stalled, as he derisively wrote, in "trade union consciousness."[2] To succeed as a practical program, Marxism necessitated a small group of enlightened individuals, a vanguard. Over the first decades of its existence, the Russian vanguard set to work rationalizing economies of production across not only material, but also cultural domains. The practical solutions they arrived at emerged not suddenly, but only through intense and prolonged negotiations. Two intrinsic features arose through these negotiations. The planned cultural economy, charged with the production and dissemination of the subjectivity-forming means of society, those symbols, values, and signs by which the vanguard would transform ordinary people's consciousness, became a major concern for the state. And the legitimacy of Marxism-Leninism as a political program came to depend on the unassailable distinction between the political-cultural vanguard and the object of its enlightenment, the state's population.

This distinction came to be woven into the institutional fabric of state-administered command economies. In adopting the "organizational forms" of the Soviet Union, Albania imported this defining feature into its economies of symbolic production after 1945. Crucially, Albanian elites perceived this feature as not a foreign imposition but a commonsense solution to the problem of their backward population, easily assimilating what to them appeared to be the natural distinction between the political vanguard and the rest of society into their local projects. In short, Marxism-Leninism provided a framework for addressing what intellectuals had long viewed as their country's most urgent cultural problem at the level of the state.

In practice, identifiable logics drove eastern bloc music economies. State-socialist economies depended on their administrators' very modern conviction in the inherent ability of all domains of life—political, economic, and cultural—to be rationalized: reformed, administered, made more efficient, or simply bettered. Yet Soviet-style cultural planning could not simply be exported wholesale from Moscow to its peripheries. While Soviet organizational forms had their own internal logics, local contexts conditioned their adoption and implementation in places like Albania.

Programs rarely worked as planned.[3] Certainly this has been shown to be true for bureaucratic projects targeting a society's material and human resources for organization and reform. But for the bureaucratic planning of cultural resources, outcomes could be even more uncertain. The goal of Albanian administrators to rationalize the cultural economy depended on available personnel, the vagaries of their daily work, and the pressing practical problems facing a small, poor country devastated by war. Yet their plans also depended on a host of presocialist ideas about beauty, progress, and the social role of art. And musical practice, a non-discursive audible domain prone to multiple, potentially incommensurate meanings, raised a host of special problems. The formation of an administered state, a state that could successfully organize and direct its symbolic economies toward the raising of the level of the people, would prove difficult. But crucially, in the minds of early administrators, it seemed not impossible.

Backwardness and Liberation, 1912–1945

What makes the practice of government so far-reaching and dangerous is its essentially recombinatory and polytemporal nature.[4] That is, historical forms of governmentality rarely have the kind of unity and coherence that the adjectives we append to them—"state-socialist" or "Stalinist," "liberal" or "democratic"—seem to imply. Socialist-era Albanian historiography depicted the boundary dividing presocialist past and state-socialist present, marked by the entrance of communist guerrillas into Tirana in late 1944, as impermeable. But in their implementation, the communists' governmental plans for revolutionizing society combined romantic nationalist ideals and discourses with socialist ones. And these plans depended on a retinue of urban men and women whose investment in administering culture and the arts preceded the uneven penetration of Marxism into Albania's intellectual circles.

The earliest events organized by the state's growing cultural bureaucracy demonstrate the intense commingling of presocialist with socialist ideas. In 1945, Albania's newly appointed Minister of Culture and Propaganda, Sejfullah Malëshova, delivered a speech on "modern culture" to the League of Writers. The League was one of a number of powerful institutions formed by Albania's new government during its first months. The government had moved swiftly. *Lëvizja Nacional Çlirimtare*, or the National Liberation Front, a well-organized group of communist guerrillas founded in 1942, inaugurated their first government council in May 1944. They marched victoriously into Tirana that November, subsequently establishing the state-socialist government that would endure until early 1991.

"One of the special characteristics of today's situation," Malëshova began in early 1945, "is the imperative, absolute need to raise a new democratic State, a modern State in a country that has by economic and cultural measures remained very backward. [. . .] We want to construct a modern economy on an advanced technical basis. We need culture. We want to raise a modern Army. We need culture. In short, we want to form a modern State, and without a modern culture this [task] is impossible."[5]

Proposed in 1945, Malëshova's vision for a modern state connected questions of security, economics, politics, and culture at the level of state policy for the first time in Albania's history. But his deeply felt concern about the country's backwardness stemmed from formative experiences as a young man in the 1920s. In 1924, Malëshova served as personal secretary to a populist clergyman named Fan Noli, the prime minister of a short-lived national government who had attempted to dismantle Albania's feudal economic and political systems and, for his efforts, had earned the mocking sobriquet "the Red Bishop."[6] Noli, Malëshova, and their self-described coterie of progressives, *përparimtarë*, lasted six months in power, toppled by a coup and their own ineptitude. Two decades removed from this inglorious episode, Albania boasted no better purveyor of Marxist-Leninist doctrine than Malëshova. Exiled after the coup, the studious young man had first traveled to France before emigrating to the Soviet Union. As World War II began, he was teaching Russian-language courses on Marxism in Moscow.

The backward population, Malëshova proposed, needed a modern culture founded "not on prejudices or obscurantism, but on science and progress." Marxism-Leninism, as exemplified in his view by the Soviet example, provided the means to attain this economic and political liberation. *Çlirim*, or liberation, figured prominently in the Albanian communists' early claims to legitimacy. They named their organization the Liberation Front, and perceived their struggle, which began with the 1939 invasion of Mussolini's Italy, continued with Hitler's German troops from fall 1943, and concluded in an all-out civil war with self-described antifascist nationalist groups, to have been a War of National Liberation, *Lufta Nacionalçlirimtare*. The communists did have some help. Yugoslav agents, acting on orders from Moscow, assisted with the group's initial organization; British intelligence funneled them material and logistical aid. But Albania's communists ultimately came to power without the direct influence of Russian infantry, a circumstance they long held as indisputable evidence of their political legitimacy.[7]

But the new government also claimed legitimacy for itself in having "liberated" its population from the social and cultural bondage of a premodern past. In northern Albania, early policies targeted urban Catholic clergy and *bajraktarë*, rural clan leaders, and in southern Albania, wealthy landowners, the feudal *beys*, dispossessing them of their extensive property and, in turn, collectivizing the peasantry that had worked their manors. So-called emancipation from these religious and social structures fomented widespread brutality in the 1940s. Contemporary accountings estimate that some 5,000 people were imprisoned or executed during this period; almost 200,000 people would be interned over the next five decades. The violence of the state's coercive strategies could be spectacularly public. Homes were torched, and prominent men tortured, their bloodied bodies paraded through town squares as bystanders pelted them with trash.[8]

Communists sought moral high ground by defining their opponents as "enemies of the People." But they also insisted on their own role as liberators freeing the population at large from an even more brutal past of ignorance and darkness, of the mental bondage of feudal social structures. Yet while the communists instrumentalized liberation as a political keyword, they did not invent it. Cultivated in a very different context, this term had initially emerged in intellectualist thought through a loosely connected series of civil society movements founded during Albania's first decades of independence. At the center of these movements' concerns was culture, and especially the Western arts of painting, literature, and classical music-making. To understand the cultural program that communists began implementing in 1945, it is necessary to first understand the genesis of these concerns in the 1920s.

"What Is Albania Doing About Music?"

In early 1924, a musician named Thoma Nassi published a newspaper editorial in the southeastern Albanian city of Korça urging the establishment of a symphony orchestra.[9] As an economic migrant in Boston, Massachusetts, Nassi had trained at the New England Conservatory and, with other members of the American colony, returned to jump-start the country's cultural development in 1920.[10] Like his colleagues Noli and Malëshova, Nassi was one of a group of progressives for whom the advancement of the country toward, as they put it, "civilization," had become a pressing political concern since its declaration of independence from the Ottoman Empire in 1912. Albania's development since then, to men like Nassi, had been insufficient.

As a leading figure in growing Korça's small civil society, Nassi directed wind ensembles, taught private music lessons to local boys, and helped to found an arts organization to promote chamber music concerts. He was not the only musical progressive active in the country. In the northwestern city of Shkodra, men with parallel aims were doing similar work. By the 1930s, both cities had blossomed into centers for Western-style choirs, wind bands, and concerts.[11] A younger cohort of musicians, singers and pianists inspired or trained by Nassi's generation, were studying abroad in Western Europe, and then returning home, as Nassi put it, to aid "in the artistic blossoming of not only Korça, but all of Albania."

"The point of this article," Nassi began his editorial, "is to give an idea of how necessary musical development is to our homeland." "We will first relate the musical condition we find today. We will then relate what other peoples have done in the past about music, what they are doing about it today, and finally, what we must do."

Written in response to a previous editorial by one of the city's "foremost music-lovers," a Mr. Paparisto, Nassi's ambitious essay traced a global history of music from the Egyptians, Persians, and Greeks, to the medieval Europeans, to the present. "All of the great cities of civilized nations have grand musical organizations," he stated. "In America, if you ask a boy or girl what instrument they play, he or she would redden and be ashamed if they had to tell you they did not know. When you pass through the roads of the cities and villages of America and Europe, you hear the sounds of pianos and other instruments playing from all sides. And you see outside hundreds more girls and boys with instruments or music sheets under their arms as they hurry on their way to or from the music schools."

"Now let us look at Albania to see what we find," Nassi continued. Albanian listeners enjoy simple Turkish-style ensembles composed of instruments derived mostly from "ancient Persian instruments" played exclusively by *jevgjë*, landed Romani musicians. "Completely uneducated," these musicians "use no written music, but while playing for days at weddings and other social events have earned a considerable technique. These musicians lead a bohemian life; they can play twenty hours or more without tiring, and after they finish their work they go to the *kafana* for a bit and get drunk."

Given this situation, Nassi asked rhetorically, what should be done? Korça must found a symphony orchestra, "the organization that best manifests the highest musical ideals" and "the highest form of activity of the musical arts." Nassi concluded his editorial by outlining a budget for outfitting the group and a plan to raise these preliminary funds. But he held out little hope that the government would contribute much, suggesting that of the 565 gold francs in his startup budget, "the prime minister, ministers, and other high persons of the State" would contribute only 30. The rest, Nassi proposed, must be raised by merchants, wealthy citizens, religious groups, and municipal employees.

Progressives defined themselves against the political status quo, dominated by landowners from the south in uneasy coalition with powerful tribal leaders from the north. Western-looking urbanites promoted civil institutions and charted education campaigns, and they called for legislation to reform the electoral system and to break up massive feudal estates, to standardize the Albanian language in a Roman rather than Turkish script, and to enforce the wearing of Western-style clothing. But in addition to editorializing, progressives also reshaped urban music-making in concrete ways. They sold gramophones and records to local music-lovers, imported Western concert instruments, and trained local students. By the late 1920s, choral societies and wind bands had sprouted up throughout Albania's cities and large towns. Korça and Shkodra became musical centers, and a growing percentage of young men and women in these cities and elsewhere achieved, at the very least, practical knowledge in terms of Western vocal production, notational literacy, ensemble performance, or part-singing. But this musical know-how unevenly penetrated Albania's population. The new guard overwhelmingly came from urban Albania's small bourgeoisie. When Nassi began organizing a youth band in 1920, for instance, he specifically invited "the best and most educated elements of Korça to participate, as occurs in all cities of the civilized world."[12]

The ensembles these young people formed in the late 1920s and early 1930s provided an avenue for disseminating new ideas about civilization, progress, and the arts. In part, these groups were heir to earlier nationalists' efforts, which often included music or theater groups. Korça's Freedom Band (*Banda e Lirisë*), for instance, a wind ensemble of forty members founded in 1908 by a French conductor, had been attached to a patriotic fund-raising organization, "Knowledge" (*Dituria*).[13] But the later groups fine-tuned their patriotic messages in novel ways. In Korça, groups promoted Western-style fine arts to counterbalance "five centuries of obscurantism," to counteract the supposedly deleterious effects of "the Turkish yoke." In Shkodra, ensembles and training were much more closely linked to the strong influence of the local Roman Catholic seminary and boys' school. Local Franciscans not only trained boys in part-singing and on instruments, but composed "elevated" symphonic works. Both Shkodran and Korçarë musicians also promoted their own, urban songs, transforming these into artsong arrangements for piano and voice or chorus.[14]

In short, a loosely organized cohort of urbanites emerged who viewed "music and the arts" as, in the words of one progressive, the country's "means of civilization and happiness."[15] Musicians in Korça and Shkodra, but also the cities of Elbasan, Vlora, Durrës, and Tirana, increasingly organized concerts for a small but steadily growing constituency of self-described music-lovers as funds and space allowed. And the children of these music-lovers were increasingly going abroad to study classical music in Italy, Romania, and France.[16] A handful of local schools formed significant nodes in this emerging network, including Shkodra's Franciscan School (1913), Korça's French Lyceum (1917), and Tirana's State Gymnasium (1922) and Queen Mother Pedagogical Institute for Women (1933). These schools all employed foreign-trained musicians who had returned to Albania. Yet organization was rarely systematic. The government, a constitutional monarchy beginning in 1928, opened the Royal Institute of Music in 1933, but this institution proved short-lived. In general, government officials tended to view the small civil society's musicians, artists, and writers as potential sources of social discontent.[17]

But these cultural movements more or less ignored certain widespread practices. Most progressives had little direct experience with orally transmitted music-making in rural areas, which Albanian scholars later termed *muzika populore*, or folk music.[18] And when urbanites did turn their attention to rural music-making, they heard it as a resource for "elevating" in classical literary or musical works.[19] Beginning in the 1920s, for instance, several musicians began using rural folk music as source material for Western-style compositions. Nassi transcribed several "folk airs" in 1923–1924, which he later arranged as short violin or flute and piano pieces.[20] Beginning in the 1930s, a cohort of operatic lyric singers and pianists trained in Western conservatories began performing and recording urban song arrangements. "Our artists interpreted opera songs and Albanian songs," noted a reviewer of one such concert. "It seemed as if they were trying to create a union between East and West, as if they were constructing a grand bridge where we see with joy an Albania that is being raised, an Albania being roused, an Albania that progresses!"[21] Enthusiasm for these trends, however, was not universally shared. Performers sometimes viewed folk music as inartistic, an obligatory exercise necessary to attract a concert-going public inexperienced with Western concert music.

Progressives attained little lasting change. Six months after gaining control of the national government in a coup in June 1924, they themselves were toppled without having implemented any meaningful reforms.[22] But they had succeeded in arguing for an understanding of Western-style theater, literature, and music as a privileged means for civilizing Albania, for reshaping and advancing its population.[23] Any attempt to pursue this civilizing process at the institutional level, they had claimed, necessitated enlightened oversight. The cultural life of the nation had been allowed to lie fallow; it now needed rigorous cultivation and administration. Oversight on the scale imagined by progressives, however, required a broad bureaucratic infrastructure. Though they argued that a Tirana-based government should support the arts, was it realistic to expect that it actually would? Nassi, for one, had answered in the negative in the conclusion to his essay on the need for a symphony orchestra. "Let us not expect anything from the government. Let us begin to establish private initiatives—and what more beautiful starting point could we make than the beginning of a symphony orchestra, the spiritual nourishment for everyone, the praise of the civilized world."[24]

Nassi's scheme to found a publicly funded symphony orchestra ultimately failed. Lacking adequate government and private support, presocialist musiclovers found themselves unable to sustain their ambitious plans. But in problematizing a connection between governance, civil society, "civilization," and music, progressives like Nassi raised the problem of the state's role in subsidizing and organizing *kulturë dhe arte*, or "culture and the arts," in a powerful new way. Drawing together diverse ideas about development, sovereignty, and culture, urbanites created a compelling vision for a new Albania. In doing this, they laid crucial conceptual groundwork for their successors after 1944.

World War II's outcome gave these successors the opportunity to implement their plans. In April 1939, Mussolini's Italy invaded Albania. Zog I, elevated in 1928 to a newly created throne as "the King of the Albanians" by these same Italian patrons, fled, living in exile in a number of places—England, Egypt, France, even considering a move to Long Island, New York—before he died in 1965. When Albanians split into wartime political factions, two complementary propositions had already become broadly accepted. First, the Albanian state desperately needed to be modernized, and its success in doing this could be quantified in terms of how well it assimilated Western civilization: its customs, manners of dress and comportment, and especially its fine arts. And second, the state not only could play a role in administering cultural progress, but it must.

The Problem of the Backward Population

The political imperative to reconcile the traditional with the modern, and to do so in a world in which the former has been indelibly constructed as linked to backwardness and the latter, to progress, represents the key problem of modernity. In the eastern bloc, the primary expression of this problem had to do with concerns about the backwardness of the individuals comprising post-1945 states' populations. These concerns in turn gave rise to novel projects to fix this condition. But these projects depended on presocialist antecedents.

"The education we received, from our families and in school, had been very patriotic," recalled Liri Belishova. "It transmitted the nineteenth- and early twentieth-century nationalists' dream for an independent, democratic, Albania, for a civilized and European Albania. And we thought that precisely this road would save Albania from poverty, from backwardness, and would make it truly independent and democratic."[25]

Belishova, a founding member of the communist resistance movement, graduated from the Queen Mother Pedagogical Institute in the 1930s. She rose to the rank of Politburo member before her dismissal and subsequent internment in 1961. Belishova's background was typical of members of the early communist movement. Her classmates had included Vito Kondi, Fiqirete Sanxhaktari, and Nexhmije Xhuglini, young partisans who became high-ranking socialist officials, married respectively to Hysni Kapo, Mehmet Shehu, and Enver Hoxha, the three men who governed Albania for much of the twentieth century. All were active in presocialist cultural movements. Enver Hoxha, who consolidated political power by the 1950s to become the most powerful man in Albania until his death in 1985, had taught French at Korça's Lyceum in the 1930s. Fiqirete Shehu was said to have had a lovely singing voice as a schoolgirl.[26] Other early communists were amateur musicians, painters, and athletes active in prewar civil society groups. In 1948, they purged from the Party's upper ranks its sole working-class comrade, a tinsmith named Koçi Xoxe, when Albania broke relations with Tito's Yugoslavia.

Albania's first communists viewed culture and the arts, bourgeois forms like novels, sculpture, and opera, not as an ideologically fraught sphere, but as the civilization that revolution would necessarily bring. In this, they were not unlike Lenin himself. They viewed "the proletariat"—understood broadly as encompassing not only the minority urban working class, but also the majority peasantry—as, in the phrasing of Carmen Claudin-Urondo, "unable to determine itself as the subject of the revolutionary process."[27] Albanian intellectuals consequently viewed their legitimacy to rest, at least in part, on their ability to fast-track the attainment of civilization in a backward country. Consider early cadres' fascination with minutely quantifying the state's ever-advancing *niveli kulturor*, or cultural level. Across scores of pages, reports chronicling the state's cultural capacity and its annual expansion calculated progress in close detail (see Table 1.1). The drive to measure progress, a 383.3 percent increase in choruses since the communists' assumption of power or a 885.39 percent increase in "artistic performances" in just four years, reveals a telling obsession of the early state. If legitimacy depended on progress, progress could be discerned in the state's ever-increasing capacity for administering, promoting, and subsidizing "the arts."

Efforts to calculate and quantify cultural progress point to the essential urgency of the country's early projects. Not only must society be modernized, but it must happen quickly. Marx had envisioned revolution as taking hold in advanced capitalist societies whose internal contradictions had reached their natural breaking points. But instead, the most committed revolutionaries sprouted up at the margins of the capitalist world. Modernist elites in diverse places, including Russia, Central and Southeast Asia, Latin America, Africa, and Eastern Europe, prepared the ground for revolutionary experiments by defining the crucial problem facing their societies as the backwardness of their populations, whether in social, political, economic, or cultural terms.[28] In areas imagined by reformers to be less than civilized, utopian dreams about transcending the bonds of premodernity proved key. As Igor Narskij writes of Russia, constructions of "backwardness not only reflected reality but also generated it, sweeping aside alternative ideologies and means of solving current problems."[29] When communists assumed power

Table 1.1 **Quantifying cultural progress**[a]

Activity	1945	1949	Percentage Increase
Culture Houses	0	11	1100
Libraries	3	11	367
Cinemas	30	39	130
Folkloric Groups	0	54	5400
Orchestral Groups	4	15	375
Choruses	6	23	383.3
Theatrical Groups	15	198	1320
Artistic Performances	89	788	885.39

[a] Excerpted and adapted from D12/1949 CAC. Data reproduced according to the original report.

after World War II, they did not find the revolutionary workers Marx envisioned. But they did find populations in need of civilizing, in need of modern culture.

Administering the Arts

Sejfullah Malëshova's 1945 speech, discussed above, may be understood as emblematic of an ambitious project targeting Albania's arts for administration. The drive to rationalize economies of symbolic production within what Allen Kassof in his classic formulation called "the administered society" was "impelled by a belief not only in the practical desirability, but the moral necessity, of planning, direction, and coordination from above in the name of human welfare and progress."[30]

That this drive posed a distinctly moral necessity might be discerned from the frenetic pace at which the small, disorganized Albanian state, bloodied by World War II and lacking the basic infrastructure of roads, electricity, and telephone lines, began organizing its cultural economy. At the center, Party officials founded and staffed new institutions to chart and implement cultural policy, including *Komiteti i Arteve dhe Kulturës*, or the Committee for Arts and Culture, hereafter the "CAC." Founded in early 1947, the CAC initially oversaw museums, a library system, international artistic exchanges, and cultural programs and campaigns. In 1953, it was absorbed along with the Committee of Radio Broadcasting into the Ministry of Education and Culture.[31] At the peripheries, the culture centers the CAC oversaw quickly fanned out across both large and small towns and villages. By 1949, eleven large Palaces of Culture served major urban areas. These centers in turn were supported by over one hundred smaller People's Houses of Reading or Red Corners, and several dozen larger Culture Houses in less populated areas.[32] By 1952, one-fifth of the state trade union's urban membership, or approximately 17,000 people, were engaged full-time by these institutions in "agit-prop": explaining government policies to peasants, circulating petitions in support of the Soviet Union, popularizing socialist work methods, organizing conferences and collective readings, distributing books, screening films, and staging performances.[33]

Without financial support and national institutions, the would-be governors of presocialist Albania had only imagined a more cultured, rational state on this scale. Their knowledge had been potentially programmatic. It enabled them to apprehend the problems Albania faced, and in turn to propose the form their solutions should take. The postwar appointment of men like Malëshova to directing positions instrumentalized programmatic knowledge, transforming plans about culture and the arts into practical, everyday concerns at the CAC. What should Albania now be doing about its music? Better organizing, administering, and planning—in short, rationalizing its production and consumption.

Early efforts to rationalize culture and the arts transformed the scale on which cultural life could be conducted almost overnight. The CAC tracked the "cultural condition of the village" in annual reports, accumulating data on not only the number of events that it organized, but also the number of participants.[34] The exponential proliferation of opportunities for a predominantly rural, agrarian population to come into contact with urban intellectuals linked previously ignored groups to emissaries of the state. These opportunities necessitated the identification and, in bureaucratic parlance, *aktivizim*, activation of urban culture-bearers, those musicians, artists, writers, and other individuals deemed to hold *një kulturë e përgjithëshme*, a general culture. Many had never visited a village, and some felt little sympathy for, never mind understanding of, the "backward" villagers they encountered there.

At the national level, a small pool of administrators with advanced training and pro-communist political credentials assumed directing positions. Appointed to the CAC, the Ministry of Education, print and radio media institutions, and national performing ensembles, these individuals administered the early economy's ever-expanding network of culture houses, workers' clubs, and libraries. Administrators were charged with overseeing this system from Tirana, and in their daily work they managed the relationship between the center and its peripheries, rationalizing the cultural and artistic life of the country by bringing it under governmental oversight. Yet as these able administrators quickly learned, the processes of rationalization they sought to implement in the planned music economy had an intrinsic logic all its own.

The Logic of Cultural Planning

In its day-to-day functioning, Albania's cultural administration depended on two complementary drives: centralized accumulation and planned redistribution. Whether in the form of books, folklore, transcriptions, music instruments, or even personnel, administrators worked in Tirana to centrally accumulate and subsequently redistribute cultural resources. The complementary logic of accumulation and redistribution paralleled the primary rationality found in the broader field of state power itself.[35] The socialist state maintained authority in part through its monopoly over allocative power. By monopolizing the capacity to distribute resources from a political center to dependent peripheries, state-socialist planned economies exercised a form of governance distinct from those found in capitalist economies. In its most basic form, allocative power depended on the accumulation of the means of production at a governmental center. In administering command economies of production, socialist states thus did not primarily seek to generate more resources, but to accumulate centrally held assets that would, in turn, enhance their capacity over time to generate future resources for redistribution.[36] And this redistribution might be termed "rational" in that it was planned, from a political center, by an expert bureaucracy.[37]

Whether directed toward the creation of new material or symbolic products, planned economies of production in the eastern bloc were driven by the centralized accumulation of the social means of production and rational redistribution. Each process could function negatively. Decree No. 1180 "On the Embargo of Materials" was ratified by the People's Presidium and implemented by CAC administrators in 1950 (see Table 1.2). The decree blocked the receipt or sale of certain materials, granting regional commissions power to confiscate "all published or recorded books, journals, newspapers, cards, and gramophone records, or [any other materials] that entered Albania before [its liberation] in November 1944."[38] Offices of Culture attached to regional committees first accumulated print and recorded materials from sellers and private citizens. Ad hoc commissions of multilingual specialists then checked these materials for certain categories of works, including textbooks, dictionaries, and encyclopedias; materials

Table 1.2 **Materials embargoed by Decree No. 1180**[a]

1. All books on history, the biological sciences, geography, psychology, pedagogy, moral-didactic education . . . all kinds of textbooks, except for mathematics, geometry, physics, and chemistry.
2. All foreign-language encyclopedias, all historical dictionaries, any dictionary of any kind.
3. All popular police fiction books; Galli, adventure stories, tales for children and young people.
4. All books on various philosophical systems, the social sciences, and political science.
5. All religious books, in every language, and especially books on doctrine and dogma of various faiths, indices of the Vatican, and so on.
6. Books by young Italian authors.
7. All books that discuss various systems (magic, hobbies, deductive, and so on).
8. Books by known reactionaries who have served fascism.
9. All books on fascism and Nazism, including *Mein Kampf*.
10. Journals and newspapers published in our country before November 29, 1944, and in any language other than Albanian.

[a] Excerpted and adapted from D1/1950 CAC.

for young people; and diverse tracts outlining "philosophical systems," whether religious, ethical, or political. Materials found to comprise these categories were then removed from general circulation and, in some cases, destroyed.

Decree No. 1180 demonstrates in microcosm the negative logic of the planned cultural economy. Centralized accumulation, or in administrative parlance, *mbledhje* or sometimes *grumbullim*, initially brought a diverse group of presocialist materials under state oversight. What did the listed materials share in common? Dictionaries, encyclopedias, textbooks, and political pamphlets all provided literate men and women a potential means for cultural production, sources for generating new artistic, philosophical, or humanistic works. By accumulating these categories of intellectual source material, *burim* in administrative parlance, the state monopolized the creation of future intellectual products. By then removing pre-, anti-, or simply nonsocialist means of intellectual production from circulation, governmental policy in theory consequently forbade the creation and distribution of works bearing non-state-approved ideas.

Planned cultural economies in the eastern bloc depended on the erasure of nonsocialist sources. But the logic of centrally planned accumulation did not primarily function negatively, to block, censor, or silence. Planning more often worked positively, to accumulate and craft a politically correct intellectual means of cultural production at the bureaucratic center. Early issues of *Nëntori*, the primary cultural organ of the League of Writers and Artists from 1954, succinctly demonstrate this positive logic. Initially, the journal's contents were dominated by translations of statements on culture and art by Lenin, Marx, and Stalin. These translations provided politically pure source material for Albanian intellectuals to subsequently create and distribute new ideas, an ideologically correct means of production for critics in the capital to exercise judgment on cultural issues.

Music bureaucrats managed this positive binary logic of accumulation and redistribution in their day-to-day work at Tirana's institutions. In 1947, the CAC administrator and musician Baki Kongoli described his ideal district culture worker.[39] This worker would collect the rural folk tunes and songs of his area "in detail and as a whole, without exceptions." After his transcriptions were submitted to administrators in Tirana, the CAC would appoint "a competent Commission . . . to separate ['pure' folk expressions] from those that have foreign influences, and to then distribute them to competent people to be arranged." The ideal fieldworker at the periphery simply accumulated material, what another bureaucrat called "*bruto* folklore," without evaluating it, a practice reserved for experts at the rational center. Work plans ratified annually by the CAC came to assume this two-step process of accumulation at the periphery followed by evaluation at the center.

Following evaluation, bureaucrats then assigned the accumulated raw material to musicians for "development" or "arrangement" into notated pieces in songbooks, or to editors for compilation into source books. In this way, these accumulated cultural materials formed the basis for subsequent rational redistribution from the center to the peripheries (see Figure 1.1). Source books filled with folk tunes and songs proliferated throughout the 1950s and 1960s, and these works could soon be found on the office shelves of working composers and culture house directors. The former group used these sources for the creation of new works, dipping into such volumes to find short musical quotations, pieces for adaptation, arrangement, or simply inspiration. New compositions based on source material could be redistributed either as works to be performed by national or regional ensembles or as recordings for national broadcast. Culture house directors used such volumes to create arrangements, suites of folk songs, or staged plays for the regional music groups they directed. During the 1960s and 1970s, compilations of songs and song texts from nationally organized festivals came to serve a similar purpose. Regional groups received compilations published in Tirana, which they subsequently employed in the staging of their own performances. This practice lasted into the 1980s.

Accumulation and redistribution had far-reaching consequences in the music economy. A short song, perhaps hastily scribbled down in the course of a chance meeting with a young villager one afternoon in the late 1940s, could provide the means to generate any number of new versions to be circulated and recirculated through songbooks and performances. Were a version to be recorded, subsequent broadcasts would continue its circulation.

But this binary logic also had significant political ramifications. The accumulation of a cultural means of production, preapproved at the center, provided

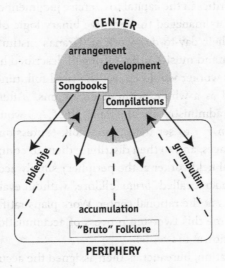

Figure 1.1 Accumulation at the center.

a powerful mechanism for ordering the country's creative life. In obligating musicians, artists, and writers to utilize the state's means of cultural production, this logic politicized non-domestic foreign sources. The borders of the music economy became remarkably rigid, keeping out non-local sonic resources while strictly circumscribing correctly "national" sounds for creative use and dissemination. In this way, the very structure of the cultural economy itself came to perpetuate the center's monopoly over the production of symbolic and ideological materials. This consequence, examined more fully in the next two chapters, enabled the producers of symbolic content to be governed at a distance, by and large unencumbered by the direct application of naked force by the state's coercive apparatus. Yet the mere existence of the binary drive toward accumulation/redistribution did not in itself guarantee the smooth operation of the planned economy. Each process had to be instrumentalized in practice.

CHALLENGES TO PLANNING

When planning worked, it often worked well. But success depended on administrators having the acumen to facilitate the economy's logic in ways congruent with logistical and political considerations. Initially, officials themselves had to balance political considerations with practical ones in appointing administrators to create and implement cultural policy. Too much concern about musicians' political backgrounds, however, often hamstrung efforts to identify qualified administrators and district workers. Without musically trained personnel, inefficiencies in accumulation and redistribution could bring the cultural economy to a grinding halt. The tumultuous politics of the 1950s also militated against efficiency. Sejfullah Malëshova, for instance, never saw the implementation of his call to create a more modern state. Purged by Enver Hoxha from Party ranks in 1946, he spent his last two decades laboring in a district warehouse. He died in 1971. Given the small size of Albania's presocialist intellectuals, their predominantly non-communist backgrounds, and the rapid growth of the post-1944 cultural economy, personnel in general almost immediately loomed as the most pressing challenge to the organization of the planned cultural economy. Consider two examples.

When fascist Italy fell in 1943, Abdullah Grimci, born into an intellectual Shkodran family, found himself studying composition in Rome.[40] Sympathetic to the Albanian communist movement's nationalist platform, Grimci interrupted his studies, returned to his hometown, and began arranging patriotic pieces for local groups. After the war, he was immediately activated within the newly created CAC. As head of its music section, Grimci did everything. He institutionalized existing ensembles and provided logistical support to regional cultural houses; he wrote performance guidelines and organized regional and national folklore festivals; and he created regional artistic commissions to iden-tify promising artists for future training. Grimci not only oversaw the collection of folklore, but he himself also transcribed urban songs, first in Shkodra and then Tirana, and edited early anthologies. When the Artistic Lyceum needed faculty, Grimci even taught clarinet and trumpet lessons. In 1953, Grimci moved to Radio Albania to organize its sound archives. The administrator prided him-self on being a jack-of-all-trades, titling his 1999 autobiography simply, "the Musician."

But a politically incorrect *qëndrim gjatë luftës*, stance during the war, dis-qualified many potential administrators from employment. Folklorist and flutist Ramadan Sokoli presents an extreme contrasting example to Grimci.[41] Born like Grimci into an intellectual Shkodran family, Sokoli too had studied in Italy. But during and immediately following the war, Sokoli, his father, and two brothers participated in the anti-communist underground; each was imprisoned.[42] A rig-orous and sympathetic researcher, musically literate and enamored of folklore, Sokoli would have made an elite administrator. But released in 1951, Sokoli found steady employment only fifteen years later. In the meantime, directors at the Philharmonic Orchestra and Tirana's Palace of Culture dismissed him from a series of low-level posts after learning of his *biografi*.[43]

Lower-level positions and employment outside Tirana usually demanded less strict political credentialing. Exceptions could be made for specialists possessing rare but necessary expertise to work at district culture houses, the Artistic Lyceum, or in performance ensembles. Instructors at the state high school in Gjirokastra, a district center in southwestern Albania, held advanced degrees from Italy, France, and presocialist Romania. "All these were knowledge-able persons . . . but they maybe had a biographical snag" keeping them from directing roles in Tirana.[44] Despite prompting continuous concerns at the CAC, pedagogues in performance retained teaching positions at the Artistic Lyceum because they could not be replaced. "There have been cases where students have accepted work for money," one report stated. "The professors do not only sup-port the old ideology, but they also demonstrate this, saying, for example, that art should represent only beauty, as this is the manner in the West, in France, Italy, and so on."[45]

Simple misunderstandings and incompetence also created inefficiencies in the music economy. Because the early administration lacked the capacity to directly oversee its plans, administrators were dependent on delegating author-ity to younger, inexperienced, or politically problematic personnel. If Kongoli directed workers to accumulate folk songs "in detail and as a whole," this rarely happened as planned. The CAC could muster only a handful of modest folk music research expeditions in the 1950s, leaving collection largely to local workers.[46] Stirred by patriotic sentiment, some musicians applied themselves enthusiastically. In the late 1940s, a young Shkodran named Tish Daija became enamored with southern polyphonic songs.[47] Named high school teacher to an area near the port city of Vlora, Daija transcribed dozens of songs from area singers. Other specialists submitted only readily accessible patriotic songs composed in a Western style, and many expressed disinterest or distaste for "*bruto* folklore," approaching rural folk music as in need of "updating."[48] Exasperated administrators scolded district workers who refused to collect material or made transcriptions riddled with errors. One, Kongoli complained, continuously "fixed" irregular meters, transforming the original folk melodies into lilting waltzes.[49]

More troublingly for administrators, cultural centers often devolved into "cafes and gaming halls," prompting sternly worded reminders about these institutions' political functions. Tirana administrators badgered district intellectuals with reminders that their purpose was to "accumulate and activate individuals of science, art, and culture for activities and scientific, cultural, and artistic production."[50] These organizational problems persisted throughout the 1950s. Yet administrators, probably correctly, perceived the widespread tendency of workers to shirk "ideo-political responsibilities" for nonpolitical, social activities not as sabotage but as ineptitude. The problem, as cultural administrators saw it, often seemed maddening. How do you organize a planned state-socialist economy without communist planners?

The Structural Limits to Planning

Despite what administrators deemed to be pervasive irregularities in the accumulation of music sources, district workers usually managed to collect a few hundred tunes and songs each year. In 1948, the CAC received 350 submissions, and prepared almost 250 arrangements of prior submissions for publication.[51] Of the 350 new transcriptions, about 150 were distributed to musicians to be harmonized for future collections. But only fifty were harmonized in Albania. Almost one hundred had to be outsourced to arrangers in the Soviet Union, Bulgaria, Czechoslovakia, and Hungary. Tirana just did not have enough competent arrangers. At its center, Albania's music economy simply lacked the capacity to fully exploit its growing means of musical production.

Defined by their concern with raising the cultural level of the People as quickly and efficiently as possible, Party officials and administrators alike found Albania's "lacks," whether in terms of district culture specialists, domestically produced works, or infrastructure, deeply troubling. Memoranda exchanged between officials and administrators demonstrate persistent worries about the cultural economy's perceived deficiencies.

One concern in particular dominated their discussions on the better organization of culture and the arts, triggering the field's first crisis. Officials understood the domestic production of "national" works, such as operas, symphonies, arranged folk songs and suites, and so on, to index the state's cultural development. This development could be visibly charted, through printed rubrics outlining the number of new works, even if their audible substance—their creativity, compositional inventiveness, and so on—could not. But administrators were predominantly focused not on the production of new works, but on the rapid systematization of preexisting resources. In the administered state's early efforts to organize culture and the arts, elites stumbled against a contradiction immanent to the system itself. Though major progress was measured by the *creation* of novel, elevated works, administrators expended most of their efforts in centrally accumulating, with much difficulty, the music economy's "raw" resources, whether in terms of transcriptions, songbooks, ensembles, personnel, instruments, sheet music, or gramophone records. Problems at the state radio during the 1950s demonstrate the apparent insolubility of this stumbling block.

INEFFICIENCIES AT THE STATE RADIO

Founded by the Italians to broadcast wartime propaganda in 1939, Radio Albania's signal reached a predominantly illiterate population in 1945.[52] Because only a small number of households owned radio receivers, the new socialist government moved quickly to erect public loudspeakers in town squares to broadcast news, political lectures, cultural programs, and music. But on assuming control of the airwaves, guerrillas found few trained specialists and a meager *fonoteka*, or sound archives. Early radio employees supplemented existing materials, initially just twenty recordings of local "folkloric" songs or dances and fifteen "stylized" folk songs performed by prewar lyric singers, with their own gramophone records of Western popular and European concert music.[53] Small ensembles, or *orkestrinë*, performed live, their performances sometimes recorded on temporary plastic records that degraded almost immediately through use.[54] A decade later, domestically produced content continued to comprise just over two hours of daily programming, and the state broadcaster relied heavily on imported recordings of eastern bloc concert music and professional folk ensembles.[55]

The lack of qualified specialists, equipment, and broadcast-ready materials caused administrators continuous headaches. Repeated instructions from the Central Committee demanded Radio Albania better its "forms of organization" by replacing unskilled personnel. But these requests often went unfilled due to a lack of trained specialists.[56] Directors even had difficulties obtaining all sorts of raw physical materials for broadcast, whether replacement parts for equipment, blank magnetic tape, or broadcast-ready recordings.[57] Inefficient communications between local institutions compounded problems. Creative solutions, however, could sometimes be found. When Abdullah Grimci, recently reassigned to head the music section, needed to buy instruments for the newly created Radio Orchestra in the early 1950s, he circumvented sluggish bureaucracy by contacting companies directly and borrowing funds from the CAC's budget to bypass the slow-moving Ministry of Trade.[58]

Domestically produced content proved a trickier proposition, though savvy administrators conjured broadcast-ready materials in ingenious ways. In 1949, Grimci arranged a Folk Olympiad modeled after Soviet festivals. He invited musicians for a series of concerts at the capital's football stadium, and organized recordings.[59] "The repertoire to be recorded includes folk music and folkloristic music from all the regions of Albania," a journalist reported. "The best groups of our country will be recorded, the orchestrinas, and lyric and folk singers, the chorus and Philharmonic Orchestra and the chorus of the People's Army. This will be done in Tirana and in some of the main districts of our country."[60] Yet even this project to produce domestic content depended heavily on Soviet aid. The recording engineers who attended the Olympiad were visiting Russians; the portable recording equipment and reels of tape came with them from Moscow.[61]

Even qualified successes were rare. Moreover, Grimci's Olympiad demonstrates the primary structural limit to cultural planning. Administrators could only identify and accumulate a finite body of preexisting, raw materials. The early state lacked the technological and human capacity, whether tape, equipment, or engineers, to professionally prepare new materials. But it also lacked the *intellectual capacity* to create new works for rational redistribution, whether due to the dearth of personnel who could harmonize raw folk materials or to the scarcity of individuals with advanced musical training necessary to compose concert music. Production in the music economy thus remained dependent on non-local subsidies. The inability to fully rationalize an independent economy became, increasingly, a pressing political problem. "The issue of original material continuously preoccupies the Radio-Committee," an official complained in 1951, "and while time after time we transmit Soviet pieces as well as those from the other People's Democracies, the lack of original pieces is felt."[62]

If administrators created some new works, their day-to-day duties conspired against more active productivity. Grimci composed small chamber compositions, as did Baki Kongoli, a fine violinist. Busy men, they were hampered by practical constraints: a lack of time due to their participation in ensembles or teaching duties, as well as impoverished technical expertise due to their eclectic or interrupted training between the 1920s and the war. Nor were cadres like Grimci or Kongoli judged on their skill in producing new works. Success for them lay in their ability to expand the music economy's capacity to generate new works by organizing its means of symbolic production. But the advanced training of personnel who could employ this means of production fell beyond the scope of the Tirana-based music economy.

THE PLANNED MUSIC ECONOMY

In the classic planned economy, a centralized state authority plans production and oversees the publicly owned means of production: historically situated *instruments of labor*, such as factories or infrastructure; *subjects of labor*, such as raw materials and natural resources; and *means of distribution*, a way to distribute products. These keywords provide a useful way to approach how state-socialist modes of cultural production worked. In general, state-socialist policies were intended to transform not only the means of production, but also the social relations to that means. The collectivization of agriculture, for instance, retooled production in practical terms by bringing it under the rational oversight of a central authority. But collectivization also transfigured social groups' relation to production. No longer wage labor or feudal serfs, workers became collective owners of the means of production, at least in theory. But while Tirana's post-1945 cultural administration fashioned a new, distinctly socialist means at the state's center, it did not target the relationship between labor and the means of cultural production. By the 1950s, this created problems immanent to the structure of the economy itself.

The centralization of a socialist means of cultural production unfolded across three sites. Initially, administrators working with Party officials and foreign advisers installed an infrastructure, or the economy's *instruments of labor*. The state repurposed available instruments, such as Radio Albania, but also founded new ones, such as the Artistic Lyceum and, later, research institutes. Radio Albania, for instance, functioned as a site for the collective production of works such as broadcasts and recordings. Until 1991, its studio was the sole facility in Albania for recording and mixing audio, in effect monopolizing the production of recorded sound. More abstractly, the Artistic Lyceum accumulated and reshaped the country's human resources. The school's pedagogical mission approached students as raw materials that, through training, literally *formimi* in bureaucratese, would be molded into ensemble conductors or culture house directors, usable forms necessary elsewhere within the cultural infrastructure. This training, however, did not directly cultivate skills necessary for creating new works.[63] These instruments also had practical limitations. Radio Albania's signal was initially too weak to penetrate much of the country's mountainous terrain; the early Lyceum was plagued by chronic shortages of instruments and teachers. And socialism's exemplary instrument, the state publishing house, could not produce polished music notation, which had to be outsourced to Bucharest during the 1950s.

Socialism's instruments depended on a ready supply of raw materials, or *subjects of labor*. Subjects included both physical materials (magnetic recording tape, instruments, scores) and abstract materials (transcriptions, "talent"). The organization of these subjects was where administrators expended most of their efforts. The CAC directed the importation of instruments, blank magnetic tape, and sheet music. It also blocked other materials, the potential subjects of non-state-administered means of production with which individuals might have generated new works, such as foreign-language encyclopedias, nonsocialist philosophical texts, foreign music scores, or Western gramophone records. Thus one of the administered state's earliest projects was to compile its own source material. Translators diligently made Albanian-language collections of Marx and Lenin, as well as Russian scholars' analyses of "the arts." Editors created songbooks, folklore collections, and literary readers.

Finally, the coordination of *subjects of labor* with *instruments of labor* depended on the smooth functioning of the music economy's *means of distribution*. The network of institutions, culture houses, libraries, and schools served as bases for accumulation. Teachers identified promising students to be sent to Tirana, while fieldworkers transcribed village repertoires to be included in administrators' edited collections. This network simultaneously served as a conduit for rational redistribution. Personnel were assigned to its institutions, arrangements of folk songs were sent to its district choirs, radio programs were broadcast through its public loudspeakers. The state's broadest campaign in the 1950s and early 1960s, *ndërtimi i socializmit* or the building of socialism, directly targeted the means of distribution by constructing roads, a rail system, and telephone lines.

In the eastern bloc, postwar cultural administrations used a host of shared techniques to oversee the reorganization of their local music economies. Between the late 1940s and early 1950s, almost all the states within the Soviet sphere founded national performing ensembles in their capitals, began organizing musical source material (cf. *izvor* in Slavic countries), and published an explosion of pedagogical and critical texts, some created locally and others translated from their Russian sources.[64] While these interrelated processes are sometimes ascribed to Sovietization, a term implying a mechanical process of colonial or imperial imposition, it may be more accurate to see them as the secondary effects of the governmental technologies of centralization and rationalization. Local contexts influenced how these processes played out initially, and how they would inflect the lives and possibilities of working musicians over time.

In Tirana, administrators' duties came to revolve around managing and optimizing the relations between the instruments and subjects of cultural labor by the late 1950s. Cultural planning relied on their abilities to deftly oversee the country's raw cultural resources and an array of existing personnel committed across diverse contexts. Administrators had to develop a second sense for balancing the political field's ideological concerns—the pro-Italian background of any one individual, for instance—with the music field's practical ones—the Lyceum's pressing need for a cello instructor. Evaluated on their success in getting things done, administrators could not also, it turned out, be realistically expected to produce new works or stylistic orientations. Calls for original works stretched administrators' responsibility to organize a potential *means* of cultural production that would enable the creation of novel works to its breaking point.

Music production in Albania's early planned economy proved a riddle not easily solved. Yet because the domestic production of original works and, in particular, complex concert music pieces like symphonies, operas, and chamber music, were deemed essential to the state's quantifications of progress, this conundrum laid bare the structural contradiction inherent in the socialist cultural economy. "Culture" that was the "property of the People" implied music, plays, or books that were accessible to non-elites. But it did not mean the transformation of non-elites' relations to the new means of cultural production. Administrators thus were charged with rationalizing a socialist means of cultural production, but they were not asked to expand the nation-state's pool of *cultural labor* by, for instance, training individuals to compose, sculpt, make films, and so on. Campaigns to educate literate readers or choristers resulted in audiences or ensembles able to appreciate or perform new works, but not the labor to produce these works. Where would this cultural labor be found?

TIKHON KHRENNIKOV'S OFFER

When Tikhon Khrennikov visited Tirana in 1949, he did not simply lecture intellectuals on installing "more correct forms of organization." He concluded by offering scholarships for courses of study abroad. A trickle of students in the arts had gone to France and Italy in the 1920s and 1930s. Now a flood entered certification programs, universities, and conservatories in the Soviet Union and its satellites after 1949. Promising performers received scholarships to conservatories in Prague, Bucharest, Sofia, and elsewhere in the region, and composers, to the Soviet Union. There, students gained expertise, but also valuable experiences. They observed the condition of artists abroad, their interactions with one another and the state. They experienced firsthand the tumultuous politics of a period that saw Stalin's death and Khrushchev's secret speech denouncing him, as well as Soviet intervention in Hungary and the construction of the Berlin Wall.[65]

By the early 1960s, the men and women who had obtained advance training abroad returned to provide the creative labor force the planned cultural economy was perceived to so desperately need. Soviet-trained students became critics and researchers, choreographers, fine artists, authors, and composers. Those who had received *drejtë studimi*, the right to study, formed a remarkably homogeneous cohort. The majority of students had been born between the late 1920s and early 1930s, by and large too young to have studied abroad before the war or to have participated actively in it. They also attended or participated in the state high schools, ensembles, or culture houses that identified promising young people for scholarships. Many came from Shkodra and Korça, the two cities with the most well developed prewar school systems. Some were chosen through national poetry or essay competitions, and their topics usually had to do with the Soviet Union, Stalin, or the Albanian-Soviet friendship. A handful used personal or family connections to Party officials, but all had "clean biographies": procommunist or, at least, nonpolitical backgrounds.

Musicians comprised an especially homogeneous group. Most were heirs to the civic music-making traditions of the 1930s, and all were deeply patriotic. Albert Paparisto, the son of the music-lover who prompted Thoma Nassi to ask what Albania was doing about music in 1924, received one of the first Russian degrees, in musicology. While many women were sent abroad for training as performers, top scholarships in composition were awarded almost exclusively to men. The Army Ensemble and Chorus, Albania's analogue to the famous Red Army Choir and directed by Gaqo Avrazi, sent a disproportionate number of these young men on scholarship to Leningrad. The Korça-born Avrazi had been active in that city's flourishing theatrical and musical life. A committed idealist, he had risked much during the war to organize performances for the communist partisans. His ensembles provided a staging ground for Albania's Soviet-trained generation. Almost to a man, the musicians who came to direct musical life from the 1960s until the 1980s passed under his baton on their pathway to the Soviet Union.

The creative labor that Soviet education provided to Albania proved to be homogeneous in one final, consequential way. Intellectually formed both by 1930s cultural societies with names like "Progress" or "Knowledge," *Përparim* and *Dituria*, and by 1950s Soviet ideo-aesthetic training, elites came to deeply understand Albanian backwardness in a new way, not in relation to the West, but in relation to the Soviet example. Their elite fraternity provided Albania a cohort of committed teleocrats: social engineers specializing in posing questions and solutions about society's future path. If administrators sought to implement the models that worked, the teleocrats had the capacity to create their own models. If administrators had a can-do attitude and the practical know-how gleaned from ideological pamphlets and their on-the-job-training, the teleocrats had read Marx in Russian translation and had studied with world-class pedagogues. Each did share the idea that the rational organization of education, art, and culture was necessary to raise the level of the backward People. But the teleocrats were able to propose novel ways to accomplish this. In doing this, the teleocrats formed a powerful, potentially divergent bloc distinct from that of the administrators, a division that came to reshape the cultural field over the course of the 1960s.

Musical Practice at the Symbolic Economy's Margins

Until the early 1960s, political officials and administrators alike continued to understand the cultural economy's so-called organizational problems to be the most acute challenge to the rationalization of culture and the arts. Yet these problems had solutions. They were perceived as gradually getting better over time. By the mid-1950s, Albania's most promising musicians were enrolled at conservatories in the Soviet Union and its satellites. By the end of the decade, the Artistic Lyceum had begun approximating its mission statement to "graduate cadres with a medium culture to fulfill the needs of the State in various sectors of art, as in the figurative arts, music, theater, and on wind instruments."[66]

But the symbolic economy itself had margins, liminal spaces in which certain cultural practices remained illegible or inaudible as domains for etatization. Music administrators understood culture and the arts in a particular way, and their quotidian practices of accumulation and redistribution reinforced this view. Work plans focused primarily on *muzikë e rëndë*, "serious music," and *muzikë popullore*, "folk music." Consider one of the CAC's first reports, a census of musicians compiled in the late 1940s (see Table 1.3). The census surveyed individual musicians' "prospects for development," collecting information on their class background, age, and "culture," meaning formal education. This survey, bureaucrats believed, allowed them to more rationally "activate" or "orient" musicians in professional folk or concert music ensembles. In effect, the census rendered a population of musicians audible for oversight in Tirana, but in doing so privileged certain kinds of musicians over others. Similarly, the Artistic Lyceum focused on training musicians only in "serious music," and students awarded scholarships to study at foreign conservatories received them on the basis of their accomplishments in the performance or composition of concert music.

But a range of musical practices coded as *intime dhe private*, or intimate and private, eluded management. Popular music-making that drew on Western dance music forms and, from the mid-1950s, Western youth culture, existed at the margins of the administered state's music economy. Certainly, foreign influences were perceived as being potentially dangerous contaminants. Soviet-style "consolidation regimes" like Albania characteristically endeavored to limit their opportunities for

Table 1.3 **An artists' census, excerpts**[a]

Name	Economic Class	Talent	Specialty	Culture	Prospects	Date of Birth
Aleko Kareco	Upper	Has	Accordionist	High school	Accordion soloist	1928
Ali Myslim Koço	Lower	Has	Violinist	Three primary grades	Limited prospects in folk music	?
Maria Kraja	Urban Middle	Has	Soprano	Conservatory	Operatic soprano	1911
Luçie Miloti	Urban Lower	Has	Singer	One grade	Unique; folk singer	1931
Rifat Shaqja	Urban	Hasn't	Tenor I	Primary classes	Hasn't	1925

[a] Excerpted and adapted from D13/n.d. CAC.

"contamination" from the outside world, understanding non-local influences to provide potential resources for cultivating dangerous ideas and fomenting disorder.[67] Popular music, however, proved inadmissible to state planning not simply for these reasons. It also slipped quietly through the gaps between institutional structures, policy, and administrative practice. But over time, the logic of accumulation and redistribution exercised a centripetal force over all cultural domains, even those seemingly most resistant to rationalization. Initially inaudible to the planners of the administered state, a number of marginal popular music practices came to be perceived as potentially administrable by the early 1960s.

FROM THE SALON TO THE STATE'S STAGES

In Albanian cities and large towns, an urban salon culture, the remnants of the civil society institutions of the 1920s and 1930s, persisted into the 1950s. Impromptu soirées often included urban Albanian-language songs composed in an elevated, Western style, as well as light classical works.

"We met at the house of Miss Ilda Melgushi, a piano teacher," recalled composer Tish Daija. "We called her 'miss,' because she was a teacher, but also because she was a bit older and was single. She played the piano well enough, was pretty, dressed well; a true bourgeois. She put the whole little house and her hospitality at our disposal."[68] In 1947, Daija invited a young colleague from Tirana, violinist Nikolla Zoraqi, to what the young men called an *mbrëmje muzikore*, a musical evening. "Nikolla displayed all his talent and skill on the violin.... When Nikolla tired, Tonin [Harapi] continued on the piano. After Tonin,

I accompanied the group on accordion as they sang some of my songs: 'Çike o Mori Çike' [O My Sweetheart], 'Me Lule të Bukura' [Among the Beautiful Flowers], 'Ndal, Bre Vashe' [Stop, My Maiden]."[69]

By the mid-1950s, groups like the one from Miss Melgushi's salon had also begun performing *la canzone italiana*, the modern Italian song that had experienced a boom with the postwar growth of that country's domestic recording and broadcast industries. At a restaurant in Shkodra, a group featuring violin, trumpet, accordion, and drum kit began regularly entertaining "the passionate amateurs of Italian song assembled, old and young, [who] listened to the beautifully executed melodies and accompanied them approvingly with applause, just like at a concert."[70] Faced with Decree No. 1180's restrictions on imported materials, the group had to be resourceful. "At that time, there was no recording apparatus," remembered one musician. "The melodies of the songs were learned by listening to the Italian radio." Accordionist Kolë Gjinaj, a passionate stamp collector, used a personal connection with a Moscow musician and fellow philatelist to secure sheet music in exchange for stamps. The sheet music ultimately traveled about 6,000 kilometers, from Italy, to Moscow, to Shkodra.[71]

With the founding of new high schools and institutes in Tirana, these eclectic salon performances migrated along with their audience to the capital. In Tirana, these evenings became student-organized parties. When Moscow-trained sociologist Hamit Beqja returned to Tirana in the mid-1950s, he found himself part of a diverse social group that cut across regional origins and professional affiliations. "At that time those things we called 'dance evenings' came into fashion," Beqja recalled. "The biggest ones were held in restaurants or public bars of this nature, or at work centers. The smaller ones we made at [any place] that had a good-sized room, for 15–20 people."[72] Student musicians gradually began incorporating more current, fashionable Western dance songs into their repertoire for these evenings, which were intended to be *dëfrim*, entertainment, for mixed-sex circles of friends. "The girls were, as a rule, students, the majority dorm students," Beqja continued. "We behaved very respectfully towards them."[73]

But *muzikë vallzimi*, dance music, could be potentially fit into certain state projects. Though not considered an element of culture and the arts, dance music was enjoyed by *Rinia*, the Youth—a social category targeted especially for state intervention beginning in 1944. Several larger culture houses, as well as Radio Tirana and Radio Shkodra, formed *orkestrinë moderne*, or modern orchestrinas, modeled after accordion, mandolin, and guitar groups that had been in vogue in towns and large villages at the end of the 1930s.[74] When young partisan guerrillas returned from fighting in 1944, local officials in Shkodra organized weekly dances with such groups for the Youth.[75] Officials at Radio Shkodra subsequently organized both folk and modern orchestrinas for live broadcast, the former presumably playing stylized arrangements of folk songs, and the latter, Western-style dance songs, patriotic songs, and partisan songs.[76] Similar groups performed semi-regularly at Radio Tirana.[77]

Modern orchestrinas sometimes played a more prominent role at events targeting the Youth.[78] At a Youth Congress held in Tirana during the summer of 1946, students formed a small group featuring violin, trumpet, trombone, saxophone, clarinet, cello, and double bass, which performed seven songs composed by ensemble members. The concert had "indescribable success," and group members "were obliged to give many more concerts to youth organizations, in work centers and . . . military depots, and at Radio Tirana."[79] As elsewhere in the eastern bloc, state agencies soon began gathering and publishing Western-style, Albanian-language popular songs. In 1957, the Central Council of Professional Unions published a series of songbooks "[w]ith the purpose to come to the aid of artistic amateur groups of clubs, culture houses, red corners, and all other cultural institutions."[80] This particular song collection was created in advance of the Sixth International Festival of Youth and Students, held the following year in Moscow. Union administrators hoped amateur music groups from work collectives would compete at regional and national song festivals to select a group to represent Albania in the Soviet Union under the direction of Bedri Dedja, a professor of education and psychology in Tirana. But these efforts remained ad hoc, falling outside the official administrative purview of the CAC.

Popular songs, however, did figure into one state-administered domain of entertainment, theater, and in particular, *estrada*, or variety show–style performances.[81] Bureaucrats applied the term *estrada*, derived from Russian practice, to fifteen small state theater companies attached to culture houses in major cities as well as in the military.[82] Estrada actors often sang, though most only had practical, on-site musical training oriented to the tastes of local audiences. Qemal Kërtusha, star of the Durrës troupe, performed light classical or popular pieces that showcased his impressive range—"several octaves, from the *do* below to two *do*s above!"—and *impostimi*, or delivery.

"I liked all the great Italian singers," Kërtusha told me. "I really liked Claudio Villa, who had such a brilliant voice. I can say I listened to him a hundred times a day. I was listening in the morning, at lunch, when I got up from the afternoon nap, during dinner, just listening, listening, listening."

Stars like Kërtusha cultivated a repertoire that included foreign showstoppers. "Granada" became Kërtusha's signature piece. His voice especially impressed the foreign-born wives of locals and visiting tourists, women from Central Europe or the Soviet Union who, he intimated, had more worldly tastes than the average *durrsakë*, or Durrës resident.[83] Yet the music performed by estrada companies remained almost completely inaudible to music administrators in Tirana as a domain for rationalization. Coded as dramaturgical rather than musical, the estrada repertoire of Western-style popular songs, partisan songs, and arranged folk songs did not concern Tirana-based administrators like Kongoli or Grimci. And institutional structures and procedures ensured that these two apparently discrete domains, theater and music, could not easily overlap within the cultural economy. When they did, the former often proved inscrutable to the administrators of the latter.

THE GROWING AUDIBILITY OF "DANCE MUSIC"

In the late 1950s, Qemal Kërtusha auditioned before a state commission composed of operatic vocalists recently returned from the Soviet Union. He was seeking a spot in the vocal program of the Artistic Lyceum in Tirana. In Durrës, Kërtusha had tirelessly sought to better himself as an artist, seeking out older singers with advanced conservatory training for guidance. He studied informally with soprano Maria Kraja, a lyric singer trained in Austria in the 1930s, and composer Pjetër Dungu, director of the local Palace of Culture. The audition required a stylized folk song, a romance, and an operatic aria, genres Kërtusha performed regularly on the estrada's stage. For the romance, he chose Dungu's "Natën Bilbili Këndon në Vetmi" (The Nightingale Sings at Night); for the folk song, "O Bilbil o More i Mjerë" (O My Poor Nightingale), a Shkodran urban song popularized by 1930s lyric singers. He concluded with his bravura rendition of a dramatic aria from Friedrich von Flotow's opera, *Martha* (1844), "Ach! so fromm, ach! so traut." Though duly awed, the singer assured me, the commission found no program for him. Kërtusha's artistic pretensions notwithstanding, estrada performers did not fit into the course of study at the state's music institutions. He returned, disappointed, to his estrada troupe.

In legal terms, the repertoire these singers performed also occupied an ambiguous status throughout the 1950s. What should these works—Albanian- and foreign-language tunes, short compositions in Western dance music meters, and even light operatic-style pieces—be called? "Entertainment music"? "Dance music"? "Modern music"? Simply "song"? Albania's first intellectual property law, drafted in 1956 in part by Grimci, did not include any of these terms. It did list the following categories: suites of cantatas; choral songs with orchestra; mass songs and marches with piano accompaniment; songs for children; choral songs; and songs in a folk style.[84] A law ratified the following year, however, set a pay scale for works recorded by "singers, actors, and interpreters" that for the first time recognized two categories called "dance music" and "light music."[85]

But whether they were called light, dance, modern, or entertainment music, these sounds at the margins of the music economy could potentially fulfill the needs of resource-strapped music administrators. In contrast to a symphony orchestra or chorale, orchestrinas demanded neither the physical space nor the technical expertise the music economy lacked. Modern orchestrinas employed only a handful of musicians performing on readily available instruments. Inexperienced musicians could even learn these songs by ear. Moreover, these groups were popular with the Youth, a segment of the population to which state broadcast policy could potentially be directed.

Practical exigencies at the state radio seem to have prompted the first push to begin bringing dance music into the music economy in a more systematic fashion. In the late 1950s, radio employees recorded several estrada stars, including the actor Rudolf Stambolla. Stambolla had been employed as an actor at state companies beginning in the early 1950s, an example of what my more professional interlocutors called, sometimes uncharitably, someone who performed *me intuitë*, intuitively. He performed in a crooning style typical of Italian and Italian-American singers of the period such as Kërtusha's favorite, Claudio Villa. Extant recordings indicate an earnest young man with a stylized timbre and an uneven vibrato; without a microphone, Stambolla's voice presumably could not have projected very far during live performances.

The songs Stambolla recorded for broadcast, along with other Tirana estrada stars such as Anida Take, the spouse of the national estrada's music director, Agim Prodani, were taken primarily from a series of three songbooks recently published by the Ministry of Education and Culture as *Muzikë Vallzimi nga Autorë të Vëndit* (Dance Music by Local Authors). Volume 3 featured sixty Albanian-language compositions written by high-level administrators, district culture house directors, and bandleaders, singers, and instrumentalists employed by state ensembles.[86] Each composition is presented as a simple lead sheet, indicating only the melody, harmonies, and meter. Without exception, each meter is a Western-style popular dance rhythm such as foxtrot, tango, rumba, or "sllov" (meaning a "slow song"), and several varieties of waltzes (*vals lento* or simply *tempo di valzer*). "Kur Gjethët Bjen në Vjeshtë" (When Autumn Leaves Fall), composed by Leonard Deda, the music director at Shkodra's Palace of Culture, demonstrates a typical example.[87] Identified as a tango, the simple minor-key piece comprises two contrasting sections: a verse of two four-bar phrases, and a refrain of three. Deda's lyric, a maudlin, first-person narration about infidelity, eschewed any attempt at realism for a weepy, rhyming sentimentality characteristic of the entire collection. "Do you remember those springs? Ah! those passionate kisses," murmured Stambolla in his late 1950s recording. "When the leaves have fallen, withered, to the ground—only then will I believe how unfaithful you can be!"

But these songbooks and recordings posed a conundrum. In practical terms, dance music recordings successfully answered one of the key problems of the early music economy, its insufficient output of domestic products. But weren't such works, notwithstanding the hopeful appellation "by local authors," somehow not socialist? Maybe even foreign? A strongly worded article published in 1960 by Dalan Shapllo, a young literary critic recently returned from training in the Soviet Union, suggested as much.[88] Yet critique did not automatically lead to silencing. On the contrary. In raising these marginal practices for discussion, critique would help to shape them into an audible domain of concern within the music field. Increasingly audible through radio broadcasts, performances, and on the pages of prominent critical organs, entertainment or dance music soon became governable as an integral part of the music economy.

Nascent institutionalization in Tirana paralleled similar processes throughout the eastern bloc. In Poland and East Germany, for instance, countries with more established traditions in composition and, as a consequence, stronger composers' unions, popular music's institutionalization was overseen by composers at these preexisting organs. In 1954, the Polish Composers' Union founded its "Creative Council for Matters Related to Dance and Entertainment Music," as did its counterpart in East Germany.[89] But at the same time, Tirana also began charting its own path. While other countries in the Soviet sphere began making efforts to carefully liberalize their symbolic economies following the death of Stalin in 1953, Albania did not. "Defying de-Stalinization," as Elidor Mëhilli describes the country's stance, Tirana began to distinguish its cultural policy from the rest of the eastern bloc by the early 1960s.[90]

Within Albania, singers and repertories that had been firmly ensconced in the Albanian music economy's margins were drawn over the next decade into its center. In 1960, a young woman named Vaçe Zela encountered the same roadblocks that had frustrated Qemal Kërtusha a couple of years earlier. As a high school student in 1950s Tirana, Zela had been a star at informal student-led parties. Her repertoire of "light music songs and, especially, foreign ones, the Spanish, French, Italian, and Latin-American ones, gave her a great popularity in artistic student circles and at the various performances that were being organized in the capital."[91] After graduation, Zela returned to her hometown, appointed general music teacher to its surrounding villages. But she soon returned to Tirana to audition for post-secondary programs. After several unsuccessful attempts, the young singer finally gained admission—not into the music course, but the acting program.[92]

But just one decade later, Zela's voice was the most recognizable and emulated in Albania. The same woman who could not pass a music audition in 1960 retired decades later, titled, an Artist of the People. And she would come to hold another, unofficial title: "the Queen of Light Music." Popular music—and its performance, composition, and broadcast—went from being peripheral to being a key stimulus in the reshaping of the music field itself, as *muzikë e lehtë*, or light music, blossomed as a domain for oversight and rationalization.

The Administered State

Beginning in 1944, Albanian intellectuals' vision for a better organized, more rational state began assuming the institutional dimensions it would retain until the early 1990s. This chapter has described that process, focusing on the rationale behind intellectuals' adoption of a state-socialist program to administer society and their early efforts to implement this program by organizing a planned music economy. The linchpin of the administered state, Tirana, provided a fulcrum for organization and centralization, the core that Comrade Khrennikov had deemed so necessary for administering culture and the arts during his remarks in 1949. In little over a decade following the Russian's visit, Tirana became the artistic "nerve center" for the entire country, a command point for planning and subsequently administering the socialist music.[93]

A tour of 1950s Tirana would begin within the monuments of this economy, the buildings ringing Skanderbeg Square in the heart of the city. An imposing marble complex, designed by Russian architects and funded by Soviet grants, housed the Theater of Opera and Ballet, the Palace of Culture, and the National Library on the square's northwest corner. Pale yellow ministry buildings, built by Italians in the late 1920s, encircled the rest of the square. The Ministry of the Interior, home to the domestic police forces *Sigurimi*, Security, and its *dosje*, files, nestled among these buildings to the east, abutting a building that would later become the National Theater. A short walk due north led to the plot that became the National Museum; further north was the train station linking Tirana to the districts. Due west along Durrës Street led to the Committee for the Arts and Culture and the Ministry of Education. A side street connected this building to a large mansion that had been reappropriated for the League of Writers and Artists and a three-story home adapted for Radio Tirana. In the late 1950s and early 1960s, this sphere began to extend south to the neighborhoods surrounding a square-mile *blloku*, the Block, which housed top Party officials. In 1956, the State University opened just to the south, followed six years later by the State Conservatory. And in 1962, Radio Albania relocated to its own purpose-built complex just two city blocks due east.

The administered state came to connect symbolic production, politics, and security in physical space, separating their institutions by mere minutes along Tirana's broad boulevards. This core in turn linked up with the rest of the country through newly constructed railroad lines, telephone connections, and roads. But this institutional web remained only as effective as the implementation of its policies, and the implementation of state policies were shaped by locally available resources, personnel, and the logic of the system itself. As a center, Tirana would come to exert a centripetal force on the lives and creativity of musicians. The center became the site from which intellectuals envisioned and audiated society in its ideal forms through their performances and broadcast media. It became a center of desire to viewers and listeners.

Molded by presocialist concerns about the backwardness of the Albanian people, the architects of the early state's cultural policies needed little prodding from Soviet advisers. The adoption of Soviet-recommended institutions, ideological lines, and forms of organization seemed less a question of politics than one of commonsense for the early administrators of Albania's postwar economies of symbolic production. The Soviet Union, after all, was the primary model of civilization for many of these men and women.

"You must remember that at that time, the Soviets had just won the war—it was of course a beautiful, exciting time," explained one intellectual who experienced the Soviet Union firsthand as a student in the 1950s. "We were studying in the heart of the Russian Empire, there were concerts, exhibitions, a whole new culture. It was a city that truly had culture."

"A whole new world for you?" I prompted.

"Exactly, a whole new world. It might be forgotten now, but the Soviets fought fascism, defeated Nazism—these are not small things."

For intellectuals like my colleague, the program to rationalize culture and the arts—and to do so along Soviet lines—represented a political and cultural imperative. The administered state manifested their quintessentially modern urge to remake society, to organize, systematize, administer, and plan a more perfect reality. But plans, and especially ones dealing with nondiscursive domains like popular music, could be implemented only through contestation and negotiation. And contestation sometimes advanced music policies in unexpected directions.

2

Debating Song

Radio Albania's music office hummed with even more activity than usual during the fall months of 1962.[1] Abdullah Grimci, editor Vath Çangu, and several colleagues were busy organizing a live broadcast they planned to call *Festivali i Këngës*, the Festival of Song. Little explicit broadcast policy existed for popular music, and the organizers sketched only modest plans, posting an open call inviting musicians to submit original compositions in July. The response, a flood of original works, overwhelmed their office. The men enlisted several colleagues, instrumentalists from the Radio Orchestra, to evaluate the entries at the club attached to the People's Theater. The ad hoc group selected twenty songs, which organizers then taught to local singers in the cramped warm-up rooms used by folk ensembles preparing for live broadcast at Radio Albania. Singers received songs in sealed envelopes, with authors' names withheld for the sake of anonymity. "But we understood," Qemal Kërtusha winked, recalling the process almost five decades later, "which composers were coming around to ask about their songs."

Initially unsure of the public's interest, Grimci invited only eighty spectators to the small conference space at the League of Writers and Artists building. Demand for tickets pushed the concerts first to the larger hall of the State Estrada, then to the Palace of Culture, and finally to Tirana's largest space, the concert hall of the newly opened Conservatory. Grimci and Çangu had two models in mind. In Shkodra, the young estrada director, Mark Kaftalli, and the music director of the Palace of Culture, Prenkë Jakova, had organized a song contest that had been well received the previous year. The Shkodra festival in turn had been modeled after the Sanremo Festival of Italian Song, established in 1953. Just like Sanremo, the Festival of Song compositions were to be performed in two variations by different singers, and a professional jury was to award prizes to the best compositions.

Grimci's event fit neatly into projects to more efficiently organize the production of socialist music culture. The Festival ultimately proved to be the apogee of administrators' work, a confirmation of the resourcefulness of men like Grimci and his colleagues. But it also proved their downfall. Just six months later, Grimci bitterly defended himself at a special plenum organized to discuss the emerging problem of popular music. Eighteen months later, he left the Radio, reassigned to a district outside Tirana. His decline paralleled the rise of a new group. By the end of the 1960s, administrators had been largely replaced at the head of the music field by *profesionistë*, a group of self-described professional composers trained abroad during the 1950s. Shaped by the planned economy's imperative to more efficiently administer popular music, the Festival—and the debates it spurred—quickly demonstrated the socialist system's immanent drive to render all domains of creative life into discursive forms governable at the political center.

By the early 1960s, Albanian-language dance music songs were proving increasingly popular with listeners, especially young ones in Tirana and other urban areas. The organization of a national music festival aimed to capitalize on this popularity. But Radio Albania's broadcast of the Festival of Song also coincided with a destabilizing eighteen months in Albanian politics. In 1961, Moscow formally broke diplomatic ties with Tirana. The ensuing tumult transformed the capital. Students returned from the Soviet Union and its satellites, swelling the ranks of the intelligentsia overnight. Radio employees, heavily dependent on Soviet broadcast materials, scrambled to find domestically produced works to fill airtime. Within this climate, Albanian-language dance music songs assumed additional significance, as well as a new name, *muzikë e lehtë*, light music.

"Before, we did not use titles like 'light music,' we said, 'singer of Albanian song,'" Qemal Kërtusha told me. "True—*mirëfillltë*—light music began in 1962, with the Festival." But with the appearance of the label came the potential for new forms of oversight. In drawing together a diverse group of non-state-administered practices, the generic label "light music" stimulated the proliferation of new critical and political discourses about popular culture in general, and song in particular. These discourses rendered informal music practices into a coherent domain audible to not only musicians, but also Party officials.

This chapter examines how musicians and officials debated light music, situating their criticisms against the Moscow-Tirana break. Fallout from the break recalibrated politics in Albania, reshaping its fields of material and symbolic production almost overnight. The break also had unforeseeable consequences. It provided an impetus for the organization of new broadcast material, seemingly reinforcing music administrators' monopoly on accumulating and redistributing a "national" corpus of materials. At the same time, the ideological break called into question the political credentials of a second group of elite musicians then returning from the Soviet Union. How could the Party trust someone who spoke Russian, had studied in the USSR, maybe even had married a Muscovite? But paradoxically, it was this latter group of Soviet-trained teleocrats who gained ascendancy over the administrators by the end of the 1960s. And this occurred mainly through highly contentious public debate over what in the music economy had formerly been an afterthought: the status of popular music.

In state-socialist music economies, policy most usually emerged not by fiat, but rather through debate, discussion, and evaluation, fashioned and refashioned through the discursive interplay among competing perspectives.[2] In this, cultural fields in eastern bloc countries were not dissimilar from those in their capitalist counterparts. As Pierre Bourdieu has theorized, such fields take shape in part through the "struggle for the monopoly of legitimate discourse about the work [of art]."[3] And musical works, whether in noncapitalist or capitalist societies, form a particularly slippery domain for monopolization. At once a fluid, non-referential form of expression, music also uses a formalized, specialized jargon that non-musicians can find impenetrable, the language of melody, harmony, large-scale form, and so on.[4] With what common language, then, can musicians and non-musicians agree that a non-discursive art form sounds "national," or "socialist," or "professional"—or not?

Socialist societies were especially prone to explosions of critical language at moments of change. In Albania's cultural field, two key events propagated widespread uncertainty for the music economy: the state's diplomatic break with the Soviet Union in the early 1960s, and the onset of a Chinese-style Cultural Revolution in the mid-1960s. As individuals in Tirana asserted and reasserted their monopoly over defining the products and goals of a music economy in flux, they simultaneously molded this planned economy into forms in which it could be governed, often in radically unpredictable ways. At moments of crisis, transactional power in the music economy became newly accessible, up for grabs by whoever could most convincingly claim it. But this occurred not necessarily through grand policy statements, but rather through the give-and-take of critical discussions about seemingly peripheral concerns having to do with "light music." And it occurred even in the face of the administered state's drives to rationalize and to encompass all creative activity. These competitive processes demonstrate how in government, "lasting inventions have often arisen in surprising and aleatory fashion and in relation to apparently marginal or obscure difficulties in social or economic existence, which for particular reasons have come to assume political salience for a brief period."[5] The history of government consequently cannot be reduced to a narrative tracing how an inexorably more rational system implements its overarching programs. For government also emerges in and through small accidents, problems that give rise to unintended trajectories in the fundamentally dynamic, aleatory state.

The Festival of Song, 1962

In late December 1962, listeners tuned the radio sets in cooperative clubs, culture houses, and private homes to the final evening of the inaugural Festival of Song. The sounds they heard crackling through speakers had just been recorded live at the Conservatory. A Radio employee legged uptown, tape reels under one arm, to make the 6 p.m. transmission from the Radio Albania building. The competition had featured twenty dance music songs over two nights, with the best ten reprised at the final third night. The jury awarded prizes to the top five compositions—three third-place awards, two second-place awards, but, with the voters deadlocked, no first-place award.

The young woman who dazzled students in 1950s Tirana, Vaçe Zela, received a special prize for her interpretations. Under the direction of Agim Prodani at the State Estrada, she was now beginning an unparalleled career. At the Festival, she performed a handful of up-tempo, lighthearted tunes. She interpreted Grimci's witty little song, "Fëmija e Parë" (The First Child), which received a second-place prize. The optimistic piece expressed a young parent's happiness at the birth of her first child. Her estrada colleague, Rudolf Stambolla, the young actor with the small register, crooned "Kam Një Mall" (How I Long), a syrupy tango composed by the director of the Artistic Ensemble of the People's Army, Gaqo Avrazi. Each work had been orchestrated for one of the Radio's smaller ensembles, and featured piano, accordion, upright bass, and guitar, with additional woodwinds, brass, and strings. They employed simple harmonies and forms, and most were composed in a specific dance rhythm, whether waltz, tango, or foxtrot.

"At that time, listeners desired and needed to have their own music," musician Llazar Morcka recalled. "Local radio stations were being established in Korça and Shkodra, just like in Tirana, that broadcast [songs] and needed light music—but above all, Radio Tirana [had this need]."[6] But even if musicians sensed the state's need for good, high-quality popular music recordings for broadcast, they had little explicit direction on what these compositions should sound like. Popular music to this point had escaped the purview of officials. The competitive field at the Festival was itself incredibly eclectic, comprising administrators like Grimci and Kongoli, as well as younger instrumentalists, bandleaders, and culture house directors. Only two Soviet-trained musicians, the baritone Avni Mula and composer Tish Daija, both Moscow-educated classical artists, participated.

The success of the Festival of Song surprised even its organizers. Grimci no doubt had an inkling as its concerts sold out, and as letters poured in to the Radio in early January his suspicions were confirmed. After its broadcast, the event took on a life of its own, its success christening the new genre, light music, and consequently elevating this domain as an audible concern for the state in ways organizers could little have anticipated.

ACCUMULATING "NATIONAL" CULTURE FOR THE MASSES

The Festival of Song exemplified the planned music economy's driving logic to centrally develop and rationally redistribute music culture. As a means to accumulate new recorded material at the bureaucratic center, the concerts succeeded admirably. The event motivated a large number of musicians to submit compositions, which an expert panel had then winnowed down to the "best" works. Its format, with two singers performing each of the twenty compositions in two variants, enabled the Radio staff to enlarge its broadcast capacity with forty unique recordings. Radio Albania broadcast these recordings and distributed copies to regional stations.

Throughout the eastern bloc, countries pursued festivalization as a key strategy for organizing musical culture. The "festivalization of culture," as researchers of late capitalist societies have pointed out, enables individuals to partake in common experiences of belonging through shared, real-time consumption.[7] Festivalization in state-socialist societies, where consumption did not play such a prominent role, functioned differently. Competitive state-sponsored festivals allowed centralized authorities to "monitor" potentially anti-state symbolic activity, as Timothy Rice writes of Bulgaria, "to exercise control at the national level."[8] "By constantly organizing such competitions and monopolizing the right to organize and publicize them," Nimrod Baranovitch similarly notes in describing song festivals in China, "the state attempts to define standards for creativity and performance, and a whole discourse of what is good or bad, or legitimate and illegitimate in popular music."[9] But in Tirana, festivalization also proved a strategy almost wholly congruent with the nature of the planned cultural economy and its drive to produce new works as efficiently and quickly as possible.[10] And ultimately it would not be "the state" that defined standards, but the musicians themselves.

Commentators initially understood the works presented at the Festival of Song to be entirely "national"—composed, interpreted, performed, and recorded by Albanians, in Albania—at a moment when the organization of a domestic music economy wholly independent of foreign materials had assumed particular salience. As Tirana severed relations with Moscow in the months prior to the Festival of Song's organization, few members of the cultural field could have expected this act's far-reaching consequences. But in practical terms, Albania had lost its primary patron. The USSR canceled aid programs and withdrew all economic support. In response, Albania expelled all eastern bloc advisers, recalled its own students and personnel, and strengthened ties with the People's Republic of China. Beijing eagerly strode in to make up 90 percent of the financial shortfall.[11] Less immediately apparent, but no less significant, was the loss of what might be called cultural subsidies: foreign-born teachers appointed to the Artistic Lyceum, students' access to eastern bloc conservatories, and the eastern bloc films, recordings, books, and other materials now considered ideologically unsuitable for domestic distribution or broadcast. In the cultural field, the break consequently precipitated a crisis in the form of a pressing need for domestic personnel, institutions, and materials. It also stiffened the borders of the domestic music economy, reframing broadcast materials from other eastern bloc countries as potential contaminants of the cultural field. Radio Albania received directives to cut or severely curtail the broadcast of such materials, and overnight its staff had to somehow make up hours of broadcast time that had previously been filled with programs created in or about the Soviet Union.

But the rupture also coincided with major structural changes to the cultural field in general that had been developing over the course of several years. In the late 1940s and early 1950s, the administered state's focus had been on the building and staffing of material infrastructure, including the ensembles, broadcast institutions, culture houses, libraries, cinemas, and administrative organs that comprised the physical web supporting the new socialist cultural economy. Soviet subsidization, whether in terms of personnel, funding, or simply advice, had made this possible. Consider one telling example. When the domestic film studio founded in 1952, "The New Albania" Kinostudio, released its first film the following year, an epic three-hour portrayal of Albania's national hero titled *Skënderbeu*, the film featured a Russian director and cinematographer. Russian actors even portrayed its leading roles, which Albanian voice actors then dubbed. And while a young Albanian composer, Çesk Zadeja, had created much of the film's soundtrack, albeit in collaboration with the Russian composer Georgy Sviridov, he too bore the imprint of the Russian system, as a conservatory student then on scholarship in the USSR.

At the same time, during the late 1950s and early 1960s the nature of planning began to change. Initially the state had depended on coercive strategies for shaping its population. Gradually the state's dominant strategy for control, a heavy dose of coercion leavened with normative appeals, shifted, not unlike elsewhere in the eastern bloc, to one based primarily on the creation and dissemination of symbols. The return of Soviet-trained musicians buttressed this evolving symbolic-ideological strategy, as did their appointment to directing positions at the newly founded State Ensemble of Folk Songs and Dances (1957), Theater of Opera and Ballet (1960), and Conservatory (1962). Yet the 1962 break also called into question the politics and allegiances of large swathes of the cultural field's membership, the very individuals who would be counted on to create the sounds and images so increasingly necessary to the state. Tirana bore the brunt of these transformations. Young artists, writers, and musicians hastily packed their bags and returned to the capital, expanding the intelligentsia's ranks and prompting administrators to reshuffle personnel at existing institutions and create new ones to accommodate the returnees. Tensions emerged. Some administrators perceived their Soviet-trained colleagues as threats. "Scandalmongers," according to the Soviet-educated sociologist Hamit Beqja, derided them as the "red professoriate," in contrast to themselves, the "whites."[12] The stakes were especially high for "reds." Framed by domestic elites as an issue of Marxist-Leninist truth, the diplomatic break reproached the Soviet Union for "revisionism" and prompted an ideological stiffening across Tirana.

Tensions were experienced unevenly across the cultural field. Factionalized into "old" and "new" guards, writers in particular sparred, and younger authors blocked from longstanding print outlets by "whites" founded new publications.[13] The rapid growth of music institutions, however, created a temporary surplus of positions and resources, forestalling similar competition in the music field. Administrators retained their posts at government Ministries and the state Radio, while Soviet-trained composers assumed newly created posts at state ensembles and the Conservatory. Yet in a system obsessed with political purity, vigilance against anti-state sentiments or plots remained the byword of the day. Soviet-trained intellectuals emerged as a social group that might plausibly be framed as politically suspect, a "useful enemy" in mobilizing unity at a moment of uncertainty.[14] But in the music field, the opposite occurred. The so-called reds, it turned out, had a practical sense for navigating the rapidly evolving music economy that ultimately enabled them to take control of the field. And they did this at first discursively, by critically redefining what national music should sound like.

CREATING NATIONAL SONG: THE TWO ROADS

Socialist systems in the eastern bloc proliferated critical discourses and counter-discourses, acting as veritable factories for the production and dissemination of words. Consequently, scholarship on the eastern bloc has often emphasized language. This is apt. "The first great socialist industry," as the dissident Herbert Zilber wrote of the Romanian state security apparatus, "was the production of files."[15] But creativity in these systems more broadly was also subject to this system-wide will to discourse, a will to potentially render all domains of reality into political language.

Immediately following the first Festival of Song in 1962, a journalist asked the music secretary to the League of Writers and Artists, Baki Kongoli, the "white" administrator formerly appointed to the CAC, for his impressions. "In the hall where the festival was held, wherever it was listened to on the Radio, there was liveliness, fiery discussions," Kongoli averred. "The cultural level of the masses is being raised. Individuals are making interesting judgments about the various songs, defending their opinions with passion."[16] Two weeks later, he published a comprehensive, two-part report that initiated six months of contentious debate.

The report appeared in the cultural field's newest organ, *Drita*, in early January 1963.[17] Kongoli again confirmed the "success" of the event and then proposed how to understand its songs as "national." Participants, Kongoli wrote, had correctly pursued two distinct strategies, or creative "roads." Certain songs employed "colors of a pronounced national style" and "utilize[d] the intonations of folk music."[18] Kongoli used the terms *folkloric* or *characteristic* to describe these songs. "Lule të Bukura Sjell Pranvera" (Spring Brings Beautiful Flowers), presented by Mark Kaftalli, the young culture house director who had helped to organize the Festival's predecessor in Shkodra the previous year, demonstrated this "road." The song had features typical of an urban Shkodran song, particularly in its harmonies. Kongoli singled out the "plagal cadence so typical of Shkodra," a simple *i-iv-ii-i* harmonic progression in the song's minor key.[19]

"Mos Më Qorto" (Don't Bother Me), presented by Vath Çangu, demonstrated a contrasting technique that, according to Kongoli, nevertheless followed this same "road." The composition quoted an instrumental dance tune collected from the northern Albanian village of Zerqani by Muharrem Xhediku, a folklorist and composer, and published in the 1952 edited volume *Këngë dhe Valle Popullore* (Folk Songs and Dances). The original snippet formed the basis for the dance tune, which Kongoli found to be a promising strategy: "The author has changed the [irregular dance] meter, reworking and developing the motive in some ways, and has made a joyous foxtrot in duple meter appropriate to the comprehensible, very attractive text."[20]

But most songs used neither demonstrably domestic compositional techniques nor folk sources. These pieces that were "not based on folk music intonations, but [which remained] contemporary and understandable," to Kongoli's ear, comprised the second successful "road."[21] Grimci's song "Femija e Parë" and Avrazi's tango "Kam Një Mall" exemplified this group, as did the fast-paced novelty song about football, "Në Stadium" (At the Stadium) by Agim Prodani. "And the pressure is strong, careful, goalkeeper! Pass it, shoot it, quickly, cross!" Despite lacking identifiably local musical signifiers, these dance music songs, Kongoli concluded, were national in the sense that Albanian authors had composed them.

The "two roads" thesis structured ensuing debate. A poet, Trim Gjata, responded first in his own two-part study confirming the "national character" of the Festival in a study focused on lyrics.[22] But the thesis also demonstrates a key principle of critical discourse for whites. Kongoli's report functioned to endorse and consecrate the material under discussion, to force the repertoire of the Festival to fit into a procrustean aesthetic scheme of his own design. But Kongoli, like the Radio employees, estrada instrumentalists, or culture house directors who submitted the majority of the compositions, failed to ask how national music *should* sound. His thesis nevertheless provided terminology for future commentators to continue the discussion—and to stake contrary positions.

In January and February, private critiques about the limits of Kongoli's analysis began mounting. Public debate then exploded in the pages of *Drita*, as a group of Soviet-trained composers, largely ignoring Gjata's discussion of lyrics, portrayed the poet's analysis as deficient and the composer's as superficial. Citing Maxim Gorky, the composer Çesk Zadeja provided the primary contours of the counter-analysis. Zadeja, by then a faculty member at the Conservatory, argued that Kongoli's perspective had entirely missed the point: "The role of light music in [composers'] oeuvre and in [listeners'] aesthetic education is not divorced from the purpose of 'serious music.' And so the 'nationality' or 'internationalness' cannot be sought differently in one genre than in the other."[23] In effect, Zadeja linked "light music" to "serious music," proposing that each should be subject to the same evaluative criteria. In undermining the credibility of analysts like Kongoli and Gjata, the composer pedantically pointed out what he saw to be their elementary mistakes.[24] And in providing evidence for his own expertise, Zadeja coined stiff, Marxist-sounding jargon, describing, for instance, one song's "psychic-national expressive force."[25]

Three months of debate about "light song" irrupted, with reds continuing to pursue an expert-ideological tone whites seemed unable to muster. *Drita* published a new rubric collecting answers to the query, "How do you understand the problem of the national character in light music?" Zadeja's former classmate in the USSR, fellow composer Simon Gjoni, replied, "The more armed the composer is with general culture, and especially with professional culture, that much more deeply will he express in art these [national] things."[26] "General culture" was a broad term that in the 1950s had meant literacy, some formal education, and knowledge of cultural touchstones. A person who could read, write, and, perhaps, appreciate classical music, fit the bill for having *kulturë e përgjithshme*. But what did professional culture mean in this context? The response from another Russian-trained composer just returned from the Soviet Union, Nikolla Zoraqi, suggested an emerging definition. "When we discuss opera, symphonies, chamber music, or song, we are overseen always from Marxist aesthetics for healthy contexts, a national base. . . . [It is a problem] that many of the young people with talent are professionally unprepared, not knowing the laws for the development of music. . . . He who desires to write light music should obligate himself to know the mastery of composition no less than he who writes operas or symphonies."[27] "Professional culture" here seems to imply a different set of criteria: facility with large-scale forms, from opera, to symphonies, but also to song; preparation in the "laws of music"; and knowledge of "the mastery of composition."

This clash portended a schism between older and younger musicians, while simultaneously serving notice of the emergence of the Conservatory as the primary engine behind the music economy. Tellingly, *Drita* published fewer responses from instrumentalists, culture house directors, and administrators, the men who had actually participated in the Festival. Those it did publish abstained from the elevated, expert ideo-aesthetic language of composers like Zoraqi, Zadeja, and Simoni, instead offering platitudes. "Our listeners thirst for art. Our People desire to sing, so let more beautiful songs be composed," answered Vath Çangu. "As [the People] want to dance, then more beautiful dance music should be created."[28] In July, debate concluded at an official plenum organized by the Ministry of Education and Culture and joined by high-ranking members of the Central Committee. Officials who followed cultural issues attended, as did comrades Nexhmije Hoxha and Fiqirete Shehu, representing their spouses, top leaders Enver Hoxha and Mehmet Shehu.

"This is an issue of prime importance," concluded the Soviet-trained musicologist Albert Paparisto, the director of the Conservatory, in his bland formal report to the assembly. "Thus we must remember the orders of the Party continuously and try untiringly to sing with the language of our People, to arrange and to develop even more this language, and to raise it that much higher to the level of a true art."[29] A high-ranking cadre charged with "cultural matters" closed with some words on the duties of the composers, and the vice-minister of Education and Culture opened a formal discussion period in which the musicians simply rehashed their disagreements from the previous months. The reds had won this battle. The composers had successfully argued against administrators for a definition of light music as not mere entertainment but art, as beholden to the same criteria as serious music, and as a domain necessitating their expert exegetical interpretation.

Reforming Song, 1963–1964

One month after the light music plenum, representatives from the Ministry of Education, League of Writers and Artists, the Central Committee for Youth Affairs, the Professional Unions, and the Theater of Opera and Ballet convened with Radio Albania officials to discuss the organization of the second Festival of Song. Attendees plotted a number of new directives, replacing the ad hoc organization of the previous year with seemingly more concrete policy, and the sole direction of Radio employees with a diverse coalition representing the cultural field's major institutions. Emissaries from the League of Writers and Artists proposed holding a formal meeting for lyricists to ensure they understood "the requirements of the time." Representatives also agreed on prize amounts, formalized guidelines for the selection of compositions and performers, and created committees to oversee each. Finally, the meeting set down an official *tematika*, or set of themes: "[Texts should] be sung not only about life, as happened in the first festival, but also . . . about the new person, our new life in our country, to the Fatherland, the creative labor of our workers."[30]

State oversight, it seems, proved almost immediately to be a double-edged sword. Targeted as a domain for administration because of its potential significance to symbolic-ideological projects, light music pushed actors at a range of institutions to weigh in on its content. But awareness did not mechanically lead to control, and non-musicians' directives failed to consider sound. Delegates declined to confirm specific compositional techniques, which remained within the purview of Festival participants. The sole definitive statement on how the songs should be musically constructed directed authors to remember that the "music must be supported in the intonations of our folk music, and [participants] must consider that it will be sung by the Masses."[31] The absence of direction as to what constituted "correct" compositional practice provided songwriters, singers, and arrangers the space to interpret this rather open statement. Yet the Festival's incorporation into the cultural field's formalized structures of critique also imposed the possibility, as certain participants soon learned, of direct state action over their lives and work.

SONGS TO "BE SUNG BY THE MASSES"

In late December 1963, Radio Albania broadcast the thirty songs a newly constituted artistic commission had selected for the Second Festival of Song. With the exception of the event's artistic director, once again Abdullah Grimci, and the Radio's general director, Petro Kito, the new commission comprised mostly those Soviet-trained musicians oriented toward the performance and composition of concert music. Yet the field of competition remained much the same as before. Administrators, bandleaders, culture house directors, and instrumentalists competed, again excepting the Soviet-trained composer Tish Daija and operatic vocalist Avni Mula. And the months of debate on the national nature of song notwithstanding, these men presented foxtrots, rumbas, and jazzy two-steps. A *kompleksi ritmik*, or rhythm group, directed by the young bandleader and now Conservatory student Agim Krajka, included an accordion, sax and brass sections, and a jazzy rhythm section of trap-set, double bass, and guitar.

The rhythm group was not Grimci's only update as he balanced opaque political considerations with the clear mandate to further popularize the state-sponsored contest. Vera Zheji, a Radio presenter, hosted along with Skifter Këlliçi, a brash young sports commentator. The two chatted on stage between songs, sharing cheesy banter in the style of foreign radio contests. "With the People in power, 'my dream' *can* come true," joked Zheji before "Ëndrra Ime" (My Dream), a jazzy waltz with swung eighth notes by Baki Kongoli that depicted the "dream" of love in "the new socialist village." The inclusion of amateur student singers also thrilled the hall's audience. Fatbardha Bengu, a ballet student in Tirana, delivered enthusiastic if untutored performances, providing a raucous counterpoint to the old-fashioned crooning of vocalists like Stambolla or Kërtusha and the belting of lyric singers like Zela. Clipping short her words in Llazar Morcka's "S'di të Vallëzoj" (I Don't Know How to Dance), Bengu's carefree, syncopated inflection complemented the song's improvisatory feel and maracas-punctuated Latin rhythm—and brought down the house.

But another amateur, Besnik Taraneshi, drove listeners into a frenzy. Taraneshi interpreted Krajka's song "Djaloshi dhe Shiu" (The Young Man and the Rain), a raucous up-tempo composition about an impatient teenager going crazy with longing as he waits for his girlfriend. Vaçe Zela performed it in its first variation, and then it was Taraneshi's turn. "Vera [Zheji] goes on stage and presents 'Djaloshi dhe Shiu,' this time sung by Besnik Taraneshi," Këlliçi later reminisced. "The hall greets him not only with shouts, but even with some wolf-whistles. That is all Besnik needs, the young joker, who begins to sing Agim's 'Djaloshi' joyously."[32] In contrast to Zela's crisp enunciation, Taraneshi's interpretation was deliberately rough. "I was competing with Vaçe, who was tops at that time," Taraneshi recalled years later. "I wanted to do something special against my competitor and as I interpreted the verse, completely intuitively, I pronounced the line '*shiu bie pikë pikë pikë*' "—"the rain goes drip-drop drip-drop," with *pikë* correctly pronounced "peek"—"as '*shiu bie pëk pëk pëk pëk*' "—pronounced "puck"—"as in the [northeastern] Dibran dialect, which is where my mother is from."[33]

The cheers lasted so long that the host, Këlliçi, came onstage to quiet the audience in order to introduce the next song, Tish Daija's "Flakë e Borë" (The Gleaming Snows). "And Besnik, intoxicated by the success, comes back on stage, forgetting that he is a singer at a festival where songs are not encored," Këlliçi explained. "It is truly a vexing situation. Luckily, one of the main Radio directors indicated I should remain on stage. So, raising and lowering my hands, slowly I calmed the unrest in a hall that is drowning in a whirlpool of clapping." On the recording I consulted at the Radio Albania archives, you can hear the audience erupt in applause throughout Taraneshi's performance and after—and imagine Nikoleta Shoshi, a precocious fifteen-year-old from Shkodra, standing nervously in the wings waiting to perform Daija's song. "I was young, a bit too euphoric, twenty-three years old," Taraneshi later recalled. "I was ready to go nuts for the applause of one girl, never mind hundreds."[34]

If the Festival songs were "to be sung by the Masses," Krajka and Taraneshi had succeeded insofar as they caught the ears of young fans. But they drew the unwanted attention of several Party officials. "The gallery rocked," as Këlliçi put it, "and its resonance crossed down into the hall below to the select guests, some even from the Central Committee."[35]

DENUNCIATION

At Radio Albania, officials' private concerns immediately drowned out urban fans' public acclamation. In early January, employees became aware of criticisms centered on its "cosmopolitan tendencies": Western-style dress, stage comportment, interpretations, and orchestrations. At their initial meeting, employees were instructed to discuss the re-orchestration and re-recording of compositions with members of the Festival jury and invited experts. They deemed two songs wholly unusable as "weak, and with foreign reminiscences."[36] Jazzy dance numbers like "Nuk e Fshehim Dashuri" (We Cannot Hide Our Love) and "Djaloshi dhe Shiu" suffered pointed criticism as "simple copies of the general rhythms of foreign songs heard on the radio." Found to be particularly troubling was "[t]he tendency of strong, rhythmic orchestral effects of brass instruments of the jazz kind"—that is, horn backgrounds and comping patterns—that "too often resulted in a deafening noise that hurts the ear." Singers' interpretations were "vulgar" or demonstrated foreign "fashions." Texts showed "a tendency for the exclamations 'oh, oh,' 'yes, yes,' 'no, no,' or 'tra, la, la,' taken especially from foreign songs."

The meeting culminated in the denunciation, *dënimi*, of the performances of amateurs Besnik Taraneshi and Fatbardha Bengu, and the censure of the Festival's orchestrators and director, Grimci. The orchestrators and Grimci responded at length with *auto-kritikë*, formal statements taking responsibility for the criticisms raised at the meeting. Taraneshi and Bengu were not invited to the meeting, but their criticisms were expanded on. "[Taraneshi] was left to his own devices and [thus] acts by imitating singers he hears on the radio. For [Fatbardha Bengu], it was emphasized the fault of [song] authors Avni Mula and Llazar Morcka, who encouraged her to interpret their songs in an ostensibly modern way, thinking this would make more of an effect. Avni, too, instructed her [personally] and secured her Western clothing and [choreographed] a stage presentation influenced by Italian movies, such as *Appuntamento a Ischia* [1960], and by television." Despite this pointed critique, Mula, the Soviet-trained vocalist, did not receive punishment. Grimci was dismissed from his post and reassigned to a kind of minor exile as culture house director in a district town. Back home in Durrës, Taraneshi fared worse. Acquaintances disappeared, and former friends ignored him when he passed them on the street. He became a nonperson.

Though circulated at closed-door meetings, criticisms no doubt leaked to Tirana's intellectual circles, especially as listeners began wondering why Radio Albania did not broadcast the Festival's biggest "hits." But in order to take effect, criticism and denunciation needed to be made public. Published analyses by Çesk Zadeja and a Soviet-trained baritone, Gjon Athanasi, translated the behind-the-scenes discussions onto the pages of *Drita*. In doing this they further refined the expert ideo-aesthetic discourses on song they and their colleagues had first posed during debate over the previous Festival. Most songs, Zadeja opined, "brought nothing new" and failed to "answer the spiritual demands of our Masses."[37] He traced the problem to "the contradiction born between melody and rhythm": the orchestrations obscured the vocal lines with too much brass and too many saxophones.

"The question then arises: what function did these instruments have?" Zadeja asked. "As we have heard often in this [kind of] repertoire, we can say: only to make noise.... As a result, an artificial dualism was created among [melody, harmony, and rhythm], which should support one another and leave always the melody in the most privileged place, as the melody concretizes the thought, the spiritual world."[38]

But Zadeja did not cite names, such as that of the orchestrator Krajka, his Conservatory student. Athanasi did, citing the "false interpretation of Besnik Taraneshi" and the positive counter-example of Vaçe Zela, who "presented herself most nobly . . . [w]ith a beautiful voice, with the timbre of the genre, with an inner force, and somewhat exact treatment."[39] These public renderings of private criticisms were soon to be translated once again, this time into policy.

DENUNCIATION-CRITICISM-EVALUATION AND POLICY

The Second Festival of Song and the fallout it generated demonstrate how critique existed on a spectrum from private to public, and from initiating less to more consequential effects. Formal published criticism followed private political denunciation, but only the latter had immediate practical effects on the objects of critique, whether by obligating an individual to make self-criticism or rendering another person politically suspect. Published criticisms followed after the fact, but this did not mean they had no influence. By translating private denunciation into public discourse, commentators like Zadeja and Athanasi also subtly transformed it. In its private form, critique had to do with "cosmopolitan tendencies" and the Festival's "vulgar" fashion for "foreign songs." In its public form, critique was remolded by an expert aesthetic language having to do with such features as a song's "rhythmic base," the ensembles' "orchestral colors," or the composer's use of "the cantilena that is so typical of our [national] melody."[40]

And critique did not need to make reference to prior statements of policy—in this case, whether or not Festival participants adhered to guidelines set forth the previous fall about thematic material, "folk intonations," or that vague idea that songs should by some measure appeal to the listening public. Athanasi even dismissed this final point in his essay. "Besnik Taraneshi, for example, *without taking account of the applause, which was not objective,* I think could sing Albanian light music—provided he did not begin from superficial effects and foreign imitations."[41] Personal relationships, too, inflected critique. Despite his almost sympathetic take on Taraneshi, Athanasi did identify him by name, something Zadeja consistently found ways to avoid when obligated to criticize works by his own composition students.

The ability to correctly "read" critiques and directives in context was fast becoming an essential skill for musicians. Many failed to develop this aptitude quickly enough. Yet the young men who wrote jazzy tunes deemed "unusable" were not necessarily flouting directives formed during the fallout from the First Festival. Some light song enthusiasts probably followed those debates, which developed mainly among elite composers and administrators in Tirana, more closely than others. Some may not have recognized the viewpoints that were politically ascendant, nor could they have known how others would interpret pre-Festival orientations. This in itself simply shows the social fact that "[a]gents positioned in some sectors of a society might be quite ignorant of what goes on in others; actors might believe that the outcomes of their activities are different from what they in fact are."[42]

But no matter how carefully policy statements about music were crafted, they could in their implementation be finessed, adapted, or even ignored. And early light song policy was not particularly tightly crafted. Broad early statements were open to interpretation, and as a non-discursive domain, light music had a potentially flexible relationship to policy in general. Given these ambiguities, what was the relation between critique, song, and policy? The jury's private deliberations during the Second Festival of Song demonstrate how policies about sound came to be formed through the process of expert evaluation itself.

Before the two final concerts, a professional jury convened by the organizing committee met to discuss prizes. Its composition reflected the ascendancy of the professional reds during the previous summer. Writer Llazar Siliqi, as at the First Festival, headed the group. But the jury now included the composers Simon

Gjoni and Zadeja; the Sofia-trained opera singer Ramiz Kovaçi; the musicologist Paparisto; and journalist Liri Çeli.[43] During their final meeting, the jury's discussion turned to prizes. Discussants considered four to be definite winners: "Dëgjo o Hânë" (Listen, o Moon), by Avni Mula; "Djaloshi dhe Shiu," by Agim Krajka, "Flakë e Borë," by Tish Daija, and "Mos Vono" (Don't Delay), by Soviet-trained violinist Pjetër Gaci. Liri Çeli, an employee at the Radio, proposed a vote on her proposition: first prize to "Flakë e Borë," first-second prize ("2/1") to "Djaloshi dhe Shiu," and second-second prize ("2/2") to "Dëgjo o Hânë."

Debate then ensued over whether first prize be given to Daija or Krajka.

" 'Flakë e Borë' is better constructed, which is the thing that makes me 'pro,' " began Zadeja, "but let's start with the melody. I do not see anything all that national there."

"The melody is typically Albanian!" Kovaçi disagreed.

"To put it bluntly," Simon Gjoni interrupted, "the problem is this—when I hear 'Djaloshi dhe Shiu,' I remember it, while with 'Flakë e Borë,' I just don't! The two songs are both national. But if we are discussing their overall effectiveness, then the technical ornamentation of Tish wins out. If we are discussing which is a hit song, it has to be 'Djaloshi dhe Shiu.' "

The jury's head, Llazar Siliqi, played a largely subordinate role to the musicians. But he did make his opinions known. "I'm for 'Flakë e Borë" because it is both modern and Albanian," he said. "Yet we must keep in mind the opinion of the public during the three concerts—though I'm not convinced that 'Djaloshi dhe Shiu' would have had that storm of applause if not for its orchestration."

In the end, the jury voted for Daija. They never settled on criteria for how to evaluate if his song, or any other, was in fact "national." Nor did they seriously consider popularity—the dance music song "Nuk e Fshehim Dashuri," by all accounts among the most loudly applauded, did not merit discussion. They did not consider "folk intonations" at all, except to summarily dismiss "Baba, Shkon Ti në Shkollë" (Go to School, Dad!), a cute ditty about a young village girl chiding her father to give up his backward ways. The only song to directly incorporate a folk melody, the composers complained it exhibited "folklorism." Instead, Daija appears to have received first prize for other reasons. "I think that what Tish gave us," Paparisto concluded, "will leave an imprint on the other composers, that it will open a kind of road to them."

The notion that the awarding of a prize could orient future light music compositions and performances permeated the jury's discussion of the prizes for vocalists. Third prize was especially contentious. Raising Bengu for discussion, Siliqi lauded her and Besnik Taraneshi. "With Fatbardha, it seems to me there is something original with her," he said. "I think we would not err in encouraging that girl."

The music specialists immediately contradicted the writer.

"If we have one like her, we'll have others!" exclaimed Selman Kasapi.

"With her way of singing she brought nothing," Zadeja argued. "She must be more controlled in her singing—and precisely to close off a road to this bad group, I am with Selman."

"We must be very careful not to legalize an incorrect interpretation," warned Gjoni, "because we have a duty to give the audience an education." The jury then awarded third prize to the schoolgirl Nikoleta Shoshi for her earnest interpretation of Daija's "Flakë e Borë." Qemal Kërtusha unanimously received second prize. Zela again received the top award, as she would almost annually over the next decade.

Jury members did not approach evaluation as a process in which they were to assess whether or not songs or performances exemplified pre-Festival directives. Not even the poet, Siliqi, raised the set of textual themes so carefully charted at organizational meetings the previous fall. Jury members instead seemed to approach evaluation itself as an important part of creating policy. By consecrating particular works or performances, the jury began assembling the body of "patristic texts," privileged models that would serve to define national popular music in Albania.[44] What compositional techniques are correct? How should one perform? In sum, how should national popular music in a progressive socialist society sound?

These are not questions that can be answered without reference to a canon. If early songwriters sometimes failed to create "correct" works, this was because they had no prior examples of national popular songs on which to model their new ones. The models dance music composers or crooners employed were effectively disqualified over time, not through direct political actions such as formal "denunciation," but rather through the cultivation of an expert aesthetic discourse in debates, discussions, reports, and juried evaluation. Yet paradoxically, the Soviet-trained experts largely did not create the new models. Zadeja, for example, presented his first (and last) light song only in 1972. Instead, they successfully consecrated particular compositions and performances. In consecrating patristic models, professionalized musicians reinforced their own aesthetic sensibilities: an orientation toward complexity; disregard for simple popularity in favor of an approach emphasizing the composer's "duty" to educate listeners; and an understanding of light music as beholden to the same "rules" as serious music.

Sounds can refer to multiple referents simultaneously, exhibiting an unbridled polysemy in accruing their meanings that both intrigued and vexed officials. In linking nationalist sentiments with socialist values, for instance, musical performances were of prime potential importance to socialist states' projects to legitimate themselves by appealing to feelings of belonging. But these same sounds, and especially ones that drew on non-local popular music, could also potentially accrue meanings at variance with state projects. Complicating this proposition for officials was that musicians in Albania as elsewhere often benefited from Party officials' inability to define what musical practices should sound like in anything but negative terms. Just as David Tompkins writes of Poland, "[o]fficials proved able to identify what was not acceptable, but they had a very difficult time developing appropriate programs themselves."[45] In this way, unanticipated and unexpected policy turns could be effected through debate within the music field. But musicians were to learn that there existed hard limits on how far debate might go, especially during moments of heightened ideological concern.

Cultural Revolution, 1965–1969

In the summer of 1967, informally organized brigades of young people poured into Albania's countryside. They destroyed mosques and churches, scratching out the eyes of saints on centuries-old frescoes. Remaining religious structures were converted to other functions, like gymnasiums or culture houses, as part of the new state ban on religion. Other individuals began posting their own public denunciations of neighbors and coworkers on *fletë-rrufe*, literally "lightning sheets," which were modeled after Chinese *dàzìbào*. Policies on circulation, or *qarkullim*, reassigned intellectuals to villages or worksites to labor alongside the Masses. Some circulated through short tours. The vocalists at the Theater of Opera and Ballet visited railroad sites, where they also performed for the workers. Other intellectuals were reassigned to district towns, in effect exiled from Tirana.[46]

Albanian elites pursued these and related policies as part of their adoption of Chinese-style Cultural Revolution. Hoxha and Mao had a complicated relationship.[47] Each had exchanged diplomatic delegations beginning in 1954. With Moscow's suspension of relations with Tirana in 1961, Hoxha looked to Beijing. In the midst of this crisis, Mao had stated that the People's Republic of China "recognized, entrusted, and admired the unwavering position of the Party of Labor of Albania in the battle to defend the principles of Marxism-Leninism"; by 1966, the Albanian paper of record, *The Voice of the People*, described Albania and China as the "shock brigades of world revolution."[48]

XV PLENUM, OCTOBER 1965

Whereas cultural policy in the early 1960s had been flexible, open to negotiation and renegotiation, it stiffened as ties with China grew. The first signs of this stiffening, however, predated the "official" adoption of Revolutionary policies. In late October 1965, Ramiz Alia delivered a major speech to the XV Plenum of the Central Committee titled "On the Raising of the Role of Literature and the Arts for the Communist Education of the Masses."[49] A Party member since the war, Alia had been elected to the Central Committee in the late 1940s, studied in the Soviet Union in the 1950s, and ascended to the Politburo in the early 1960s. He was relatively younger than other top officials, and on account of his age, his appointment overseeing cultural affairs, his family background in Shkodra, and his Soviet training, he soon enjoyed close relationships with many younger members of Tirana's intelligentsia. Alia addressed members of the Central Committee as well as a group of invited artists, writers, and musicians, a group that left the plenary session ill at ease. Though members of the intelligentsia had been increasingly successful in creating space for themselves to direct the cultural economy, the cultural field itself remained always embedded within the broader field of power. And, as intellectuals learned during the revolutionary state's short-lived experiment with Maoism, the cultural field was ultimately beholden to directives and edicts formed in the broader field of political power within which intellectuals were located.

Singly, the orientations Alia outlined had largely rehearsed older ideological statements. But taken as a whole, the report signaled a major change in policy, as well as a significantly more prominent role for the Party in artistic life. Intellectuals, Alia proposed, must better strive to "present a deeper and wider reflection of life."[50] They must "correctly represent" the positive aspects of this life, with special attention to its "positive heroes."[51] In doing this, their works were of prime social and political significance. Because the Masses were bearers of "ignorance" (*padituria*), they required enlightenment through artistic works. "Tastes," Alia reiterated, "are learned."[52] This orthodox statement echoed earlier conceptions of the intellectuals as society's vanguard. In educating the Masses, intellectuals were to be "vigilant against foreign influences," to create "true values," and to base their works on "the People's creativity" rather than "the cosmopolitan." The content, form, and execution of artistic products, Alia concluded, depended on intellectuals' cultivation of "a deeper knowledge," *njohja*, of Marxism-Leninism, but also on their "knowledge" of the true condition of the People.

And here Alia introduced into Albanian cultural politics a novel twist. If the ignorant Masses required enlightenment, so too did the intellectuals. Intellectuals exhibited their own form of ignorance, which he termed *mosnjohja*, or the non-recognition of the true conditions of the People. Only by acquainting themselves with the real nature of social reality—engaging in physical labor, living in rural areas, meeting with non-intellectuals—could intellectuals dispel their own darkness. Intellectuals' elite status as the educators of society had to this point sometimes been raised for debate, particularly among working-class or rural members of the Party, but never seriously challenged. Alia's challenge, the subordination of "intellectual labor" to "physical labor," would ultimately have far-reaching effects. Writers, artists, and musicians were assigned to work brigades; physical labor and military training were introduced into the educational system; workers were assigned to supervise intellectuals in *kontrolli punë-tor*, or "workers' checks"; and the coveted social status of the intellectual was called into question.

The plenary report raised several concrete orientations that anticipated the coming Cultural Revolution. Alia demanded that intellectuals, and especially those employed by the ensembles and institutions comprising the cultural economy, be better overseen by the Party. The quality of works, especially in the popular spheres of theater, the estrada, and song, was to be bettered or, in Alia's term, their "artistic mastery" was to be raised. Works were to more explicitly treat political themes in general, and to portray the "positive hero" in particular. The "aesthetic tastes of the Masses" were to be better educated. Finally, amateur artistic movements were to be better organized and integrated into the fabric of the planned cultural economy.

In more abstract terms, Alia's address radically destabilized the once-firm position of the intellectuals vis-à-vis domestic consumers, the objects of their enlightening works. But were the Masses and the People synonymous? What was their relation to each other? To the intelligentsia? The People, Alia seemed to be claiming, could exercise a directing force over intellectuals as the primary source material for their works. But these works in turn educated and elevated the tastes of the Masses. How could the People/Masses be simultaneously a source for cultural works and their object?[53] Over the course of the next two decades, this paradox reshaped the cultural field. But in the years following Alia's report, intellectuals faced a more pressing problem: How should you navigate these new, disorienting directives? Or if not successfully navigate, how could you at least avoid running afoul of them?

A REVOLUTIONARY FESTIVAL OF SONG, 1968

In 1966, Albania formally began its intensive three-year experiment with what elites termed the Cultural and Ideological Revolution. The Fifth Festival of Song of December 1966 had been organized before orientations began to be implemented, and so the three Festivals held in 1967, 1968, and 1969 demonstrate how revolutionary directives affected the music economy at this event. Today, these orientations are often used as evidence for how state-socialism narrowed artists' options. But a closer examination of the Seventh Festival of Song, broadcast in December 1968, demonstrates the unexpected consequences of the implementation of ideological directives, and the growing skill with which certain musicians navigated even the most revolutionary of political demands.

As employees began organizing the Seventh Festival in summer 1968, they contended with major policy changes that affected the event's content. First, the event's *tematika*, or thematic material, reflected its radical politicization. Each Festival during this period contained songs about specific ideological campaigns; martial themes and, especially, the National War of Liberation; and "the positive socialist hero." Second, the event began incorporating more "amateurs," a direct response to Alia's orientation in October 1965 and part of a growing campaign to redistribute power within the cultural field. Third, a new, grander aesthetic emerged, as what participants called *këngë epiko-lirike*, epic-lyric songs, began to predominate. And finally, composers began to more explicitly incorporate folkloric materials into their songs in response to directives that all works be based "on the creativity of the People."

The most striking feature of these events was their politicized *tematika*, as all song texts were now expected to have explicitly political content. Guidelines distributed in March listed the kinds of themes composers should set: "The songs of the Festival will express in all their aspects the revolutionary will of our People, the heroism of the working class, as well as our Youth, the revolutionary solidarity of our People, [and] the joy of their labor and of their life."[54] (A "boy-meets-girl" lyric would still be fine as long as he met her in a factory.) In September, the general artistic committee made the initial selection of songs, which were then forwarded to a special committee concerned with texts. Some submissions were simply lead sheets with a melody and chords but no text, while others just had a note scrawled in the margin as to what kind of text would be appropriate.

The primary goal of the texts' commission was to create a well-rounded *tematika*, a collection of songs that balanced martial or ideological themes with social ones. The set of songs approved for the Seventh Festival demonstrate how this occurred in practice (see Figure 2.1). A handful of songs treated ongoing ideological campaigns, including the "building of socialism," a campaign then in its final stages to rally the construction of infrastructure, and "north/south relations," a newer nationalist campaign to discourage regional divisions. Another category of songs concerned romantic relationships, and another, World War II and patriotism. Finally, two prize-winning songs concerned "positive heroes": "Komisar i Kuq" (The Red Commissar), by Nikolla Zoraqi, and "Mësuesit Hero" (To the Hero Teacher), by Limos Dizdari and discussed in more detail below. In practice, these categories overlapped. Was the lyric "U Njohem në Digë" (We Met at the Dam) about the social theme of love or the ideological theme on the building of socialism? Moreover, prizes tended to be awarded to works that fell on

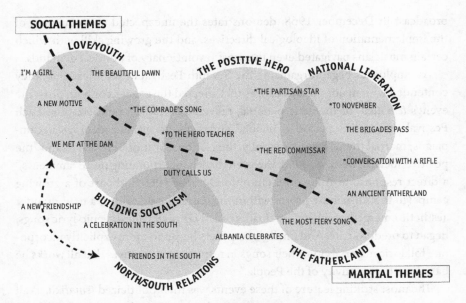

Figure 2.1 A balanced *tematika*. An asterisk indicates songs awarded prizes.

the martial, rather than social, end of the spectrum. But significantly, organizers checked to ensure that the overall *tematika* was balanced, meaning that it included a wide range of lyrics on both social and political themes, as well as lyrics on specific campaigns. By the late 1970s, Festival themes had become so standardized that the resident texts' editor, Zhuljana Jorganxhiu, simply wrote short phrases on each lyric sheet she approved, such as "for the Youth," "the building of socialism," or "the Second World War."

Festival organizers also introduced measures to recruit so-called amateurs. In July, Radio employees met to discuss and encourage non-professional composers in Tirana and, at the end of the month, held a competition to recruit nonprofessional singers. Employees recorded these singers over the course of several concerts and, on the basis of these recordings, generated extensive lists of potential invitees. One invitee was Ema Qazimi, soon to be enrolled at the Artistic Lyceum. "I was first discovered at the age of twelve," she told me. "A birthday party had been organized, and I sang a song. My voice was discovered, and they recruited me for an amateur group. Afterwards I left that group, and when I was fourteen I participated in the Radio competition, called 'New Voices.' Accompanied by a small amateur group from the Palace of Culture, I sang a Vaçe song. She was even on the commission." In addition to the open call Qazimi describes, the organizing committee invited two amateur choruses recently formed at state enterprises, one from the Durrës Seaport and the other from the Textile Plant "Stalin," a show factory on Tirana's outskirts.

Yet despite efforts to encourage nonprofessional composers, few were found. Instead, organizers publicized the inclusion of Conservatory students, many on the cusp of graduation, as "amateurs." Competition among these mature students was fierce, and several received top prizes during the late 1960s and early 1970s. Composer Limos Dizdari, the winner of the Seventh Festival of Song, was one such student, a rising star who had just then completed his first major work, a film score for *Horizonte të Hapura* (Open Horizons, 1968).

Dizdari's epic-lyrical composition, "Mësuesit Hero," portrayed the positive hero Ismet Sali Bruçaj. Bruçaj, a young teacher, had recently died while attempting to reach his pupils in a remote mountain district during a storm. Dizdari incorporated thematic material from the recently completed film score, which portrayed another socialist hero, a young dock worker named Adem Reka. Each work shared a three-note motive, *fa-mi-fa*, a heroic leitmotif evoking a bugle call, an impression reinforced by the piece's brass-heavy orchestration. "With the use of [the film's] intonations in the song 'Mësuesit Hero,' the author has sought to make a generalization of the figure of the hero of our days," wrote Dizdari's classmate, Kujtim Gjelina, who analyzed the piece as part of a thesis directed by Zadeja in 1969.[55]

Like other epic-lyrical pieces, Dizdari's composition was less *një këngë*, a song, than, in composers' parlance, *një vepër*, a work. "I was not necessarily taken with *këngë*," the composer told me at our first meeting. "I have always been more oriented toward other kinds of works, especially film music, *vepra* concerned with larger themes that many different kinds of people could enjoy. Not just intellectuals, but the People as well." "Mësuesit Hero" reflects this orientation toward song as a kind of complex work. An introductory swell of strings precedes a recitative-like verse over sustained chords; the opening material successively develops over the course of the verse leading into the refrain. "[The composition] begins with a figure in the double basses, which prepares you for something heroic that comes later," Gjelina wrote. "[Dizdari] here inserts material from the vocal line for the clarinet. . . . We later see in the trombones the figure the double basses played, but more developed and fragmented, with smaller note values that raise the pulse and emotion of the work, until the explosion of notes at the culmination."[56]

Epic-lyrical "works" like "Mësuesit Hero" dominated the revolutionary Festivals, garnering prizes and prestige for their composers. But at the same time a new kind of smaller, *intime*, or intimate, song employing "folk intonations" also emerged. The Festivals needed these compositions, composers often told me, not only because they were popular with listeners, but also because a balanced *tematika* required songs about love and social issues. In Tirana, it has become a cliché to point out that such songs never received top prizes, and that Agim Krajka, who graduated from Zadeja's composition studio along with Dizdari in

1968, won more second prizes than any other composer in the Festival's history. "If twelve songs were about ideology," Krajka told me, "two would be about love. And even if the Festival [jury] was obliged to give first prize to the Party"—that is, according to Krajka, to songs with explicitly ideological lyrics—"I'd get second or third. And I got eighteen of these."[57]

Krajka's early Festival songs, created in collaboration with his longtime lyricist, theater director Haxhi Rama, had been popular and, in their arrangements for his rhythm group, sometimes controversial. But by 1968, Krajka had successfully transitioned from "dance music" musician to "composer" as a graduate of the Conservatory. At the Seventh Festival of Song, Krajka hit upon a new formula. "Jam Një Vajzë" (I'm a Girl), written again in collaboration with Rama, became a model for integrating "folk intonations" in an aesthetically and politically correct fashion. A simple verse-refrain tune, "Jam Një Vajzë" is constructed on a simple pentatonic riff presented in the introduction in piano octaves. The riff indexed "the intonation of the South" for contemporary commentators, referencing the "national" folklore of southern Albanian polyphonic vocal music. Krajka's vocal line subsequently develops the same pentatonic scale, and in its performance by young amateur singer, Justina Aliaj, demonstrates what the student-critic Gjelina called "the dynamism and optimism of the Masses."[58]

But pentatonic material, of course, is not only found in southern Albanian polyphony. My sense is that Krajka found a way to incorporate "folk intonations" within a structure that, in reality, differed little from Western popular music in its use of a five-note scale and its arrangement around a single riff or "hook." And Krajka foregrounded the "national element" so obviously, the opening five bars simply outlining a pentatonic scale, that critics could not fail to note its basis in "folklore." Though he did not receive a prize for "Jam Një Vajzë," other young composers quickly began imitating this new patristic model for what were soon termed *këngë ritmike*, or "rhythm songs."

A PRACTICAL SENSE FOR REVOLUTIONARY POLITICS

Despite the implementation of the Cultural Revolution's orientations, participants did not necessarily experience the Festival of Song's increasing politicization as simply a narrowing of their creative space. The composers, lyricists, and performers who were selected by expert commissions shared a practical sense, or a "feel for the game," that enabled them to deftly maneuver among the ever-evolving revolutionary edicts governing the music field.[59]

Participants could strategically refuse to engage certain edicts. Consider the growing "problem" of untexted song submissions to the Festival committee. Some composers, a critic claimed in a 1968 article in *Drita*, submitted untexted tunes because they wanted to first receive the organizing commission's approval before making efforts to contact a lyricist.[60] Only once the tune had been accepted would the composer "immediately pick up the telephone and, after some cooing and caresses, which both sides expect—like 'Please! I don't have time!' and the reply, 'Come on, you can do it!'—at last come to the decision that the text will be figured out that afternoon at [the intellectuals' hangout in central Tirana] Café Sahati, or first thing the next day. The poor song."[61] Savvy composers could potentially beg non-expertise over texts in order to extract themselves from potentially sticky, ideologically charged issues concerning themes. While this created more work for text editors at the Radio, it came with one significant perk. Untexted or half-finished submissions enabled editors to better craft a balanced *tematika* by assigning them "missing" themes.

But it would be wrong to see non-engagement as participants' primary strategy. Individuals did not simply refuse, maneuver around, subvert, or disengage from increasingly politicized Festivals. In part, this is because Festivals of Song had become too significant to the music field, albeit against long odds. Following the Second Festival of Song, several composers had even suggested canceling the event scheduled for December 1964.[62] Preparations for the twentieth-anniversary of Albania's liberation that November, they said, would make its organization too difficult. It is not difficult to imagine that they might also have had unspoken concerns about the previous year's denunciations. But if the Festival were canceled, Zadeja had then stated, conclusions could be drawn that its organizers were afraid to answer the problems raised by its first two editions. The music field's highest profile event after just two years, the Festival could not be abandoned. And by 1968, the Festival had begun to be viewed as the site at which members of the music field could become *afirmuar*, or affirmed. Participants were now competing for their peers' approval, the prestige of prizes, and to express their core creative self on what had become Albania's biggest stage.

Affirmation, competition, and self-expression, explored in detail in the following chapter, largely guided participants at the Seventh Festival. Krajka viewed his use of "folk intonations" not as a result of politics, but as arising from his training and his own creative nature. "All my pedagogues had graduated from conservatory in Moscow—the whole system we had was totally, completely Russian," he told me. "But *ama*, really, we were taught to use the theme of the People."

"Yeah, but why?" I interjected, apparently stupidly.

"What do you mean, 'why!' We have the most wonderful folklore in the world, second to none! Twenty-four thousand square kilometers, three million people, different rhythms between zones, villages, and so on, more diverse than anywhere else!"

In explaining how he had felt about policy, Dizdari invoked a discourse that, over the 1970s, became woven into the fabric of the music field. "I am oriented" toward particular styles, he explained to me, and *orientimi* comes from within. Composers of Dizdari's generation came to internalize the sense that to compose in a way that was not "their own" would be unnatural, "false," as well as creatively bankrupt. Dizdari claimed that his personal creative orientation toward "the grand" or "epic" themes lined up with, but did not derive from, political directives.

As did Ema Qazimi's *orientimi*. After 1968, she became a fixture at the Festivals, winning prizes and, ultimately, assuming Vaçe Zela's mantle as light music's leading star by the 1980s. The revolutionary fashion for epic-lyrical songs, Qazimi told me, had "swept her up." She had been in the right place at the right time as a young woman with a large range, strong voice, and dramatic delivery. The composers who initially championed her, coaching her and requesting she perform their works, "were not simple song specialists, but were overseen by the motive of the *work*," meaning pieces that were "not simple ABA, or strophe-refrain-strophe" forms, but classical in their construction. Qazimi found herself prepared for this moment because she had been emulating Zela, whom she called her personal *pikë referimi*, or reference point, for the previous six years.

The trends described above diverged sharply from those found elsewhere in the eastern bloc.[63] The boundaries separating other state-socialist societies from one another and from the Western world became more permeable, with media flows cutting across previously impassable borders following Khrushchev's repudiation of Stalin in the late 1950s. Inspired by their counterparts in the West, young people in the region pursued their own forms of cultural revolution during "the socialist sixties."[64] The Soviet Union, the Central European countries, and the rest of Southeastern Europe began experimenting with tolerating Western culture in general, and American popular culture in particular. At the same time, these countries also directed significantly more of their domestic resources toward creating local alternatives to Western popular culture. The refusal to de-Stalinize the cultural economy and dalliances with Maoism forestalled such experimentation in Albania until the early 1970s. And practically, there had existed little demand for a local alternative to Western popular culture from Albania's predominantly rural population. But as Albania urbanized and its young people increasingly gained access to domestic and foreign media, officials would begin to view what they called "the demands of the Youth" in a new light.

Professional Spoilers

In 1970, composers did not conceive their popular music compositions to be in competition with foreign popular songs. Instead, even young composers defined light music in relation to concert music.

"A song is not at *all* a simple thing. In three minutes, to express a clear thought—how is this possible when the composition is over before it has even begun?" Shpëtim Kushta, a composer who graduated from Zadeja's studio just a couple of years after Dizdari and Krajka had, was lecturing me on the difficulties of creating a popular song. He did not think I understood what he was trying to say, so he gave me an example.

"For my diploma, I created a cantata. Okay, with four movements, what happens if you do not create a clear thought in the first movement? You develop it in the second movement. And if it is not fully realized there?"

"The third movement?" I answered, hesitantly.

"Okay, so there is a third movement. And again?"

"A fourth?"

"So you finish it in the fourth movement, you crystallize the musical thought. But if you do not arrive there? You have a finale. And it is not finished there, still? Okay, you have the coda. A piece like this has 'waves,' do you understand this word? It is a metaphor, of course, I mean a composition has waves, going up and down, until you reach the end. Like the sea, you have the entire ocean to construct one clear thought. But this is why, no other reason, that a song must be a professional work."

Then, tapping his finger on my notebook, he directed: "Write down three big P-s. Okay, now what does this mean? It means PRO-FES-SIO-NAL"— again, tapping out each syllable—"professional. This is how a song must be created: professionally."

Despite professing his expertise about light music songs, Kushta composed only a handful over the course of his long career. He peaked with his first composition, "Mesnatë" (At Midnight), which received first prize at the Ninth Festival of Song in 1970. He collaborated with poet Fatos Arapi, another member of Tirana's younger guard, and orchestrator Robert Radoja, a virtuoso pianist and classmate at the Conservatory. Vaçe Zela, who had a second sense for prize-winning songs, as one composer bluntly told me, interpreted the work by the two students.

The piece was truly symphonic in its conception, a real professional work. A methodical, *rubato* verse became metered and faster in its second iteration with the addition of a double bass and piano figure; the bridge featured an accelerando leading to a climactic *a tempo* at the refrain. Melodically, Kushta developed in the bridge an upper neighbor figure, first foreshadowed in a wistful figure linking the first verse with the second, as it built to the culminating refrain. Kushta was harmonically adventurous, too. The verse featured a flash of chromatic color via a prominent passing tone, and the conclusion to the refrain juxtaposed a minor sonority with a brilliant major chord. Zela's voice soared over Radoja's orchestration, which employed the full complement of the Radio

Orchestra: woodwinds, horns, brass, *divisi* strings, timpani. "Side by side, the two of us silently walk," Zela quietly intoned at the beginning of the second verse, "Just as at our first meeting / You are magnificent tonight."

In this paean to the pure love of two young Albanians can be discerned a remarkable shift that occurred in just under a decade. The dance music ditties penned by culture house directors, administrators, and instrumentalists at early Festivals had given way almost without exception to the elevated works so carefully crafted by professionalized Conservatory students. And the practical concerns of men like Grimci and Kongoli with accumulating repertoire for broadcast and redistributing songs to district ensembles had given way to discussions focused primarily on innovation and aesthetics. Did the composer, colleagues now asked at the post-Festival debates organized by the League of Writers and Artists, "bring anything new?" Several discussants lauded "Mesnatë" for its "clear form" that "created an impression of a full, concrete emotional force."[65] Others debated if it was truly a light song, or an "aria, romance, or cantata." One of Kushta's pedagogues, Tonin Harapi, worried these "concert types" would not be "understandable" outside Tirana, suggesting such elaborate pieces were more suited to "academic evenings" than Festivals of Song.[66] By 1970, commentators with such misgivings were in the minority. The debate about light music had been decided.

Discussion itself enabled the flowering of new aesthetic orientations during the 1960s, orientations over which professional composers and their students progressively managed to monopolize. Fluent in a Marxist-Leninist language of aesthetics, Soviet-trained intellectuals forged a position for themselves at the head of the music field by translating the so-called problem of popular song, its position vis-à-vis other forms of local musical creativity, into expert language understandable to their peers and Party officials alike.[67] How did they do this? In part, by employing the narrative of progress that officials believed to be so essential to their political legitimacy. Like political elites, composers and their students deeply internalized the *telos* of Marxism-Leninism, adopting the future-oriented language of five-year plans and industrial production. In critical discourse, compositions were "produced" by "culture workers," each new work demonstrating "a step forward," *një hap përpara*. Postwar creativity, critic Dalan Shapllo proposed in an exemplary statement, has "passed from the simplest songs, to musical tableaux, to operettas and operas, to [tone] poems and cantatas, to instrumental pieces and the first symphonies in the culture of our art.[68]

In measuring musical progress in terms of its increasing formal complexity and then interpolating light music into this scale, composers successfully reframed song as demanding their self-described "professional culture." This kind of language proved legible to political elites who themselves understood music as a domain necessitating expertise. By invoking expertise, or in local parlance, their professionalism, composers like Zadeja and the young men and women they trained asserted their distinction from administrators. At stake during debates about light song, however, were rarely specific compositional techniques. The key struggle centered on the redefinition of light music as real art rather than mere entertainment, as works rather than songs. Over time, these notions could be made commonsense through educational institutions, broadcasts, social networks, and the everyday practice of creativity itself.[69]

Composers succeeded in their struggle to redefine the genre of light music as an "expert object," its songs as things that "require help in interpreting even though they may appear legible to a layperson."[70] By debating song, composers enacted their expertise in ways that had specific effects in the music field.[71] This did not go unremarked by their contemporaries at the time. "There are some composers among us who present themselves *with words* as champions of the national character in music," Abdullah Grimci had complained at the plenary session on light music held in July 1963. "I am sorry to say," he continued, "that some comrade composers and musicians do not judge our works by their real artistic values, but from the name [of the] school from which the composer graduated."[72]

But the professional composer did not only assert control over the field "with words." Composers became adept at preserving their position in the music field by effectively preventing other groups from advancing. In part, this derived from the development of the position of "composer" as a kind of self-regulating guild, not unlike elsewhere in the eastern bloc.[73] But it also derived from a peculiar affinity between the composer's sense of self and the socialist state itself. The socialist state's strength, in Jan Gross's classic analysis, rested in part on its ability to incapacitate or "spoil" potential sources of competition.[74] The spoiler state prevented the creation of alternatives, whether in the form of sacred or secular institutions, inhibiting, criminalizing, or strictly regulating its potential competitors. Composers acted as "mini-spoilers," and not only through their strategic deployment of expert aesthetic discourses. By ascending to directing positions within the music economy, composers could effectively spoil others' opportunities in more direct ways as well.

Why, for instance, did so few amateur songwriters present works at the Festival of Song, even at times contradicting direct political objectives? In part, composers blocked amateurs by redefining "song" as necessitating professional technique, and this technique, as gained through expert formal study at the Conservatory. "There are many amateur musicians in work and production centers who, inspired by our socialist life, write songs in which their talent is apparent," began a 1967 article in the popular magazine *Radioprogram*.[75] "How should these comrades begin their work?" "It is essential that the musician know, play, and study folk music, to be educated to feel and to love it, to study all of its intonational rhythmic, harmonic, and polyphonic characteristics," the author answered. "Simple classical works of world [concert] music and, especially, the best creations of our composers, must be listened to and studied closely."

So how do you succeed as an amateur? In effect, by becoming a composer. "Amateur composers must work doggedly for the education and development of their taste, which will then be reflected in the works that they write." In actuality, few amateurs ever cracked broadcasts. At a meeting held in 1968, an instrumentalist employed by a district culture house complained that the Radio's staff actively discouraged submissions: "Often when [amateurs] send their songs [and are rejected], they do not receive an answer about why they are worthless, or what changes can be made to better them.[76] A vocalist from a large district city continued, saying that the Radio's music office made no visit for several years. When their team did come, the recordings it made were of such poor quality that they could not be broadcast.

One of the major ironies here is that the men who played such significant roles in reorienting the music economy by debating light music often did not even compose songs. Zadeja, like his students, was oriented to "grand works." Few of his colleagues were as involved in dance music as individuals like Grimci, Avrazi, Kongoli, and others had been. Yet the Festival of Song became a site anchoring the music economy that Zadeja and his Conservatory colleagues had come to direct. Requiring the activation of a number of intellectuals, major artistic events obligated members of the intelligentsia to come together in collaboration and critique, organization and evaluation. The Festival of Song consequently became a gauge officials could use to ascertain the general health of the cultural economy. This rendered the Festival's songs and participants audible as potential objects of government.

The Aleatory State

In state-socialist societies, the significance of symbols primed music policy for contestation. But for the musical products of policy to be contested, these audible symbols had to first be made legible through ideological and aesthetic language. Yet different domains of life were subject to contestation in different ways. The domain of the audible proved a special case, as Sadik Bejko, a writer and poet who worked at Radio Albania editing texts from the early 1960s until his dismissal in 1973, explained to me.

Sometimes, Bejko explained, Party officials, even those occupying its upper echelons, called the Radio personally directly to complain about works they had heard broadcast. Bejko's job was to make sure they had no reason to call. When folk or light music lyrics arrived, Bejko checked each one over carefully to make sure it had correct ideological content, that the texts "sounded good." Most often he would fix words, elevating the language in places and correcting grammar. His supervisor, the Radio's general director, Thanas Nano, carefully approved these changes before they were recorded and broadcast. But to the poet's knowledge, no one ever called to complain about the music. "The words were handcuffed," he told me, "but the music was free."

As Bejko spoke, I sensed he had rehearsed this statement with other interviewers. It sounded familiar, and I later came to realize why. Among intellectuals, this idea had become part of the postsocialist "Party line" about culture during the socialist period. But this aphorism also points to an essential insight about music and its control under socialism. Control was a question of knowledge. And knowledge about musical sound often eluded officials.

"The music library? There wasn't one," composer Limos Dizdari told me. I had been asking if his cohort, trained in the 1960s, ever tried to obtain "subversive" scores while they were in school. I followed up by asking if these materials were even available. "There was a small music library at the Conservatory, created with the contributions of whatever we had, whoever had records shared them, whoever had scores shared them, and around this time, they began to order new things and those things came, but even so they were few, not enough, insufficient. That's why we did not know, we did not know what to look for, we did not know what to enjoy!"

My line of questioning concerned how officials decided to prohibit certain scores. But these questions, Dizdari patiently explained, began from a flawed premise. "The State did not interfere very much with those things because, well, first of all it did not know what to say about music. And *we* did not know that the composers and works we were interested in were prohibited. If *we* did not know this, then the state did not know anything at all! *Shyqyr*, thank goodness, when the state did not know something, the state could not clearly control it, and thus there could be no prohibition."

The architects of the administered state had dreamed of planning everything, from chromium production, to birth rates, to the number of ballerinas trained each year. But as this chapter demonstrates, cultural policies and orientations did not develop according to blueprints found in the works of Marx or Lenin. Music policies were particularly susceptible to an inherent quality of socialism, what Janos Kornai has called the "curious natural selection" by which "new [elements] easily reconciled with the nature of the system take root."[77] Certain developments could at times be contradictory. As officials demanded that music be made more accessible to the listening Masses, a cohort of expert professionals pursued not simplicity, but an aesthetic of growing complexity. Were compositions like "Mesnatë" able to be performed by non-specialists outside Tirana?

Not without a culture house ensemble boasting orchestral instruments and a singer able to navigate its soaring vocal line.

But the ascendancy of the professional composer lined up with an even more enduring, structural feature of the socialist system. Professionals like Zadeja, Kushta, and the composers they later trained as faculty at the Conservatory succeeded in monopolizing not only specialized musical knowledge, but a more fundamental, programmatic one: intellectual knowledge. Over the course of the 1960s, the professionals were successful in claiming for themselves a monopoly within the music field over intellectual knowledge, the governmental form of knowledge-power "concerned with values that a society deems pertinent for orienting and regulating the behavior of its members."[78] The kinds of programmatic questions the Party claimed absolute privilege over ("What is good? What is bad? How are we to act?") depended on intellectual knowledge. Intellectual knowledge in turn legitimated the primary social division on which governance in postwar Albania rested, the distinction between a leading vanguard and the broad Masses. By claiming expertise over questions about not only the aesthetic content but also the social import of music, professional composers forged, and claimed, directing roles for themselves in the cultural field.

But these ad hoc developments, the unintended consequences of critical debate and subsequent practical reforms, were certainly not planned in the sense of being products of the logical advance of the field. Such developments might better be described as aleatory. In the short term, direct policy could effect immediate change. A demand for amateur participation led to the creation of amateur ensembles; an edict that works address the "positive hero" yielded songs about fallen teachers, heroic dockworkers, revolutionary schoolgirls, and larger-than-life war heroes. But over the long run, the aleatory state proved a place where the sum total of its agents' strategies and positions-taking, leavened by chance, conditioned outcomes in the planned music economy, unforeseeable outcomes that proved difficult to control from above. At any moment, however, the Party could assert control through the naked exercise of repression, something the music field soon came to comprehend firsthand.

3

Cultivating Individuality

"I did not participate in the Tenth Festival. The Eleventh Festival, this was the point at which I suffered. But thank goodness, I was not imprisoned."

A guitarist and dance music enthusiast, Alfons Balliçi had matriculated in the Conservatory's composition program with men like Agim Krajka and Limos Dizdari in the 1960s. On graduation, he was assigned to head the music section of the culture house in Elbasan, the nearby district capital where he grew up. "In Elbasan, I began a small guitar course with a few pupils. It became a guitar quartet, and later I added an organ and drum kit. Around 1972, someone"—a big name, Balliçi implied—"at the Radio-Television heard about the group. He came three times to hear the group, and thought he might do a piece for them to perform at the Eleventh Festival. But then someone else said, 'No, you, Alfons, should write a piece.' So I wrote 'Rruga e Dibres' (The Road to Dibra), which Sherif Merdani performed. The group was really appreciated!"

"And then what happened, well, that happened afterwards. I was denounced because of the Festival, and I lost my right to creativity, *drejtë*, for three years."

"Denouncement—*dënimi*," I cut in, "what did that mean for you?"

"Well, it was really a form of internal denouncement. So, I submitted a song for the Twelfth Festival. It was not accepted. I submitted a song to the Radio. It was not broadcast. I would write a song in Elbasan—which the district needed! I was the only one there, I was the artistic director, the music head, and the district really didn't have a lot of people—I would write something, and my name wouldn't be put on it. Another person's name would, but I had written it. So it was clear that I was banned from creative work. It was official, but it was not public. And the strange thing was, before the Eleventh Festival, there were people at the Radio who had raised my group to the sky. 'Bravo, Alfons! Great job! This is really light music, this is true music!'"

I later learned that Balliçi was rehabilitated, as my consultants put it, only after the composer and Tirana's leading conductor, Ferdinand Deda, found him a pathway leading back to the national stage. "Dita më e Lumtur" related a young girl's pride, the "happiest day" of the title, on entering the ranks of the Party. A short political piece "with a predetermined theme," a kind of light music reply to just criticism, the composition was accepted four years after the unpublicized-but-official denouncement.

The composer's answers above related to my direct questions about his personal experiences of repression. But when our talk turned to the creative process itself, or the manner in which he generated new works, the political keywords of denouncement, rehabilitation, and so on disappeared, and a new one, individuality, emerged. It appeared as Balliçi discussed his early attempts to write light music songs.

"For sure, they are not crystallized," he told me. "But they have my face, you understand?"

"Do you mean they have *individualiteti* or *origjinaliteti*?" I asked, trying to apply the professional jargon my other consultants used and which, I think, Balliçi may have worried would stretch my heavily accented Albanian to its breaking point.

"*E saktë*, exactly—my individuality. While listening, you hear the melody and harmony that pertain to my face, to my individuality. Every song has its own melodic line, has its own harmonic bed that belongs to me."

"In the sense that you have *created* an individuality?"

"Look—," now impatiently, beginning to mix metaphors even more freely: "Does your son resemble you?"

"Yes."

"Okay then, this is something that is passed down, right? Do you understand the comparison? It is the same. The way a composer has been prepared determines the fruit he bears. His style. I mean, even in my early songs I reflect myself, my face, in my works. This is what it means to say that I created my individuality."

The idea of *individualiteti* was so self-evident to my consultants that many, like Balliçi, became exasperated with me when I asked them to explain its meaning. As plain, the composer claimed, as the nose on your child's face.

In Albania, the eleventh edition of the Festival of Song (1972), a self-conscious attempt to produce *moderne* popular music, has been its most closely scrutinized. Commentators today discuss the Eleventh Festival as a potential opening to the rest of the world, and its spectacular denunciation, as the catalyst for the naked exercise of state power to silence opposition. This narrative has the ring of truth. In a major departure from prior editions, the Festival promoted Western- and American-style pop sounds. Its broadcast initiated a string of major political speeches in 1973 and 1974 on the dangers of internal enemies to the state, speeches that resulted in punishments that swept first through Tirana's cultural field before enveloping, in turn, its military and political fields. These events led to a radically isolationist turn.

The new 1976 Constitution changed the country's official name, adding the word "Socialist" to distinguish the People's *Socialist* Republic of Albania from revisionist pretenders worldwide. Following Mao's death in 1976, Tirana suspended even relations with Beijing, pursuing an ultimately ill-fated path toward self-sufficiency. And a new defense policy, hopelessly quixotic to outside observers, resulted in the construction of thousands of concrete bunkers from which guerrilla fighters might repel attacks from the capitalist and Soviet worlds.

This schematic history explains the silences of this period but not the sounds. Dominant paradigms on musical creativity in the eastern bloc have too rarely examined the everyday creative processes of ordinary musicians. Commentators accord a disproportional significance to spectacular moments of repression— for the most part, exceedingly rare—when artists either snubbed their noses at the system in which they worked or were silenced for doing so. But recent works on everyday life in state-socialist societies more generally have revealed a shift in techniques of control that began from the 1960s, a broad turn from external forms of coercion to internalized techniques of discipline.[1] This change held even for intellectuals in demonstrably more repressive states, like Albania, where the specter of state coercion remained relatively closer to society's surface into the 1980s. To examine this duality, this chapter contains two parts tracing the play between external and internal techniques of control from 1971 to 1985. These complementary techniques comprised two facets of Party officials' governmental projects to administer consumption and production within the planned cultural economy. The first part explores how young consumers of state-subsidized popular music came to be targeted as a group necessitating renewed concern in the early 1970s, and how this policy shift inflected the work of musicians; the second part, how producers came to govern themselves between the late 1970s and 1980s.

Each bundle of techniques points to how illiberal states, not wholly unlike their liberal counterparts, depend on what may productively be described as indirect forms of control. Adapting Bruno Latour's notion of "action at a distance," Miller and Rose have proposed "the analysis of 'indirect' mechanisms of rule that are of such importance in liberal societies: those that have enabled, or have sought to enable *government at a distance*."[2] I take this to mean an ensemble of techniques that do not act upon social bodies directly, but rather concern the shaping of the *conditions* by which such bodies are able to be rendered administrable in certain ways and toward particular ends. The geography of symbolic production in Albania made possible indirect mechanisms for the control of creativity. In the 1950s and 1960s, expert planning and the rational redistribution of musical resources from the bureaucratic center resulted in the emergence of a spatialized logic distinctive to noncapitalist societies. This structuring of symbolic production subsequently allowed bureaucratic calculations about broadcast policy to become enmeshed with the expressive practice of individual composers working in Tirana and elsewhere.

This interlinking of broadcast policy, creative practice, and musical subjectivity occurred, to return to the coinage by Miller and Rose, at a distance. That is to say, individual composers did not perceive their creative agency to stem from or to be determined by policy, nor did they ascribe to their creative products the taint of official oversight. Rather, composers came to understand their lives and work, their very senses of self, almost exclusively in reference to an ideology of self-expression, named *individualiteti*. In the long run, fear and repression alone could not shape social life, even in the most repressive of societies. Desires and dreams too molded creativity, as did internalized senses of duty and obligation to listeners. In Tirana, desire and duty joined at the point where musicians, their creative work, and listeners intersected, something my consultants often stressed to me.

"It was always, 'The Artist Must Serve the People,'" lyricist Jorgo Papingji explained over coffee. "This was the system's principle." Seated to his left, the light music singer Bashkim Alibali clarified this quotation in an aside, concerned I might not understand the reference. "So you know, this was *një parullë*, a slogan from that period."

The lyricist interrupted. "No, I am saying it was *not* simply a slogan. It was executed, like a law, by the People itself. If I went with a group to a village, if they had one chicken, then it would be cooked for our dinner. We were given accommodations. People recognized you, and adored you. Even though the salary for an artist was minimal, the love of the People was great. If Bashkim went to Korça, everyone recognized him and would talk to him. There was a great love for artists."

A Festival of Song for the Youth, December 1972

Microphone in hand, Zija Saraçi stood, flanked by electric guitars and drum kit on one side and a women's chorus on the other, preparing to begin "Sonte u Përkasim të Gjithëve," the opening song of the Eleventh Festival of Song in late December 1972. The artistic director, Mihallaq Luarasi, waited offstage with its two presenters, the soprano Edi Luarasi, his wife and one of the most fashion-forward women in the capital, and Bujar Kapexhiu, a young humorist. The choir began, intoning untexted syllables—"ua, oh!"—and Alfons Balliçi's small pop-style guitar group entered, the drummer measuring out a pulse on his ride cymbal and the electric guitarist strumming chord changes in a twangy surf style. As the applause died down, Luarasi and Kapexhiu walked on stage to explain the newly democratized voting procedures.

The Eleventh Festival appeared to have turned policy within the planned music economy upside down. Voting, before the domain of a specialized jury at the center, was to be conducted *direkt*, tabulated from special juries of amateurs at the periphery as well as listeners in the hall. Composers eschewed completely their prior patristic models of epic-lyrical works for foreign pop models, models so audibly non-national that no amount of discursive gymnastics might have argued otherwise. Even older members of the Conservatory faculty competed to show how up-to-date their works could be, willfully suspending, for one event at least, their recent and hard-fought claims to professional distinction of the 1960s. The dean of composers, Çesk Zadeja, presented a riff-based jazzy composition with saxophones in his Festival debut, a tune that featured a solo saxophone break following the first chorus and concluded with brass backgrounds leading to an unprepared modulation at the coda. Tish Daija composed a lounge-style blues performed by Vaçe Zela.

Daija and the other middle-aged composers had perhaps less of a feel for contemporary pop styles in 1972 than their younger counterparts, who presented riff-based, heavily syncopated works indebted to American and Italian rock and pop. But each group sought to proffer listeners audibly modern credentials by foregrounding compositional elements they perceived to be emblematic of an imagined West: brass sections and sax breaks, jazzy modulations and "blue" notes. But the live performances by younger musicians, and especially non-professionals from outside the Conservatory establishment, really shook listeners. The beautiful controlled technique and smoothly articulated pronunciation exemplified by the award-wining interpretations of Vaçe Zela had characterized the field's vocal sound ideal for the Festival's first decade. But among the Eleventh Festival's singers there now emerged a more idiosyncratic, personal style. Singers had previously been subordinated to the work of the creator, or *krijues*, as its interpreter, *interpretuese*. Through the personalized grain of their voices, this Festival's singers—like rock and pop vocalists in the West—marked each piece as their own. A young radio employee, Justina Aliaj, took on Agron Xhunga's song "Në Ekranin e Televizorit" (On the Television Screen) with small whoops and little hiccups, and even Zela cast aside her *bel canto* technique for the broadcasts, playfully pushing and pulling on the notes of Daija's straightforward blues.

Taken as a whole, the songs of the Eleventh Festival widened the acceptable melodic, rhythmic, harmonic, and formal subjects of music production in general. By the end of the 1960s, composition had come to privilege a Tin Pan Alley–style model. Composers submitted piano scores, which expert arrangers, often the Radio's ensemble directors, then orchestrated. The "work" itself, however, remained the melody line, harmonic progression, and text. So even as rock music had rendered this model old-fashioned in the United States, Western Europe, and much of the eastern bloc, the notion of song-as-work had continued to undergird Tirana's music field into the 1970s. By expanding the acceptable range of who should be activated for the 1972 Festival and how they should participate, organizers marked out new sonic space for novel forms of authorship after Western practice, crafting a program that diverged radically from the aesthetic status quo.

And in promoting contemporary Western models, the Eleventh Festival's programming seemingly questioned the very status of popular music as a professionalized domain subject to the laws of art music. Some songs had been collectively authored. A two-bar pentatonic riff provided the foundation for "Mbremja e Fundit" (The Final Evening), student-composer Enver Shëngjergji's paean to university students celebrating their graduation night in Tirana, performed by Bashkim Alibali. The ensemble's director, Aleksandër Lalo, was officially credited with the piece's arrangement, but the song really came together organically, violinist Bato Gashi told me, during the rehearsal process. Similarly, Françesk Radi, a Conservatory student and guitarist, presented a Bob Dylan–style, singer-songwriter protest against the Vietnam War. "So I wanted to do a song, I had heard a song from Italy, a pacifist song against war," Radi explained to me. "A group of young people—this is the idea, or narrative—they were singing in a park or public garden, and their song was an echo against the war." If the ideal collaboration had comprised composer, lyricist, and interpreter, the non-professional model of the singer-songwriter elided these positions.[3]

In sum, the Eleventh Festival presented a break with prior Festivals, as well as a potential challenge to the organization of the music field. Absent were the epic-lyrical works, operatic in their scope, that had characterized the late 1960s. The music economy that had formerly depended on defining and monopolizing national resources had been deterritorialized overnight, with organizers opening the Eleventh Festival's borders to admit Western pop and rock aesthetics and practices previously disallowed, and musicians self-consciously nodding toward British and American artists in their performances. Within six months, a number of these singers had been denounced, exiled from Tirana, and silenced from broadcasts. One, Sherif Merdani, was imprisoned. The Party purged the architect of this liberal turn, the Radio-Television's general director, Todi Lubonja, from its ranks, interning him and members of his family along with a playwright, Fadil Paçrami, for purportedly fomenting anti-state intrigues. How had this brief period of liberalization, which culminated in the Eleventh Festival, come about? And why did it end so abruptly?

THE DEMANDS OF THE YOUTH

In the decades following the Second World War, young people occupied a key position in debates about society, education, and media in both the First and Second Worlds.[4] In the eastern bloc, young men and women comprised an especially significant group to be enlisted for state projects. Viewed as relatively free from the backward mentalities of older, rural citizens, the social category that Tirana intellectuals and officials called *Rinia*, the Youth, was understood to comprise exceptionally flexible subjects ready to be molded by schooling, media, and ideological campaigns. And during the two years preceding the Eleventh Festival of Song, young listeners were elevated as a key target for governmental concern within the cultural field. In this brief window, the status of the Youth subtly shifted. When intellectuals asked what the Youth wanted, their question was no longer a formal rhetorical gesture. Instead, officials really wanted to know: what did actual students and young workers who composed the Youth seek from their media? And how could the cultural economy be reformed in order to meet these demands?

Radio organizers had debated what listeners sought from the Festival of Song without reaching a firm conclusion in the 1960s. Preceding the Fourth Festival in 1965, for instance, organizers discussed adding factory workers to the professional jury and soliciting listeners' opinions through ballots in order to make the prizes "more correct and more democratic."[5] Organizers raised plans like this for discussion almost each year. But in practice, organizers, if they did anything, placed listeners on a jury with "a consultative character, [with] the final decision for prizes given by the Radio Office in support of the proposals of the jury."[6]

Yet because cultural events gradually came to be predicated in officialese on having "met the ever-rising demands of the listener," listeners' participation as "popular critics" potentially endowed jury results and composers' winning compositions with a measure of ideological legitimacy. But the inclusion of "popular critics" or "amateurs of light music" would also have entailed ceding authority to individuals outside the music field. This concerned professionalized musicians. In a thesis written under the direction of Çesk Zadeja in 1969, one musicologist summarized the problem. "[W]e must not transmit without any criteria the immediate demands of one category of amateurs, as we simultaneously influence them in the development of aesthetic tastes. Before the music office's employees stands a difficult duty: on the one hand, to fulfill these [listeners'] demands (which are many), and on the other, to educate the radio listeners' taste toward the widening of their musical horizons."[7]

Moreover, informal discussions among Conservatory faculty and their students on the correct role of art in society often contradicted 1960s efforts to recast the "light music amateur" as a meaningful critic. In discussions with me some four decades after the fact, composers recalled the passion with which they had debated the social role of art as students.[8] These professionals viewed musical composition as a process wherein the composer, inspired by the creativity of the People with "its own inherent values," "selects" from among these values. The "values" one might choose for a three-minute song needed to be "clear and easily communicated, because there is not enough time to develop them further," and the success of a song's development depends on "the selection and elevation of a distillate of values." Conceptualized as a distillate of values, song in this formulation depended not on listeners' appreciation, or even acceptance, of the light music song-as-artwork, but rather the composer's aesthetic intention and technical skill in working its *vlera*, or values. At the same time, composers came to understand a successful song as one appropriately fitted to the average listener's preexisting cultural level. They perceived most listeners at that time to have not yet attained the level to appreciate, for instance, an opera. And this was why in their minds light music songs held such significance. Songs provided easily comprehensible music for "simple listeners" who might have struggled with advanced symphonic fare, while at the same time preparing them to appreciate more "elevated" forms in the future.

By the end of the 1960s, Conservatory graduates had imagined into existence a generic light music amateur, an individual they conceived as the object on which their own, elevated music values was to be exercised. And paradoxically, the Cultural Revolution's politicization of amateurs had obligated young composers to think about and discuss the relationship between their own creativity and its target, the simple listener. So while listeners' judgments about light song often remained a formalized exercise, these specialists' notion of light music as an edifying instrument to be exercised on the Masses became increasingly integral to their self-definition as professionals. Did these "simple listeners" actually exist? And did epic-lyrical songs guide them through their first, tentative steps on the path to operettas, suites, chamber music, and symphonies? Such questions were becoming moot by the early 1970s. At the same time professionals were elaborating discourses on the enriching effects of popular culture, and consequently their own significance in producing this culture, ongoing demographic and technological changes had been progressively reshaping actual young people's tastes across Albania.

THE EMERGENCE OF NEW STATUS GROUPS

Among the performers at the Eleventh Festival of Song were a number of young urban men and women for whom the private consumption of Western media provided important, albeit unofficial, vehicles for imagining novel social realities. Zija Saraçi, who debuted at the Eleventh Festival, looked self-consciously to Western popular music. An amateur fan of 1950s and 1960s radio stars like Zela and Qemal Kërtusha, Saraçi, like Kërtusha himself, at first had emulated Italian crooners.[9] But unlike Kërtusha's generation, Saraçi soon found inspiration in the American star Elvis Presley, as well as the Italian Elvis, rocker Adriano Celentano. Growing up, he passed through a phase "when—in a completely instinctive way—demands toward myself emerged, [a question of in] what direction I would position myself." "I imagined myself as a film artist, or even a boxer, especially when we—the neighborhood guys at the time—played [1952 American film] *The Ring* in the street and began to box, two by two. And when I was winning, I'd say to myself: 'Perhaps? Could I become a famous boxer?'" Whether the singer might have become a boxer of course does not matter. The point is that Saraçi was one of a growing number of young Albanians who were using foreign media to imagine a potential future beyond the borders of the nation-state.[10]

As elsewhere in the eastern bloc, young people's media dreams did not necessarily prove incompatible with socialism. One woman explained this to me by relating the following story. During her summer break in 1968, *Mirela, then a Lyceum student, excavated trenches at the Rrogozhinë-Fier railroad construction site in central Albania. Sending students on *aksion*, small-scale work projects, formed part of a broader governmental project to recruit the Youth as active members in the campaign to build socialism. As Mirela retrospectively put it, she believes these policies succeeded in helping to "form a generation": "All young people in Albania shared the same experiences, survived under the same conditions," she told me. "Everyone went to *aksion*, everyone had the same schooling, the same clothes."

Though compulsory, young urban students' experiences of *aksion* tend to be recalled today with fondness. In fact, Mirela had recorded her experience in notes she was preparing for her children. "I was sixteen years old," Mirela began reading to me, "and memories of my just-completed year at the Lyceum were in my head. We slept on mattresses lined up in rows on the floor, one after the other, and the heat in our dormitories was overwhelming. Every night mosquitoes swarmed over us, biting. The wake-up call was at four in the morning. We rose, washed, ate, and collected our tools to go to the work site. There we worked next to one another, laughing, joking, and singing. I remember one very beautiful moment, singing a song by [popular Italian artist] Orietta Berti."

Mirela was one of a growing number of students relocating to Tirana and other major cities. The movement of students comprised part of a larger rural-to-urban movement that reshaped the country's demographics within a generation. Between 1945 and 1965, Albania's urban population increased from 21.3 to 33.2 percent, a figure that only incompletely describes the ongoing change.

Approximately 45 percent of the 1945 population lived in communities of fewer than 500 individuals; by 1960, this had been halved. In the meantime, the 8 percent urban minority previously inhabiting several large towns more than doubled.[11] Tirana changed dramatically, swelling from 10,000 occupants in 1923 to 150,000 by 1964, as other major prewar towns more than doubled or tripled in size. The population of neighboring Durrës, Zija Saraçi's hometown, increased an astonishing tenfold.[12]

As the Albanian population urbanized, campaigns to wire their homes for sound and image intensified. Thus not only were newly urban youth groups forming, but as Mirela's story emphasized, they were forming around media. And media content was not always domestically produced. Infrastructure previously hampered consumers' access to films and radio-television broadcasts, whether domestic or foreign, and thus their potential media dreams. In even large villages or district towns, public loudspeakers were sometimes the only outlet for radio broadcasts into the 1960s, as few families owned expensive imported receivers. When the precursor to Television-Albania, the Experimental Television Center, began broadcasting three programs per week in 1960, no households outside the uppermost Party ranks owned television sets. But this situation had changed by 1970. Over 150,000 transistor radios now received broadcasts from six national radio stations powered by fifty-two transmitters. The state television broadcast a short daily program to 35,000 homes with television sets.[13]

For officials, the modernization indexed by technological progress signaled the state's success. New patterns of media consumption in general, and the consumption of foreign media in particular, however, were this progress's unintended consequences. For young consumers, access to *moderne* technologies, and especially television viewing, began to powerfully register social distinction.[14] Control of this consumption most often was not subject to clear-cut policy, but as Mirela found on her return to the Lyceum in the fall, to the whims of certain individuals.

"During my second year, it became a fad to collect pictures," she recalled to me. "We collected them, traded them with one another, looked at them. I had about a hundred, but I might be exaggerating. I remember having Johnny Holiday, Brigitte Bardot, Rossana Podestà—she played Helen of Troy."

"These were pictures you cut out of magazines? Albanian magazines?"

"No, no! Out of foreign magazines, newspapers. But then one day the director for the school gathered us together, because someone had noticed that we were doing this. He thought it was *një shfaqje të huaj*, an alien manifestation, and we were told that if any of us were caught with the pictures, our parents would be denounced."

"Why your parents?" I prompted.

"Because we were just kids, too young to be denounced, but they had allowed us to do this. I went home that afternoon and looked at all of my pictures one more time. Then, tearing up, I ripped each one into little tiny shreds, so that you couldn't even tell what it was anymore. And as soon as I ripped the last one up, I looked at the mess, and I regretted it. 'Why did you do this!? Who is going to come check in your house, in your room? Why didn't you just hide them!? No one would have any idea if you just kept them secret, kept them for yourself!' But I was afraid, I was afraid that my father could be denounced. But I didn't think I was doing anything wrong."

Individuals like the school's director could and often did initiate small acts of repression. Hierarchical organizational structures enabled some to wield their authority in ways many perceived to be absurd, arbitrary, or cruel. But at the same time, these small acts of repression were not subject to an overarching policy about the Youth, but rather enabled by the small spaces that existed between efforts to target young people through educational institutions, media and cultural policy, campaigns for the building of socialism, and so on. Nor were all young people potential objects for repression. Different people held contrasting levels of access to the economy of distinction based on media consumption, an informal economy often allowed to run unofficially in parallel, unmolested, alongside the planned cultural economy. And this informal economy thrived because the trendsetters in 1960s Tirana were the children of Party officials. These high school and university students lived in and around the Block, a closed neighborhood housing top officials and their families; they accessed foreign media and products unavailable elsewhere through special shops or their parents' travels abroad.

"If a part of the Youth aspired to go to the East in the 1950s, the 1960s were years of closing off and isolation of Albania, but at the same time, years when the introduction of Italian television was experimented with," explained Fatos Lubonja. The son of Central Committee member Todi Lubonja, Fatos was a university student in the late 1960s. "[T]he Youth sought to leave, via imaginative means, through foreign, Italian radios, with music. . . . [W]e lived in a virtual world in our own way, in that world of music, in that Western world of song or what we saw on television."[15] Unabashedly oriented toward the West, these young consumers rarely followed domestically produced media. Lubonja claims his elite Tirana circle found light music and the Festivals of Song to be in "bad taste."

Yet tastes for Western-style clothing, foreign films, and American and Italian popular music gradually brought the children of political elites into contact with a wider social network that included musicians from the Lyceum, University, and Conservatory. The singer-songwriter Françesk Radi made friends easily with the children of officials, trading albums, singing, and even receiving a tape recorder an elite athlete had purchased while abroad. "We were marketable!" he told me, recalling the admiring high school girls and young men with whom he had socialized. "The son of someone at the Ministry of Defense would be there at the Radio-Television for Festival of Song rehearsals," the composer Aleksandër Lalo told me. "The son of [top-ranking Politburo member] Rita Marko would be there, too. These were just our friends, and our group made no distinction about what your parents did." Unsurprisingly, little political will existed to regulate the behavior of these groups, never mind repress them.[16] But as young people's tastes increasingly spread beyond these rarefied circles to students in Tirana and young urbanites throughout district capitals, officials began to perceive the need to respond.

COLONIZATION AND THE MUSIC ECONOMY

Beginning in the late 1950s, officials throughout the eastern bloc began turning their cultural economies toward the production of songs, films, literature, and art that might better compete with Western-style popular culture. This shift represented a novel technique mixing remunerative strategies with symbolic-ideological ones in order to better manage new urban populations through their own private consumption. As Gleb Tsipursky writes of the Soviet Union, officials aimed to "ensure that young people did not long for consumption goods that the [state] could not satisfy due to economic restraints, or was not willing to provide because of ideological limitations, such as rock and roll music."[17] Officials often had to carry out complicated cost-benefit calculations as they "made deliberate decisions to deny products in high demand to the population, balancing popular displeasure and economic needs with ideological requirements."[18] In the USSR and Central European countries, this led to the institutionalization of robust popular culture sectors, including standing artistic commissions charged with producing domestic works along Western lines, like the *Lipsi*, East Germany's version of the Twist, and new state-subsidized opportunities for musicians, such as conservatory-trained rock ensembles, euphemistically termed "Vocal Instrumental Ensembles."[19]

The strategic appeasement of consumer desires stemmed from a structural property of the planned economy: the centripetal force it exerted over non-state-administered domains as administrators sought to bring to the center all facets of creative life for oversight and management. In this sense, cultural administrators sought to colonize consumer desires, to bring demands peripheral to and unorganized by the state into the domestic economy of cultural production. While this occurred in most state-socialist societies beginning in the late 1950s and early 1960s, colonization techniques did not fully blossom in

Albania until 1970. Forestalled by the country's overwhelmingly rural demographics, the music field's traumatic break with the Soviet Union, and officials' short-lived experiments with Chinese-style Cultural Revolution, colonization emerged abruptly in Tirana, first through small, localized trials, and then as part of national cultural policy.

In early 1970, the Soviet-trained choreographer Skënder Selimi received a phone call. Best known for his classical and folkloric works at the Theater of Opera and Ballet, Selimi was surprised by the caller's request.

"'We want a dance, a modern dance,'" he remembered the caller telling him. "'We want one that is completely modern, but one that is also completely Albanian. For the Youth. What do you think? Is this something that could be done?'"

"'With pleasure,'" Selimi had replied, "'this is something I'd very much like to do!' You see," he continued to me, winking, "the idea was that we would counter the American 'Twist' phenomenon. To have an Albanian version, a modern dance that had an Albanian scent."

Forward-thinking cadres at the Ministry of Culture and League of Writers soon scheduled Selimi's popular couple's dance, the Alba, for test runs at district culture houses. Powerful individuals—*me pozitë*, he told me, with serious positions—had a hand in organizing this new initiative. Nevertheless, organizers immediately bumped up against institutional roadblocks. Neither the Ministry nor the League had an official choreography section to approve the dance; it was ultimately sent to the Central Committee of the Youth Organization where, Selimi assumed, someone with authorization to approve it did so. The dance caused a sensation in previews, and Selimi was asked to choreograph a second dance, the Shqipo, for the following year.

Colonization expanded quickly apace after initial successes. In 1971 and 1972, university students received permission to organize two popular song festivals. A composition student, Aleksandër Lalo, directed one, staged "in the style of contemporary foreign festivals," he told me, after Sanremo and the Eurovision Song Contest. Students wrote the majority of songs, which closely followed international pop trends, and singers fronted an amateur group featuring brass, saxophones, and electric guitars. Radio Albania itself began a new initiative, *Anketa Muzikore*, or the Music Poll. A call-in show, the Poll debuted a new song each Sunday evening, and listeners voted for their favorite at the end of each month.

But Comrade Todi Lubonja's appointment as general director of Radio-Television proved the most significant institutional change. Lubonja replaced the conservative Thanas Nano, a fixture at the state media for over a decade. Whereas Nano used agents to track his employees' outside working hours, Lubonja welcomed collaboration. And whereas Nano cast a wary eye over any deviation from pre-established broadcasting norms, Lubonja arrived with a mandate to update programming. Radio-Television Albania broadcast the Eurovision Song Contest in spring 1972, as well as the Olympic Games in Munich that summer; other broadcasts included international football matches and even American pop music.[20] Lubonja's crowning achievement, the Eleventh Festival of Song, followed soon after.

This brief period, described in retrospective accounts as *një fllad* or soft breeze, has been a major point of contention for postsocialist commentators. People I interviewed sometimes viewed it as deriving from the heroic efforts of young people to resist state repression. But evidence increasingly suggests that the impetus for change came not from below, but from the highest ranks of the Party. In April 1971, Agim Mero, the Secretary to the Central Committee of the Youth, received a summons to meet Enver Hoxha to discuss the Youth. Perceiving an opening, Mero spoke frankly. Students, Mero related to Hoxha, listened to Radio Roma instead of Radio Tirana. "Only with difficulty can [students] secure an orchestra, because they have to pay a good sum of money for this. They don't have tape recorders, nor does Radio Tirana transmit dance music for the Youth, at least not more than one or two times a week. When I spoke one time about this problem with the Radio director, Comrade Thanas Nano, he answered that the Youth don't even really like this [dance] music that we put on."[21]

"It seems to me," Hoxha had responded, "that Comrade Thanas might not be in a position to understand correctly the demands of the Youth." Mero in turn boldly questioned "the predisposition of *anyone* in [the Party] to understand the Youth."[22]

Efforts to better meet "the demands of the Youth," and especially the urban, increasingly media-savvy young people in Tirana and other cities, became part of a diffuse strategy to colonize their desires. These consumer desires had, by the early 1970s, become the de facto markers of a vigorous, non-state-administered economy of social distinction that existed next to the state-administered symbolic economy. By targeting this informal economy of distinction, officials sought to reconstitute the Youth as an object for management through the consumption of popular culture.

As a technique, colonization resulted in the widening of the domestic cultural economy's borders to encompass new resources for symbolic production.[23] This represented a major step for officials who, to a far greater extent than their counterparts elsewhere in the region, had continued to fear the contaminating effects of outside forces on domestic life. And so colonization occurred not without complications. A conservative cadre in Shkodra, for instance, ordered the brief suspension of Selimi's dance before higher-ranking officials stepped in. Most significant, the intensity of the desires of Albania's young consumers frightened some Party officials, particularly in districts outside Tirana. The reaction of these conservatives to the Eleventh Festival of Song brought this experiment in colonization to an unexpected conclusion.

Spring Ends

Changes to media policy between 1970 and 1972 seemed to portend major reforms to the symbolic economy. In part, this perception derived from the performative nature of broadcast in state-socialist countries. Control over the airwaves, paradoxically, heightened viewers' savviness in interpreting even minor changes—the inclusion of guitarists or saxophones at a performance, the wardrobe or appearance of political figures—as foreshadowing broader reform. If all symbolic representations were closely policed, then any deviations should be perceived as potentially meaningful. But deviations could also be misleading. Without structural reforms to Tirana's planned economies of symbolic production, change remained illusory. And structural change never came. Officials experimented with allowing certain listeners to have a say in symbolic production only within narrow limits. Briefly, young urbanites were allowed to impersonate consumption by dictating the nature of the enlargement of planned production's *subjects*—that is, the sounds, images, gestures, and so on that music professionals might be permitted to use in creating modern Albanian culture.

The apparent choice that enabled the music field's incorporation of non-local subjects of symbolic production created opportunities for certain musicians. The aesthetic-professional discourses during the 1960s on "correct" musical practice had been targeting these musicians as non-professionals. Only incompletely incorporated into the music field, this loose cohort neither followed nor recognized the emergent "rules" governing compositional and performance practice in the 1960s music field. As an instrumentalist, for example, Françesk Radi had studied outside the Lyceum's theory track, which fed into the Conservatory's composition program. Nor were the Eleventh Festival's most popular singers, like Zija Saraçi, Justina Aliaj, and Sherif Merdani, professionalized like state-employed performers Vaçe Zela or Ema Qazimi. It was these non-professionalized individuals who would bear the brunt of the fallout from the Eleventh Festival.

At the wistful conclusion to "Kur Vjen Pranvera" (When Spring Comes), the winning composition at the Eleventh Festival of Song, Tonin Tërshana sang, "Someone close to me said: 'Spring came'/But I did not believe it." Ostensibly a love song, addressed to a girl "with that blonde hair, that fine blouse/covering her young shoulders," the composition by violinist Pjetër Gaci and poet Fatos Arapi might have been interpreted as an oblique reference to the period's fresh breeze or *fllad*. But as it turned out, Gaci and Arapi had instead provided an ironic elegy for this short period.

Officials' concerns about the Eleventh Festival seem to have mounted quickly. The singer Bashkim Alibali had an appearance in Shkodra canceled just days after the broadcast and before any statements were announced. Radio employees received instructions to stop broadcasting Festival songs in early January, though a short newsreel they produced, but presumably never aired, does exist. The first public statement on the Festival came in mid-January 1973 during Enver Hoxha's address to the Presidium of the People's Parliament. "[D]irectors in the cultural field [claim] that the youth like these creations, that these are 'innovative' creations, appropriate to our times, to the rhythms of our development, to the dynamism of our life."[24] Yet viewers in the districts, Hoxha claimed, had been sending heartfelt letters criticizing the Festival for its foreign tendencies. The Festival thus demonstrated the dangerously wrongheaded ideas being bandied about by intellectual in the capital. "As the television [audience] is today widening," Hoxha added, "these problems take on a special acuteness, especially in the first phase of [television's] spread."[25]

Culture houses began organizing critical discussions on the "problems" that had surfaced at the Eleventh Festival. Proceedings often quickly devolved into personal attacks, as critics queued up to score easy political points against young songwriters and singers. Radi recalled to me the atmosphere as tense, ugly, as even some music colleagues criticized him. In a rare lighthearted moment, however, a few students asked to hear his song played back several times—"to better criticize it, Comrade," they ironized to the Party official directing the session. As criticisms spread, the united front of artists disintegrated. One younger member of the music field was recruited to publish several damning analyses of the event; a few, one composer suggested to me, sought to capitalize by enthusiastically allying themselves with hardline conservatives.

Criticisms peaked at the Party's IV Plenum in July 1973. Here Enver Hoxha railed against enemies who, he claimed, challenged the state from within the Party ranks, and especially from within its economy of symbolic production: media specialists, artists, musicians, and writers. "Pseudo-theoreticians," "so-called learned intellectuals," and some young people in the capital, Hoxha argued, were trying to demonstrate that "capitalism has superseded its contradictions, that bourgeois society has gotten better, that now capitalism and socialism are converging toward the same society, that there is no longer a place for class struggle, no more a place for revolutionary coups, no more a place for communist ideals, and so on."[26] These dangerous sentiments could be discerned in popular songs, literature, variety shows, and theater, all of which promoted *shfaqje të huaj*, alien manifestations. Dangerous elements, Hoxha claimed, spearheaded these insidious efforts from within the ranks of the Party itself. Politburo members Fadil

Paçrami, a playwright and the Minister of Culture, and Todi Lubonja, general director of the Radio-Television, were called to make self-criticism, expelled from the Party, and subsequently sentenced to prison.

Smaller figures were also formally excised from the symbolic economy, relieved of their duties at its center and reassigned to its peripheries. Zhani Ciko, the Theater of Opera and Ballet's music director, a virtuoso violinist and kind of wunderkind in the music field, was reassigned to Patos, a small city in the district of Fier, as its music teacher. Choreographer Skënder Selimi was reassigned to a mountain district town not for the Alba, but for choreographing bourgeois works by composers like Strauss. Dritëro Agolli, a poet and journalist, replaced Dhimitër Shutëriqi as head of the League of Writers and Artists; young composer Feim Ibrahimi, trained by Tish Daija, assumed the post of music secretary. Over the next two years, successive purges enveloped the economic and military fields.

No major composers received punishments for their participation in the Eleventh Festival. Peculiarly, only singers suffered, despite simply interpreting, rather than creating, approving, or staging the performances in question. Singer Justina Aliaj was fired from the Radio-Television and banned from future performances. Radi, who had graduated from the Conservatory that spring, received an assignment to a remote post in the village of Fushë-Arrëz. Villagers were starstruck by their new music teacher. But some viewed his arrival as an opportunity to garner information for the secret police. Radi remained on constant alert against "provocations": "Someone would say, 'Hey, what did you think about the Sanremo Festival? About the latest Eurovision song—beautiful, right?'" Sherif Merdani received the stiffest punishment: a prison term, followed by internment. In effect, officials directed the ritual cleansing of the music economy, purifying its center in Tirana through the symbolic removal of alien elements. This act reasserted the Party's prerogative over the cultural field. But crucially, the purge did not compromise the domestic music economy's capacity for production.[27] New singers could easily be found, but composers needed specialized training. These professionals represented a substantial investment in symbolic-ideological strategies for governing society. As cultural politics reset after the failed experiment in colonization, returning broadcast policy from "answering the demands of the Youth" back toward readdressing the cultural level of the People, officials viewed composers as essential.

Writers, Artists, and the Party

In that the purview of intellectuals encompasses what shape society should take, their work necessarily has to do with the subjectivity-forming means by which this future shape might be achieved. Artist-intellectuals consequently occupied a fundamentally equivocal position vis-à-vis the Party officials who depended for their legitimacy, at least in part, on symbols. Absolutely essential, intellectuals were at the same time inherently dangerous.[28] Fear of their symbolic power, spurred by the response of would-be consumers to this work, pushed conservative Party members to retake the political field by reasserting intellectuals' subordinate position në emër të Partisë, in the name of the Party. Yet the proximate fallout from the Eleventh Festival did not create this shift, but rather intensified preexisting schisms. It enabled conservative officials in the districts to attack urban ones at the center, raising the former group's profile at the national level.[29] This process ultimately portended nothing less than the reorganization of relations among the Party, intellectuals, and the population, as officials renegotiated which social groups were to be addressed by cultural policy over the course of 1973 and 1974.

Renegotiations culminated in a policy statement titled "Artists and Writers in Aid of the Party," presented by Enver Hoxha to the Secretariat of the Central Committee on December 20, 1974. In his address, Hoxha expanded on the "lessons" arising from the previous year's IV Plenum, positioning Albania at an ideological crossroads.

"During the entire course of history the kingdom of capital, of religion, of the aristocracy, and of the bourgeoisie has clashed with the progressive forces, with progress itself, and has lost many limbs in these wars," Hoxha said. "Now [capitalism] has reached the stage of its final decay. . . . [Y]et we must not think that in the face of the defeats it is suffering, world capitalism has laid down its arms. In its objectives, it relies precisely on its barbarous attacks and on predatory imperialist wars against the liberation of the peoples from its yoke, but it also counts on that world outlook and on those remnants that burden the consciousness of men and have kept them as its slaves for centuries."[30]

"Writers and artists have an exceptionally great role," he continued, "our People and the Party need them." By creating "Art in the Service of the People," intellectuals must work to replace "those remnants that burden the consciousness of men" with healthy, enlightening, politically correct works. In this way, Hoxha's statement formally reinstated the previous decade's contradictory, overlapping relations of symbolic production: the People over an intelligentsia beholden to develop the resources of the former; the Party overseeing the intellectuals "in the name of the People"; and the Intellectual as the People's voice. Yet instead of dismissing, resisting, or rejecting the notion that Art should in some way "serve" the People, over the next decade individual artists came to embrace it. I examine how this came to be in the final sections of this chapter. But it would misrepresent the years between 1974 and the mid-1980s to ignore the significant role that baldly coercive strategies also played during this period.

In the following pages, I take a brief detour to examine exceptional cases of repression, state violence carried out against musicians for the sake of security.

SECURITY AND CULTURE

From the mid-1970s, officials redoubled efforts to craft a mixture of coercive and symbolic-ideological techniques to govern domestic consumption. Television sets produced by the domestic electronics factory in Durrës, opened in 1974, blocked transmissions from neighboring Yugoslavia or Italy. This and other social policies provided Western journalists compelling evidence to characterize a dystopian anti-democracy: "The long-haired or full-bearded among [foreign visitors]," one anecdote informed the incredulous Western reader, "are forced to shed their displays of bourgeois decadence at the airport barbershop."[31]

In the name of a new political keyword, *vigjilencë*, the 1976 constitution effectively criminalized those forms of social organization that, like the taste groups described in the preceding sections, existed outside the administrative purview of the state. "The creation of organizations of a fascist, anti-democratic, religious, or anti-socialist nature," its infamous Article 55 stated, "is prohibited."[32] In practice, authorities invoked Article 55's language on "agitation and propaganda" to effectively criminalize all non-state-administered forms of assembly. The 1976 constitution further decreed a national policy of self-reliance in Albania's "efforts to complete the construction of socialism": no foreign troops could be stationed on Albanian soil, nor could the people's representatives in government make "concessions to, accept any credits from, or even create foreign or joint financial or economic institutions with capitalist, bourgeois, or revisionist monopolies or states."[33] Rejecting all outside influence, Hoxha adopted an attenuated form of protectionism, breaking relations even with China in 1978. The sum result of these changes hardened all borders, whether physical or symbolic, in the name of security.

Protectionism elevated the role of the domestic intelligence agency, *Drejtoria e Sigurimi të Shtetit*, the Directorate of State Security, hereafter "Sigurimi."[34] Established in 1943, the Sigurimi's ranks exponentially expanded in the 1970s, along with Albania's network of prisons and internment camps that were soon holding increasing numbers of citizens deemed *armiq të popullit*, enemies of the People. To intellectuals and non-intellectuals alike, repression could seem at times to be pervasive, the warp to the weft of the fabric making up everyday life. Anyone could potentially be informing for the Sigurimi. High estimates claim one in three Albanians collaborated with the Sigurimi in some way during the 1970s and 1980s; I often heard astounding stories from citizens of the capital about the reach of agents. "I came into the apartment, and my mother looked nervous," one woman told me, relating her recollection of the day in April 1985 when Hoxha died. "She made me go into the bathroom to wet my eyes. 'Why!?' I said, 'I'm not sad!' But she was right. A neighbor came around to check, to make sure we were all appropriately upset."

In the mid-1970s, the Sigurimi developed its Section of Institutes of Higher Education, charged with "the protection of the intelligentsia, the youth, and cultural-educational institutions and objects."[35] Today many people believe the Department of the Interior to have kept files, *dosje*, on all citizens. But during the late 1970s and early 1980s, a period seen by intellectuals as one of particularly intense surveillance, the Sigurimi listed 260 "suspects" in Tirana's cultural field. Concerned not with "liberals," agents pursued "the old [guard] intellectuals who were used in the initial postwar years, especially in the raising of institutes and other upper schools, but who carried a 'danger' for the 'spoiling' of the intelligentsia with their thoughts." Only after 1982 were a number of formal investigations opened on major cultural institutions in Tirana, including the Radio-Television.[36]

By the early 1980s, over 150 intellectuals, using code names like Romeo, the Pen, the Researcher, Lahuta (a one-stringed folk instrument), or the Painter, were themselves surreptitiously working as active informants in the cultural field. But my sense from talking to musicians is that agents did not widely suppress their colleagues' rights as much as foster an atmosphere of suspicion. Some informed for opportunistic reasons. Most probably informed because they themselves had a "black mark" on their past, perhaps a family member in prison for "agitation and propaganda," which had provided a pretense for their recruitment by Sigurimi agents. As a coercive state practice, security depended on the perception that the artist was always potentially subject to its exercise. Yet not everyone experienced this atmosphere in quite the same way. "Fear," as Katherine Verdery suggests for the region in general, became "integrated into state-making variably across time and space."[37]

But intellectuals' own organizations did not initiate repression. These institutions served as vehicles for formalized censure after the fact of accusation. "[Artists] were not denounced by the League [of Artists and Writers]," Dritëro Agolli, the general secretary appointed in 1973, has stated in interviews.[38] "The League itself was even criticized by the Central Committee, that it was not vigilant. These things were fought out first of all in other *instanca*, and only then did [officials] notify the League that 'you don't publish so-and-so.'" Intellectuals within the state's instruments of cultural production, whether at publishing houses, the Radio-Television's Editorial Office, the Kino Studio, or performing ensembles, then enforced exclusion by banning the dissemination of materials made by "enemy elements" or refusing to "activate" individuals for state-sponsored events. But because of their positions and their inside knowledge of shifts in the political winds, these same individuals often served as bridges to "rehabilitate" individuals. This, for instance, was how Alfons Balliçi, discussed in the opening to this chapter, recovered the "right to creativity" with the help of conductor Ferdinand Deda. Deda, a gregarious, savvy, and compassionate man with many connections in Tirana, seems to have been especially well placed to help musicians with questionable political credentials regain access to the resources of the planned economy.

Agolli has also explained the relationship between state institutions, denunciation, and creative works at some length in postsocialist interviews. "The League," he has said, "was truly an instrument under the command of the Party, but it was not the one who decided. When we received news that someone was arrested, it came to us completely unexpectedly [...]. Many [arrests] were made for agitation and propaganda. Persons that spoke with one another, an agent heard and said, 'this is what they said to me.' Even when you were at a table with a writer, there was no assurance that he was a writer, not a spy. [...] Afterward, after the spying, it was seen if this one had sent a book for publication. 'Let's take a look at it, to see if he perhaps has these thoughts in a book, too?' they told us. This other thing was [then] added [to the original charges]. This is how it was, because there was no way to [trump up charges] in a book to start with, so first [one is identified] by [spoken] words, [and only] later with the written ones."[39]

THE BANALITY OF REPRESSION

A full ethnographic and archival rendering of the negative effects of state power over artists in Albania remains to be written. But though I lack the knowledge and space to do that here, I may still indicate something of my impressions about how repression, in most cases, seems to have been typified less by its calculatedness than its ugly triviality, its foul incoherence. The most prominent of a handful of examples of repression in the music field, the arrest, abuse, and imprisonment of singer Alida Hisku, exemplifies the inherent banality of state violence over certain artists.

Hisku first came to national prominence at the Thirteenth Festival of Song in 1974 with her interpretation of composer Enver Shëngjergji's "Vajzat e Fshatit Tim" (The Girls of My Village). An eighteen-year-old who had participated in regional festivals before debuting at the previous year's Festival, Hisku had been added by the Festival commission as an afterthought. Her simple, straightforward performance of Shëngjergji's folk-inspired piece, however, charmed listeners and received first prize. The daughter of a politically correct and connected family, Hisku continued to perform while pursuing a political career. For university, she received a coveted spot in Tirana's Party School, directed by headmistress Fiqirete Shehu, the wife of Albania's second-in-command, Mehmet Shehu.

"At that time," Hisku recalls, "the most popular artists, those who stood out, they invited them to the Block to do the music for birthdays or other parties, according to the tastes of leaders. I sometimes went. There I met Fiqirete Shehu and her family. I tried to use contacts with her to find a good job according to my preferences. Even though I liked music, and though I had also begun studies for music, I was not only a singer, but also was looking for an [upper-level] position in the cultural field. Well, by this time nobody could be named to these kinds of positions without a Party card and advanced political schooling."[40]

The political fortunes of the Shehu family, however, soon collapsed. In December 1981 Mehmet Shehu committed suicide after being charged with espionage; Hoxha later spectacularly claimed Shehu had been a quadruple agent reporting to Yugoslav, American, and Soviet secret services. Assigned to a southern village following her graduation from the Party School, Hisku was arrested by Sigurimi agents in June 1983 and charged with agitation and propaganda after a roommate submitted her diary to the local Sigurimi office. Rumors spread throughout Tirana: she had rejected a powerful suitor, had interpreted foreign songs, even had worked for the "enemy Shehu group" formally denounced the previous year. Employees at the Radio-Television sound archives received an order to pull Hisku's recordings from broadcast rotation. In a country that pressed no recordings for mass domestic consumption, this effectively erased the "enemy" artist's voice. At trial, Hisku was found guilty of crimes against the state and consigned to psychiatric hospitals. She emigrated in the early 1990s.

A district security officer whom the young woman had previously spurned arranged her arrest. The diary, which provided evidence sufficient for her initial detainment under his guard, was a mere pretense not mentioned in trial proceedings.[41] Such agents "surfaced openly with the most varied tricks," Hisku has said. "Initially with an invitation for coffee, to 'clear up' some delicate circumstances, then directly with their bastardly offers. I remember especially well their presence during the television festivals [that is, the Festivals of Song]. At that time, they were not only the most important cultural events, but also served as a beauty pageant"—a dating service for powerful or sadistic men.[42]

Creativity and Self-Expression

At Festivals of Song in particular, and the Radio-Television more generally, musicians encountered narrowed creative horizons after 1974. Following Lubonja's dismissal, Hoxha reappointed Thanas Nano, the conservative who, just sixteen months earlier, had "failed to correctly understand the demands of the Youth."

Among employees there emerged a humorous couplet, "spoken in hushed tones": *Iku Todi Italia/Erdh Thanas çiftelia.*[43] "Todi Italy left/Here comes Çifteli Thanas." To the urbane, the *çifteli,* a two-stringed folk instrument that accompanies northern Albanian men's epic-historical songs, represented conservatism and backwardness. In audible terms, songs increasingly featured musical themes borrowed or adapted from folklore. *Kontrolli punëtor*, workers' brigades composed of district workers and farmers and first developed in the 1960s, also proliferated at the Radio-Television to oversee content. And most significant, the commissions that organized high-profile events like the Festival of Song began including high-ranking Party officials.

According to one popular narrative, Tirana's post-1973 music field came to be dominated by Party hacks, toady pseudo-musicians who exercised their powers of censorship according to personal whims cut with an equal measure of cultural illiteracy. Yet it would be incorrect to view even renewed oversight to have been fundamentally debilitating or silencing. Repression alone, the naked and direct exercise of the state coercive apparatus on individuals, can little account for the substance of the creative labor of politically correct music-making at the Festivals of Song between 1974 and the mid-1980s. This work can be understood only by closely listening in to the musical decisions composers made as they navigated artistic commissions, broadcast policy, and—in my analysis, most crucially—their own internalized orientations toward the field.

During the socialist period, oversight remained channeled primarily through artistic commissions and editorial offices staffed by respected members of the cultural field. "According to the regulations of artistic creativity's preliminary control," the intellectual historian Jakup Mato has written, "every important work had to be approved by . . . specialists and employees of state and party apparatuses involved with the administration of art."[44] Artistic commissions, or *komisionë artistike*, provided a potential means to censor works, to enforce broadcast policy by rejecting works either penned by undesirables or expressing undesirable content. But in practice, commissions habitually functioned as a peer-review system that enforced field-specific aesthetic codes.[45] "The control and administration of creativity had two consequences," summarizes Mato. "Some authors of works and well-known artists have been clear that creativity generally profited in its creative values from the discussions in artistic councils and commissions, where specialists primarily participated. . . . In this case, the artists and participants comprising the artistic councils and commissions played the role of a qualified public. Since the work was still in process, this enabled some additions, changes, and shortening of pieces or details. Other times, however, interruptions of various commissions have seriously influenced some works, threatening their true artistic values."

These consequences influenced musicians, writers, and other kinds of artists unevenly. At Festivals of Song, an artistic commission of composers and bandleaders reviewed compositions, while another commission of writers reviewed texts.[46] The composers first read through piano-scores submitted for consideration, keeping or disqualifying submissions based on musical criteria as well as the submitting composer's reputation. Zhuljana Jorganxhiu, a poet and the successor to Sadik Bejko, then edited accepted songs' texts, and found, commissioned, or composed new lyrics for the pieces composers submitted without one. An editor with a keen sense for ideologically correct language, Jorganxhiu inserted lines or words deemed necessary to "fix" a lyric in political terms. Finally, the editorial office commissioned orchestrations and advised a singers' commission in the distribution of pieces to vocalists. Following four weeks of rehearsals, Festival organizers staged a dress rehearsal for the *komision i përgjithshëm*, the general commission that included top composers, writers, and several Party officials, usually Tirana's Executive Committee Party Secretary and the Minister of Education and Culture. This final commission *bënte vërejtje*, made observations, and in the hours before the Festival's live broadcast, perhaps requested one or two song lyrics be revised.

Of the composers I interviewed, several complained about politically motivated changes to lyrics that hampered their finished works. But none recalled to me any concrete examples of musical changes requested by commissions. More surprisingly for me, nor did composers claim that they exercised self-censorship in creating light music songs for competition. In part, the definition of a professional work itself militated against certain kinds of problems. Because a professional composition had by the 1970s come to be defined as one produced in conscientious collaboration with a poet-lyricist, to be performed on stage by a state-employed interpreter, and arranged in close collaboration with the musician-bureaucrats at the Radio-Television offices, little opportunity existed for composers to encounter political problems. The only possible window for problems occurred when the composer first submitted a lead sheet to the organizational committee during the summer preceding the December Festival. At that point, the work was evaluated by peers who, in the unlikely event that a political problem might have arisen, would probably have quietly taken the composer aside, months before any performance in front of officials on the general commission.

Instead, notions of correct or professional values largely structured creativity from within the music field itself. To explore this phenomenon, I will examine three distinct strata, the privileged, elite, and district-employed composers, that came to comprise the music field from the 1970s. These categories roughly derive from how my consultants discussed themselves and their socialist-era peers. They also have to do with my understanding of how the field came to work—or more accurately, with how people worked in their day-to-day lives as members of the music field. No doubt composers exercised a measure of restraint at times, especially when writing for popular genres. Yet censorship by the state apparatus figured to a far lesser extent than individuals' cultivation of techniques for artistic self-discipline, the self-expression of *individualiteti*. A set of personal-aesthetic obligations, artistic individuality conditioned any one individual's role within Tirana's state-socialist mode of cultural production, both capacitating the composer and situating him or her within a professional-aesthetic hierarchy.

The Privileged

Të privilegjuar, or "the privileged," comprised a small group of powerful men who held top titles such as Artist of the People and occupied directing positions within the symbolic economy. In material terms, their privileges sometimes included international travel, easier access to goods, comfortable homes. From the 1980s, these top musicians and writers lived in a series of large modern apartments in the center of Tirana, right behind and north of the Theater of Opera and Ballet, the most spacious of which, my consultants claimed, supposedly had chandeliers. In economic terms, these musicians had the privilege of nearly open access to the planned economy's resources. Privileged composers were usually oriented not to light music songs, but to large-scale concert works, for which they needed the capital's large and well-trained performing ensembles. In part, this was due to the peculiarly circular logic of prestige. To gain titles and privileges, a composer needed to have created a reputation in the field of concert music. Once gained, titles and privileges in turn obligated that composer to create major concert music pieces for high-profile events or anniversaries. Çesk Zadeja, the dean of composers, would be commissioned to compose a choral work on the Nth Anniversary of an Important Party Event. Busy with more "serious" projects and oriented toward the concert hall, Zadeja rarely composed for the Festival of Song.

But the Festival of Song's profile as the most significant event in popular music necessitated the full symbolic participation of the music field. Participation signaled the field's unified support for the state's initiatives, but little else for privileged composers, who could gain no further prestige from the event. To men who enjoyed access to more prestigious national events and state resources, the Festival came to be perceived as a burden. The bigger burden, however, rested on Radio-Television employees, who often had to badger the privileged composers to submit compositions. These works often arrived late, usually without texts, which editor Zhuljana Jorganxhiu then generated, without exception, on political themes. In the 1980s, privileged ones began submitting *këngë përshëndetje*, short greeting songs, performed outside of competition and at the request of the Festival organizing committee.

But some privileged composers relished the challenge of polishing *një xheva-hir*, a small gem, constructing elaborate, "beautiful" songs based on the development, *zhvillim*, of folk motives. These tightly crafted works could be complex artistic-political statements integrating the cultural field's highest professional-aesthetic demands. Such works usually followed careful collaboration with top poets and elite vocalists. With his 1981 composition "Krenari e Brezave" (The Pride of Generations), Artist of the People (1989) Feim Ibrahimi presented an artfully conceived, metaphorical paean to the Party and Enver Hoxha. The lyric, by leading poet Gjokë Beci, revolved around the figure of a soaring eagle, and the composer developed a short folk-inspired motive in an irregular dance meter throughout the piece. First set in the contrapuntal introduction, this figure resurfaced in the orchestral accompaniment to the verse and in the conclusion of the vocal line in the refrain, just as a figure in a concert work might be developed over the course of the composition.

Ibrahimi often worked with Beci, whose "elevated" texts overflowed with poetic devices, and especially metaphors: "over the white waters goes the eagle," "our people [like children] are brought up each day by the Party," "a pure and beautiful life we construct [that is, as one would a building or railroad]," "we make the country bloom," "the Party speaks." These poetic figures served primarily to personify the Party and Enver Hoxha, as well as to describe the actions of the People, a collective "we" voiced in this work by elite vocalist Ema Qazimi. The balanced formal structure of Beci's lyric followed a literary style then in vogue (see Table 3.1). Each couplet shares the same elegant internal structure, as line 1 begins with the verb "they come," and the next verb comes at the end of line 2, "they caress," similar to the switch that occurs in lines 3 and 4—the symmetrical pair *we see/the present*, with *we meet/the future*. Beci also incorporated literary words, such as *ledhatoj* and *i/e ndritur*, and artistically alternated the narrative between different points of view. In lines 1–2, the speaker describes action in the third person, switching in lines 3–4 to the first-person plural to symbolically draw the listener into the narrative leading up to the refrain. Here another, more detached, voice emerges, addressing to the listener a quick succession of stylized statements about the Party. "When the Party speaks, hearts

Table 3.1 **A "little gem"**

1	Ja <u>vijnë</u> nga puna *të* qeshur në vatrat,	<u>They come</u> from their work *laughing* people to hearths,
2	*Foshnjat* me gaz <u>ledhatojnë</u>.	Their *infants* with joy <u>they caress</u>.
3	Ne <u>shikojmë</u> *të sotmen' ndritur*,	<u>We see</u> the *enlightened present*,
4	*T'ardhmen e bukur* <u>takojmë</u>.	The *beautiful future* <u>we grasp</u>.

take new strength/Its light is the light of all years," Qazimi sang. "All Albania weaves unending song/For you are the pride of generations."

The Elites

Immediately below privileged composers existed a distinct stratum of elite composers, or *elita*. To my consultants, privileged ones referred to a very small cohort of top artists, and elites, a much more diffuse group that individuals could ascend into over the course of their careers. Employed at the Conservatory or activated for sought-after work at high-profile institutions like the KinoStudio, the Radio-Television, or the State Estrada, these savvy individuals had a strong practical sense for navigating the cultural field and hands-on experience at its center. Oriented toward both concert music as well as "elevated" songs on grand themes, elite composers held creative-professional credentials and connections enabling them to realistically aspire to climbing the career ladder to directing positions in Tirana. Though an elite might compose a song on a political topic in order to, as one composer told me, "score points," many accrued prestige not by strategizing, but simply by expressing an individuality oriented toward the "grand" or "epic" political-social themes most often rewarded with Festival prizes and recognition. By the 1970s and 1980s, a cohort of elite love song specialists, including Agim Krajka, Aleksandër Lalo, and, later, Vladimir Kotani, figured in this stratum as necessary experts on rhythmic or youth songs, *këngë ritmike* or *rinore*, treating intimate or beautiful subjects.

To elites oriented primarily to song and film music, the Festival of Song represented their year's premier event. These composers competed annually, and some began work on their submissions in the weeks following the previous Festival's conclusion. Rarely were song specialists censored. The Radio-Television, as one former employee explained to me, had a "need" for songs with lighter subject matter as a counterweight to "grander" themes, and these composers knew which compositions would be well-received by artistic commissions as audibly national expressions. The song specialist collaborated with a small group of carefully selected lyricists and vocalists with whom he might work as a team over the course of several Festivals. Moreover, as pedagogues, *estrada* employees, or bandleaders in Tirana, song specialists often had a remarkable sense for finding and grooming unknown vocalists on the cusp of stardom, either in *estrada* groups or at the Lyceum.

Elites oriented toward concert music genres also submitted compositions to the Festival, for reasons ranging from an artistic-ethical sense of duty to move the listener through elevated pieces, to strategic calculation to raise one's personal profile through participation among other elites and privileged ones at the national level. Like song specialists, these elites developed folkloric resource material as part of what they viewed as their professional-artistic duties. And different levels of "development" indicated varying levels of professional distinction. In my interviews, this group of composers spoke most explicitly and at length, usually without my prompting, about professionalism, values, or the "laws" of composition.

"The first method is to take a motive and to put it into the song," composer Gazmend Mullahi explained. "What I mean is, to take a phrase or a melodic figure from a folk song that already exists and to use that as the basis for the song. I did not use this method as much as the next one. The second one is to utilize the intervals that are most characteristic of Albanian music, to insert these as the foundational elements of your song, as the melodic material that you utilize for the song. We might say that the first way, the citation of a piece, is a method that is less professional, that is even primitive. The second demonstrates a more serious professional manner. This is the basis of a professional creativity, how a professional creates music. So that we are clear: what I am talking about are the cells of folk music, its basic parts, which serve as the structural framework for folk music. Utilizing these 'cells,' as we might call them, such as intervals or modal material, the professional creates all genres of music."

In this manner, Mullahi went on to explain, one might "bring something new" by creating works that "sound original," or "do not sound like anything else." The paradox, of course, is that a composer could only "bring something new" in the correct, professional way, by utilizing the very same sonic material, the raw subjects of domestic music production, as everyone else. Obsessed by notions of professionalism, this segment of the elite stratum most closely policed Tirana's means of cultural production through critical discourse to ensure its subjects remained rooted në taban, literally in national soil, and unpolluted by either nonprofessional or alien elements from outside the planned economy's borders.

"Gonxhe në Pemën e Lirisë" (Buds on the Tree of Freedom), presented by Limos Dizdari with a text by Robert Shvarc, and performed by Vaçe Zela and the leading opera singer Gaqo Çako, received first prize at the Sixteenth Festival of Song in 1977. Like Dizdari's other grand works, "Gonxhe" featured several dynamic and tempo changes, and a late romantic, lyrical aesthetic. Shvarc's historical text depicted Tirana's prewar girls' school, which produced many of the early communist movement's female members, and later provided Party leaders with politically suitable wives. Historical pieces attracted Dizdari, and when we spoke he was particularly proud of how the vocal line of "Gonxhe" paralleled its epic-lyrical subject matter. The first half of final stanza of "Gonxhe" exemplifies the corpus of common artistic-political keywords, italicized here: "They are of your age, our girls, o star and light! / Today raised in freedom, they construct life itself—they create it and protect it with love."

As a topic for a light song, Nexhmije Hoxha's school enjoyed, as Dizdari put it to me, "a kind of dualism." That is, the theme had political overtones, but also (to him) apolitical, "patriotic" ones. But Dizdari denied having made any explicit *kallkullime*, or calculations, in selecting this topic.[47] He instead felt that his own personal musical style lent itself to these heroic historical themes. If this meant he created pieces with political resonances that the Radio-Television not only programmed, but also rewarded with prizes, Dizdari claimed, this stemmed from a variety of fortuitous factors.

Directors

Rarely titled, though usually respected by their peers as culture house directors in major towns, district music specialists comprised the field's largest stratum overall but presented the smallest percentage of Festival songs. In their daily work, district composers oversaw, prepared, and rehearsed folkloric ensembles, organized local or regional festivals and events, and more generally convened district cultural activities. For these directors, the Festival of Song provided an opportunity to participate in musical life at the national level. Directors thus sought to demonstrate the professional credentials they had earned in study with elites and privileged ones at the Conservatory, but which rarely figured in to their routine district work. But at the same time, directors often told me they lacked an internal orientation toward grand, heroic, and epic themes or complex concert music. Again, a kind of tautological reasoning overdetermined this. Were a director to have demonstrated an orientation toward grander works during her Conservatory training, she might have been assigned to a more prestigious position on graduation in the first place.

But while directors shared with elite creators the field-specific discourses on individuality and motivic development described above, their peripheral positions outside the capital handicapped aspirations to leading roles at the economy's center. Yet Conservatory training ensured district composers were not only able to compose large-scale works in addition to the smaller ones deemed requisite for district areas, but also often aspired to this elevated form of creativity. Many directors certainly felt themselves genuinely oriented toward more intimate genres, embraced their district role, and prided themselves in being able to "do it all." But others felt stifled.

"You have to realize," one director told me, "the conditions were extremely difficult. Each composer was expected to create works in many different spheres. But does it make any sense that I, as a composer, would also be expected to be in charge of all the folk costumes? To collect them, figure out which ones to use, hand them out to people? I was not trained to be a traditional costume researcher!"

For directors who chafed at their perceived lack of opportunity, the Festival provided a means to demonstrate how they might, given the opportunity, have deserved a higher position in the field. Many district musicians submitted texted compositions annually, and while in a given year their submissions might not be selected, directors employed at the largest urban centers usually made the final cut. And through compositions with wide, sweeping melodies, the district composer demonstrated a correct sense for "the beautiful" and "the national." As a working guitarist in Elbasan and, later, as its Culture House director, Alfons Balliçi had gained a mastery of local urban repertories. On his return to national broadcasts from his ban, he began presenting beautiful, lyrical pieces drawing on regional folklore. In his 1977 composition "O Moj Shamishpalosura" (O My Scarf-wearing Girl), for instance, Balliçi set a soaring melody in what he termed an "Elbasanese melodic mode," an urban scale similar to the Turkish mode *nihavend*. Balliçi always arranged his own pieces, and viewed himself as both a creator and expert craftsman. The orchestration for "O Moj" to me sounded very much like an elevated version of an arranged urban folk song from Central Albania, especially in its use of a single violin to double the vocal line during the verse, and woodwinds (oboe during the introduction, and flute doubling the vocal line at several points). The orchestration also called for a women's choir to thicken the texture on long held notes behind vocalist Afërdita Zonja's lyric refrain. Balliçi often worked with Zonja, an excellent singer who, like the composer, existed at the economy's periphery in part because of her position outside the capital, in the city of Korça.

Festival juries never rewarded district composers with top prizes. Steeped in local folk styles, district musicians often drew on resources experts at the center deemed regional or non-national, such as Balliçi's "Elbasanese mode." And less ambitious composers, or ones more deeply invested in the arrangement of folk materials, sometimes based their songs too closely on folk motives, even "citing" a preexisting melody. When Sabrie Nushi graduated from the Conservatory in 1975, she was assigned to her hometown of Pukë in northern Albania. There Nushi became the region's first female virtuoso on *çifteli*, the two-stringed folk instrument. As a researcher, ensemble director, and folk music arranger, Nushi rarely submitted songs to the Festival of Song. In 1979, however, she received a telephone call from the Radio-Television concerning a composition, "Seç Më Fton në Stan" (He Invites Me to the Pasture), that she had submitted for a lower-profile program several months before. "They told me, 'This is a very beautiful song, but let's get rid of the text'—which had been done by a district writer from Puka—'and put in the text of a poet, a writer.' The theme was the same, but they used a text from the well-known poet Zulaha Puci. The song even made it to the final night, but all this really surprised me!"

In "Seç Më Fton," Nushi had cited a local folk song, quoting the melody for the verse and creating a countermelody based on that quotation for the refrain. Nushi demurred when I asked why she thought she had been invited. As a consummate professional, there is no reason why she should not have taken part, though she believed that the need to include a woman composer might have influenced the invitation. Few women composed, though Nushi stressed to me that she did not feel that she had been discouraged from the Conservatory's composition track. Yet the Festival provided Nushi a means to exercise what she self-effacingly called her pretensions to creativity. "The Festival was the culmination, most important activity of the year. I mean, it was a dream for me, and when it was achieved, I felt: 'Wow, I was evaluated among the greatest composers, like Avni Mula, like Çesk Zadeja,'" she said. "I had brought a song that was chosen, that had touched an emotion."

A BODY OF COMPOSERS

The shared understandings composers held about aesthetic practice had, by the 1980s, become remarkably coherent. In part, this coherence was the product of the ascendancy of a particular group of men during the 1960s and their subsequent monopolization of discourse about the correctly professional way to create new works. But the homogenization of aesthetic practice also derived from the field's peculiar path to institutionalization. Beginning in the 1950s, composers elsewhere in the eastern bloc inhabited an increasingly variegated aesthetic landscape. Composers traveled within Eastern Europe and sometimes to the West; some state-socialist governments even, as in Poland's case, funded international centers that created official avenues for dialogue between domestic artists and their Western counterparts. In this sense, Tirana's planned music economy represents an outlier, the audible expression of the state-socialist administered society in its purest attenuated form.

By refusing all attempts to liberalize the domestic symbolic economy after 1974, Albanian politics fostered the creation of remarkably unified social bodies within the cultural field. I use the metaphor of the body advisedly, as my consultants invoked this very image. Willfully adapting metaphors, one composer began describing for me a creative lineage, from grandfathers, to fathers, to sons, as inhabiting *një trup*, one body.

"Composers like Zoraqi, Zadeja, even Ibrahimi, who did not study abroad—these men trained in the 1950s and early 1960s were the head. Further down," he continued, gesturing towards his chest, "you have myself, Aleksander Peçi, Limos Dizdari, Kujtim Laro—we were the students, the children of those composers that studied in Moscow. After that, of course, come others, like 1980s-trained Ardit Gjebrea, or Shpetim Saraçi. These are the three generations, the three sets of children that have created light music over the past forty or so years."

Individualiteti, an ideology of self-expression, articulated the limbs, torso, and head of this patrilineal body, fleshing out and defining membership in the compositional field of production—to mix metaphors after the fashion of my consultants. In a workaday sense, commentators used the term *individuality* to describe an author's sound or style. You can praise a song for the "simplicity of its [folk-derived melodic] figure and its compact development, which give a special color so characteristic of the author's individuality." This exemplary phrasing comes from conductor Ermir Krantja's review of the composition "Fest' Ka Sot Shqipëri" (Today Albania Celebrates), presented by composer Agim Prodani and Zhuljana Jorganxhiu at the Eighteenth Festival of Song in 1979.[48] Conscientious analysts might uncover individuality "in the notes"—*me nota*—of a work. Criticizing my project, the composer above, for instance, suggested a more mature approach would have been to analyze the "three best songs" of top composers in order to uncover the creative profile of each.

"This is a project," he exclaimed, "that does not take twelve months, but forty!—and what do you have left, four, five months?"

"Eight months."

"Not enough time, not enough! To really *know* these songs—how they were created."

To composers, individuality represented the normal self-expression of an interiorized, artistic core. To express your individuality is to compose in a way that resulted in creativity that, as Balliçi related to me in this chapter's introduction, *të ngjan*, literally looks like you. This notion held for popular song and concert works alike. The ideology of expression naturalized a commonsense link between an artistic selfhood and its products, between subjectivity and creative practice. But it also normalized the professional link between the composer and the music field, between the individual and the social body of professionals. To express an individuality meant to be a professional creator; to be a creator entailed membership in the music field. This metaphor, of course, presents obvious problems. It does not account for what has happened since the end of socialism, what comes after the "feet." The "head" lines up with the privileged ones, the body, with the elites, but directors remain outside. Nor do women seem to fit into this patrilineal line, this gendered body that my primarily male consultants also unsurprisingly (and unimaginatively) sometimes described using metaphors of insemination.

Crucially, individuality had a dual nature. Its expression simultaneously determined a composer's position within the music field, while at the same time helping to give form and stability to this body. In this way, the emergence of this form of selfhood, a specifically state-socialist creative habitus, came to have key artistic and political consequences for Tirana's artists.

Governing the Music Field

The accretion of composers' aesthetic choices, to my consultants simply the audible expression of each individual's creative sense, gave the music field the form it came to hold by the 1980s. This could occur because not all individuals had the same internal sense or orientation toward artistic production. Among composers there emerged a hierarchy of distinction around a cluster of keywords concerning originality, creativity, and professionalism. This hierarchy at once depended on the structure of the planned economy and shaped its products. Because the state monopolized the capacity to produce new symbolic works, composers had to access centralized resources in Tirana in order to receive a hearing at the national level. But to gain access to resources at the center, a new musical work had to first be recognized within the music field. And for a new work to obtain recognition, its composer had to have demonstrated his knowledge of correct compositional techniques. Among professionals, not all practices—from development, to quotation, to arrangement, to mere duplication—were perceived to be equal. At the apex of the field worked composers oriented toward developing and elevating source material, especially in large-scale concert and popular music works; toward its bottom, directors oriented toward arranging smaller-scale works and organizing groups to interpret other composers' creativity.

Over time, the creative field perpetuated itself. Individuals best able to demonstrate their professionalism received more prestigious appointments, to Tirana or major district centers, positions relatively closer to the economy's center. Composers who failed to gain such recognition received assignments at the economy's periphery. The logic of the planned economy in turn reinforced these practical distinctions. Individuals nearer the center received more broadcast time and, as described in the previous chapter, their works became patristic models to be emulated not for their political correctness, but for their aesthetic qualities. Individuals nearer the economy's peripheries were concerned largely with their day-to-day work organizing the groups that would interpret, rather than create, new works.

In sum, the music field became rigid, shaped like a pyramid (see Figure 3.1). Those individuals at the field's apex who enjoyed almost open access to the economy's means of production created models for the rest of the field. Individuals at the bottom of the pyramid competed for recognition within the field in order to potentially gain access to Tirana's centrally located resources through promotions that brought them progressively closer to the center. But musicians at the peripheries often found themselves hamstrung by their very positions, which emphasized performance, teaching, and arrangement, the less prestigious practices of duplication rather than creation. And in this way, the field's structure itself largely foreclosed questions of resistance or dissidence, the very problems

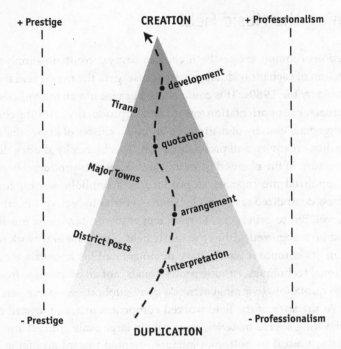

Figure 3.1 The music field.

so often at issue in music scholars' works on the eastern bloc. Because access to centralized resources depended on producing works that demonstrated field-specific values indexing "professionalism," composers had little or no incentive to adopt non-local techniques or materials. And because the economy rewarded those individuals best able to secure centralized resources with directing roles as faculty, broadcasters, and so on, over time, the overall profile of the music field tended to skew toward individuals invested in reproducing, rather than challenging, the status quo.

The spatial logic of the pyramidal music field could condition musician's opportunities in contradictory ways. "Living in a district town, you had a hard time breaking in to the Festival," one composer said. "Singers were accumulated from all over at that time, and assigned to composers. I was lucky to have found *Pranvera in my town, because she was an excellent singer, liked my songs, and did well at the Festivals. But it was a rare thing, and difficult, to get a good singer. Of course, someone like Krajka was right at the source where all the best singers were collected, in Tirana, and had a much easier time of it. I think it would have been very difficult for him to have found good singers if he had lived in my town." Needless to say, composers at the center usually dismiss this kind of criticism, believing themselves to have occupied the positions they did simply because they deserved them. At the same time, a position in the district town, the composer told me, had "saved" him. By living outside Tirana, he felt his works were not as subject to close scrutiny as those of his peers in the capital. This had preserved him, he said, after the Eleventh Festival of Song, when he passed under the radar of formal criticisms in Tirana.

Given the complicated and potentially very high stakes of participating in the music economy, why did composers, whether at the center or the periphery, submit compositions? Participation largely derived from *detyrim*, broadly meaning duty or obligation. In one sense, composers felt themselves to hold a professional obligation to be skilled enough to "create in all musical genres," with the idea that you might "specialize" in one sphere over another viewed as somewhat suspect. The ideal professional, as one composer put it to me, could "work on a symphony for breakfast, arrange a folk suite for lunch, and create a light song for dinner." But professionals felt obligated in a second sense, which a violinist encapsulated for me. The socialist period, he theorized, had engendered "a kind of intellectual competition, an artistic-cultural competition. You wanted to be the best, to distinguish yourself from others. Not for money, or for privileges, because we were all equal from the point of view of money. No one had more, or less. But we were not all the same in terms of this *garë*, or competition." For composers, the Festival of Song provided Albania's highest profile site for this competition for distinction. The individual seeking to raise his or her profile to obtain a better position or creative opportunities might *bie në sy*, or stand out, at the Festival of Song. After not submitting a composition in the early 1980s, one composer told me an older colleague had chided him: "'Why have you not done any song?!' You had to do one, because at the Festival you shined for everyone, and you needed it because it was the most followed event by both the powers-that-be, as well as the People."

This final sense of obligation, to the People, brings this chapter's discussion full circle. Initially, composers surprised me when they referred to listeners collectively as *Populli*, or the People. But I soon came to view this as part of their commonly shared creative habitus. As government policy transitioned from addressing the Youth back to addressing the People, composers came to deeply feel this sense of duty toward listeners. And the self-expression of individuality enabled them to mediate between themselves as individuals, their creativity, and the object of their enlightening works, the People. In this way, the belief in an individuality that expressed a stable core identity came to indirectly govern intellectuals' approaches to symbolic production. Claims to intellectual status became coterminous with ones to individuality, even as individuals recognized individuality as a "natural" property both divorced from the practical constraints of one's position in the field and discontinuous with the political exigencies of creativity. For composers trained between the late 1960s and early

1980s, the notion that one has an individuality to express remains so common-sensical that the opposite seems unthinkable. This suggests Bourdieu's insight that the deeper a person's imbrication in a field's codes, "the greater is his [sic] ignorance of all that is tacitly granted through his investment in the field and his interest in its very existence and perpetuation and in everything that is played for in it, and his unawareness of the unthought presuppositions that the game produces and endlessly reproduces, thereby reproducing the conditions of its own perpetuation."[49]

To gain membership in the field, composers were obligated to hone a creative individuality. In expressing this individuality, however, they contributed to the field's perpetuation. Given this situation, what could be musician's prospects for dissent from the aesthetic status quo?

MUSICIANS AND THE ROAD TO DISSENT

Following an interview at a small café behind the National Museum in Tirana, a popular meeting spot for intellectuals, I stood chatting with a lyricist before departing for home. Talk turned to a composer with whom he had collaborated in the 1970s, and a recently broadcast interview where the composer had made claims about his covert resistance against the state *në atë kohë*, at that time, a euphemism for the socialist period. The lyricist became increasingly exercised, asking rhetorically, "Where was this dissidence? Where did you demonstrate it? In what work?": "No one says, 'My dissidence is obvious, I refused to create good works.' Have you heard that? A work for the Party, a song, from the text, to the music, to the interpretation, was obliged to be excellent. You gave your best. And everyone gave their best work when asked. You should not now be at fault for this! But then, where is the dissidence?"

In early April 1985, Enver Hoxha suffered a major heart attack and died at the age of seventy-six. As political power transferred to Hoxha's handpicked successor, Ramiz Alia, the state media began a broadcast blitz of speeches, wreath-laying ceremonies, performances, and of course the funeral itself. Eight months later, the Twenty-fourth Festival of Song memorialized Hoxha in a number of songs. Elite composer Agim Krajka, the rhythmic song specialist so beloved by the Youth for his dewy-eyed, blossom-filled paeans to the dynamism of young love, presented his first and last politicized song, "Partia Ime" (My Party), based on a text by the state's foremost novelist, Ismail Kadare. Krajka, naturally, received a prize for "Partia Ime." So too did the emerging elite composer Haig Zacharian for his composition, "O Enver, O Yll e Dritë" (O Enver, O Star and Light), an epic-lyrical work paired with a text by Radio-Television editor Zhuljana Jorganxhi.

"This song," its composer told me, "came about more or less from the demands I placed on myself, to say something different. Because here we come to 1985, and my [creative] maturity is a bit different."

Writing now, I remember at first not entirely following Zacharian's train of thought as he spoke. In fact, I had assumed he would evade or dismiss the question. Just weeks earlier, one of his colleagues had refused an interview with me, fearing that my questions about the socialist period might get her in trouble. An older woman, she feared a younger administrator had put me up to the interview to find evidence of hidden "communist" feelings in order to justify her dismissal from a government position. A friend later explained this had happened before at the postsocialist Conservatory. But Zacharian, an honest man who understood my project a bit better, was exceptionally candid with me.

Zacharian submitted compositions each year. Oriented toward concert music, the composer (I sensed) did not often expend too much effort on his Festival song. He rarely collaborated in depth with a poet, usually indicating only the composition's main idea, theme, or just a few couplets. Jorganxhiu then completed the lyric or found a new one in order to complete the Festival's *tematika*. This, he told me, was how he remembered the paean to Hoxha taking shape. "Not finding another song that would fit a text like 'O Enver' they asked me, 'So, do you have a text? No?' And they used this text."

In interviews, composers sometimes revised earlier positions or seemed to misremember "politicized" works they had created decades before. In passing, I mentioned this vignette to other composers, leaving out Zacharian's name. Composers who had been closer to the economy's center, whether at the Conservatory or Radio-Television, thought it probable; those in the districts, that the composer had been conniving, or maybe now was conning me; and one younger, non-intellectual person, that the story was a flat-out lie. But my sense is that Zacharian's own individuality and position in the field, as oriented toward large-scale works rather than songs, yet without the prestige necessary to choose his own themes, put him in line for compositions such as "O Enver." Such a profile in turn brought with it privileges. In 1986, Zacharian applied for *profesion të lirë*, an extended sabbatical from teaching and administrative duties, which was granted with full benefits. Leave provided him a formal institutional affiliation in Tirana, reduced faculty service hours, and time for composing the concert music works toward which he felt himself to be oriented. He had recently turned thirty-three.[50]

For singers, the economy functioned most efficiently in purging suspect models to its peripheries and endorsing correct ones at its center. In early January 1973, a young Bashkim Alibali had sat on the hard wooden seating of the Culture House in his hometown of Shkodra to face criticism for the Eleventh Festival. One by one, critics stood to denounce the young man's performance. Alibali's dress had been too flashy, mannerisms too brash, style too foreign. At last the culture house's music director, Leonard Deda, rose to spoke. The young man's critics, Deda cautiously acknowledged, had correctly demanded he no longer perform light music. But a proper denunciation would allow Alibali to continue his career, albeit with the stipulation he sing only the music of the People, folk music. The commission accepted Deda's proposal, and Alibali, who had previously shown neither the talent nor the slightest inclination toward arranged folk music, became a folk singer. Clad in the heavy woolen stage costumes used by professional folk singers, he performed first at local and regional festivals and later at national ones. After seven years he returned to the light music stage and, ultimately, to the Festival of Song in the 1980s.

The performances of Alibali and his colleagues at 1980s Festivals of Song are remembered nostalgically, as truly Albanian. But they are also pointed to as a potent representation of the essentially repressive state's infiltration into the very bodies of its subjects. Rigid, betraying almost no movement, large smiles plastered on their faces, light music singers' performances from this period seemingly exemplify the debilitating effects of the state over artists. Stock-still, lower body rigid, hands blandly arranged at his sides, the singer carefully avoided foreign mannerisms. He expressed himself not through the body, but through his voice and, with studied precision, a raised eyebrow here, a careful tilt of the head there. Never would a singer dare touch the microphone like a Western star, the cliché goes, nor would he dare move a muscle without absolute forethought. The repressive state almost seemed to have entered the very bodies of performers.

But despite the neatness of this idea, not to mention its attractiveness as a retrospective way of thinking about late socialism, Alibali and his contemporaries did not conceptualize their experiences in ways that juxtaposed repression with freedom. When I met Alibali in 2010, we almost immediately began discussing his "punishment." To him, the years he spent singing arranged folk songs had provided the professional basis for his mature career. The 1970s taught him control, but of a different sort than implied above. The training taught him how to handle his voice, how to manage his body on stage. It taught him the professionalized discipline of self-expression that he retrospectively deemed to have been essential to his artisthood.

More usually, singers learned to discipline themselves through a process singer Ema Qazimi described as *me intuitë*, intuitively, in which rehearsal sessions comprised "work linked by a chain" between creator, conductor, and interpreter. Initially, the singer learned her song with the composer at the piano, before then rehearsing with longtime Radio-Television conductor Ferdinand Deda. The consummate professional, Deda imprinted the Festivals of Song with a sense of purpose and order. "Singer A will be in the small studio at this time, then with the orchestra in the rehearsal hall at this hour, and everyone was very exact," Qazimi described. "It was extremely professional, and necessitated a huge amount of discipline. There was no question of coming late or not being prepared. Everyone there was very professional and put in late hours of work."

"Deda would not let you leave that piano until he was convinced you had learned each phrase. I mean, with the most extraordinarily detailed details. And he would himself sing, demonstrate. The composers would, too."

Rote repetition, drills, imitation, these building blocks inculcated in singers like Qazimi and her contemporaries an internalized artistic disposition. She felt able to express this in words only with some difficulty and, I believe, after reflection some two decades later.

"A kind of—how do I put this?—a kind of scheme was created."

"But not 'scheme' in the negative sense of the word?" I asked.

"No, no. In the sense that, I mean, in the beginning, you have an identity that is not trained, or that needs work. And then you train your individuality, or you create your profile as an interpreter. Through work, through songs, this was how your profile of individuality was created."

Yet in casting musical practice, whether composing or interpreting song, as a professional issue of artistic expression—that by correctly creating works one represented a "physiognomy," or "sounded like oneself"—musicians forestalled possibilities for voicing political, anti-hegemonic statements. Highly developed field-specific artistic codes thus did not mechanically police individuals' conduct, but rather framed individual instances of potentially disruptive symbolic behavior (for instance, an aggressive vocal style, or a repetitive melody) as non-professional rather than subversive. Similarly, the notion that one might have had a practical sense for formal, melodic, or gestural expressions indexical of politicized themes signaled neither coercion to compose such pieces nor strategic calculation (such as "point-scoring"). And in a field governed by aspirations to complexity, melodicism, and grand gesture, professional-aesthetic values often resonated with political ones. In this way, the nexus between the structure of the economy, broadcast policy, and individuals' sense of themselves as artists facilitated an illiberal form of government at a distance.

This is not something my consultants expressed in interviews, nor could they reflect on the broader intersections between the audible politics of creativity sketched above, political power as exercised by Party officials or Sigurimi agents, and the semantic content of state media broadcasts. Most ignored or corrected my questions. Some hesitated, searching for the words like Qazimi above, working hard to articulate what had not been able to be articulated at that time.

"Look, you have to understand, at that time it was, in some way—normal. Maybe there was no other road, you just accepted it," Zacharian told me. "Because—hmm. It was the only way of living, there was no other way." And then, perhaps anticipating my unasked follow-up, he continued. "*Shyqyr*, my goodness, I don't know. I don't know how we *could* have been dissidents then."

The Repressive State

Was the Albanian state essentially repressive? A few months into my fieldwork, a talk show televised an exchange between two composers. I missed the original broadcast but later read its outline as recalled in memoirs written by Agron Çobani, the longtime Radio-Television journalist active beginning in the 1960s and named its first postsocialist general director after the end of one-party rule in 1992. "During the first years of this decade, [socialist-era] creativity has been insulted and denigrated," Çobani wrote in 2010, "it seems almost as if it was torture to take part in the Festival."[51] He then reproduced the televised exchange between the two composers point against point:

—"Now, censorship! I find this difficult to talk about. No one ever told me, 'take away that and put in this.'"
—"Songs for the Party? For those these were direct orders."
—"Nobody ever ordered me to make a song for the Party. Those songs were usually composed by those who desired to gain something."

"The conversation continued long," Çobani summarized in conclusion. "And through it I understood the essence of discussions about history that you hear today.... [E]ach writes it according to his own feelings, and the others learn it as they want it to have been."[52]

As astute an observer as Çobani was before passing in 2012, I do not think this is only what has been at issue. Over the past two decades, certain intellectuals, like their counterparts in the late Soviet Union, have strenuously denied even "the possibility of mixing the language of power with their own language: their own language [was] in some way not affected, it [was] a free space to be extended through struggle."[53] This division has its roots in the socialist period itself. If rapid discursive change and competitive positions-taking based on claims to professionalism typified the 1960s, extraordinary stability came to characterize the period between 1974 and 1985. By the mid-1980s, the composers' pyramidal field had undergone a remarkable ossification, as creative discourses, practices, and a shared sense for correct musical expression ultimately instantiated and then maintained equilibrium among musicians. Even while culture became progressively politicized, composers began to view themselves as divorced from politics and creatively free from state strictures. Only those other intellectuals "served the State." The nature of symbolic production itself grounded this system. Strict prohibition of non-local performance models or non-national subjects ensured all individuals accessed the same raw materials of musical production, which in turn encouraged the efflorescence of forms of discursive and practical professional micro-distinctions. Obliged to work and rework the same corpus of melodic-rhythmic resources, individuals could distinguish themselves only through increasingly fine degrees of aesthetic difference.

Agents do not pursue their creative lives outside political and economic structures, nor must these structures necessarily constrain, silence, or suppress their work. Economic structures, like all social structures, exercised positive effects in subsidizing, promoting, or otherwise shaping aesthetic practice. This chapter has claimed that the practice of creativity and performance are, at least in part, economic practice, and as such must be contextualized within their specific economies of symbolic production. For particular economies of production mold not only aesthetically meaningful musical output, but also socially and politically meaning musical subjectivities. As political power became capillary in entering the body of composers, these composers found ways to form and reform themselves as artist-subjects. Their practices over time gave the music field its particular shape, made particular positions within this field available, and ultimately allowed for a distinctively rigid set of positions-takings and creative trajectories.

The audible practice of making song helped to structure hierarchy within the music field in ways that simultaneously depended on and perpetuated the shape of the music economy itself. Because 1970s politics rendered this economy's borders so strict, there existed no outside in which musicians could gain alternative forms of prestige, subcultural or economic capital beyond the gaze—and ears—of the state.[54] And because access to resources—Albania's sole recording studio, broadcast time, singers and ensembles, and so on—depended on your position vis-à-vis the planned economy's center, a position that in turn depended on how well you had previously expressed values congruent with those of the field, change proved difficult. But could such an economy, so dependent on the strict erasure of foreign contaminants from symbolic production at the center, be sustained over time? And what would happen to musicians were the borders of the planned economy to be breached?

4

Voicing Transition

When Enver Hoxha died in April 1985, Ramiz Alia, the veteran Party member long charged with overseeing the cultural field, succeeded him. As a leader, Alia was fundamentally different from Hoxha. He held little mystique, as Albania's unipolar political universe had admitted little competition. Sculptors erected no Alia statues, poets composed no panegyrics, and folk singers arranged no songs. Alia soon announced his so-called continuity policy, meanwhile signaling that reform, if it came, would be directed by his office. Over the next few years, the Albanian leadership largely maintained its protectionist policies, outwardly condemning *perestroika* in the Soviet Union and, at least publicly, forswearing rapprochement with the capitalist world.

In the 1980s, Tirana's cultural field proved no less stable than the political field, with the aesthetic equilibrium forged through the humdrum practice of creating and broadcasting culture to the Masses acted as an unseen hand in governing symbolic production. But from 1988 to 1992, the symbolic and physical landscape of cities and large towns began undergoing a series of rapid mutations, from the everyday to the spectacular, which Albanians retrospectively called *tranzicion*, or transition.

"Around 1992," *Genti told me, "I was walking on the beach and I found a bottle of spring water, washed up on shore, with an Italian label. I remember, I took this empty bottle home—"

"You mean a plastic bottle?"

"—yeah, a plastic bottle. And I put it on the shelf, in my grandmother's living room. Like it was something to look at, just an empty bottle. Can you believe it? We left it up there until 1996, '97! That was how I thought, like it was something valuable, like a vase. But that was the *mentaliteti*, or mentality."

Another consultant remembered the older students at his school whistling the opening to "Wind of Change" by the Scorpions by 1991. A paean to *glasnost'* in the Soviet Union, the power ballad became a global hit for the German rock band. Young guys with shaggy hair used the tune to greet friends and passing girls.

In comparison with these mundane flows into living rooms and adolescent life, the transition's other flows were spectacular. Tirana swelled as citizens from its district peripheries began migrating, precipitating a series of crises first at its foreign embassies, which began to accept asylum seekers, and then the country's borders, as thousands passed clandestinely into Greece or commandeered ships for Italy. At the same time, the planned symbolic economy began faltering, its borders likewise compromised. Protesters pulled down the capital's massive golden statue of Enver Hoxha, the system's master political signifier, and then its bronzed Stalins. Radio-Television employees hastily adapted, liberalizing broadcast policy by allowing novel forms of political and musical expression.

These breaches prompted a range of reactions among intellectuals. The sociologist Hamit Beqja began a new research project asking how the Youth, given these rapid social changes, should behave.[1] Fine arts students organized contentious discussions.[2] The arts weekly *Drita* began printing a series of contradictory articles. Some individuals called for "full and creative freedom of expression," while others debated even the state's most basic symbols.[3] But reactions to *tranzicion* did not result in the mechanical dismissal of the socialist past. On the eve of a historic visit in by the U.S. Secretary of State James Baker in June 1991—to "welcome Albania to the free world," as headlines in Western newspapers put it—most of Albania's Lenins remained on their pedestals.[4] But like the Hoxhas and Stalins, these too had to go, especially as foreign journalists swarmed Tirana "to see and describe, to film, to photograph the statue-corpses," the "symbolic witness to the end of a tragic epoch" (see Figure 4.1).[5]

Among mainstream reactions there stands out a remarkable essay, "The Intellectual Before Today's Duties." Penned by Sali Berisha, a cardiologist and Party Secretary then quickly becoming a leading voice for reform within the establishment, the 1990 essay pondered the definition of *intelektuali*, the intellectual. What role must the intellectual take during this period? Moving forward, what should it mean to call oneself an "intellectual?" At one point in the essay, Berisha asks what new forms of knowledge would be necessary to nourish the new intellectual.

"This sustenance," Berisha wrote, "must contain knowledge of primitive man's initial, naïve drawings; the works of Homer, Shakespeare, Fyodor Dostoevsky, Ernest Hemingway, Gabriel García Márquez, and Albanian novelist Ismail Kadare; the discoveries of Archimedes, the theory of relativity, and research by Theodor Schwann, Charles Darwin, Hendrik Lorentz; the symphonies of Beethoven and Tchaikovsky, the songs of both Luciano Pavarotti and Whitney Houston, the interpretations of Charlie Chaplin; the bravery of Neil Armstrong; vaccines, hormones, light, laser, nuclear fission, genes, protein synthesis."[6]

Figure 4.1 "Statue-corpses" standing behind the National Arts Gallery, 2010.

Berisha's problematization of intellectuals' "sustenance" intuitively linked science, the arts, and politics as sharing the same challenge. His call for reform centered on the limits bounding intellectual resources, diagnosing the intellectual as constrained by structural problems inherent in Albania's domestic economies of material, scientific, and cultural production. The curtailment of access to non-socialist intellectual resources, Berisha suggested, had limited the intellectual. The commonsense solution to this problem, he proposed, would be to expand the domestic economy's borders: to freely adopt, engage, and experiment with non-domestic and nonsocialist resources, the best of the West, whether Ernest Hemingway, Ludwig van Beethoven, or Whitney Houston.

In a state where legitimacy had depended on strictly managing the cultural resources intellectuals might employ in crafting the symbolic stuff of belonging, this problematization implicitly proposed the necessity of radical reforms to domestic economies of intellectual production. Foreshadowed by small reforms to state media policy during the final years of Alia's time in power, change came quickly with the accession to power in March 1992 of Albania's first opposition organization, *Partia Demokratike*, the Democratic Party.[7] Headed by Berisha himself, the Democrats embraced major political and economic reforms as a means to reintegrate Albania into Europe. But despite political rhetoric to the contrary, this process did not entail the simple introduction of new freedoms for intellectuals via the lifting of prior constraints. It proved to be, as elsewhere in the region, complex, fundamentally uncertain.[8] This chapter examines how musicians navigated the audible transition from a state-socialist rationality predicated on organizing the arts to a postsocialist one concerned with defining relationship between art and freedom.

The notion that the primary problem facing artists concerned *liri*, or freedom, quickly entrenched itself in local thought. But this has less to do with the self-evident nature of freedom as an artistic *sine qua non*, a universal common good to be sought out, expressed, and preserved, than with the wider practical significance of "freedom" in the late twentieth century as "the principle of so many political dreams and projects."[9] In the modern world, states are evaluated according to their management of freedom, their health assessed by their protection of a bundle of concepts that include the freedoms to associate, to exercise speech, to express oneself artistically. As a political principle in Tirana, freedom became implicated in new forms of musical and media practice aiming to remold Albanian citizens, communism's former "captives," into the rights-bearing subjects of a "normal" state. But this process was not without contestation, as well as dead ends, internal contradictions, and paradoxes.

Efforts to sound out freedom enveloped major symbolic events like the Festival of Song because of the status symbolic representations held in the socialist state. Indeed, the very beginnings of popular resistance to the Party, a March 1990 protest, rested on its protagonists' understanding of the significance of symbols. "We call all those who are convinced that our communist propaganda is from head to toe a deception," three young men wrote in a pamphlet distributed in Kavaja, a district capital. "Let's gather together with our unified, energetic voices at the match on March 25 Partizani—Besa and at the 80th minute of the game let's raise our fingers while yelling loudly and without break: 'Freedom, Democracy.'"[10]

When Minister of the Interior Simon Stefani submitted his confidential report on the protests to the Central Committee two days later, he too foregrounded the failures of cultural policy. Suffering from high unofficial unemployment, food shortages, and electricity cuts, Kavaja, he said, had been a political powder keg waiting to explode. And its lack of cultural outlets had exacerbated the danger. "With the exception of a palace of culture and cinema," the minister stated, "there are no other recreational or entertainment places for youth."[11] Protesters' chants, *Liri dhe Demokraci*, quickly spread, becoming key linguistic signifiers across the political and cultural fields. And the sounds with which these keywords came to be paired in the music field point to the sonic dimensions of the transitional state, as an emerging media policy did not passively render preexisting political changes audible, but actively contributed to imagining the transition's endpoint beyond Albania's borders in the West.

"How to Write a Schematic Song," 1985

In 1985, a young humorist named Artan Dervishi published a rubric titled "Five Points for Writing a Schematic Song."[12] He identified two song "schemes," and listed mock-serious advice for aspiring lyricists. "Schematic Song A must have a general title," and must include lyrics "about life, work, defense, and *aksion*, and through lyrical-theoretical-epico-phyliosophical explication must achieve 'grand' and 'powerful' ideo-emotions." Schematic Song B, Dervishi continued, should be smaller, more "intimate," and its "primary motif 'me and you' or just 'you' must arrive—following its lyrico-lyrical explication—at 'the two of us' or 'together.'" The verse should treat "beautiful nature filled with greenery, flowers, fruit, and vegetables, until in the refrain they 'blossom,' open their 'petals,' and 'open flower buds.' Ready-made figures such as 'the rays of the sun in the morning' or 'dewy roses' can be used, too."

But Dervishi also included advice for composers. The composer should begin style A "by citing the motive of a folk song, later 'arranging' it to create something between song, march, or ballad"; it should conclude "with a high, held note almost unsingable by the singer." Likewise, the more "intimate" style B should begin with a folk song motive. "Later, by simplifying it and lightening it an 'original' motive is achieved. (And since everything about this song remains light, it can thus be classified as light music.)" "It is not advisable," Dervishi added in a short postscript, "that the composer of the schematic song have inspiration before writing the song. And he may compose it quite simply without having its text [beforehand], as it is sufficient to bear in mind the above points and to choose the scheme one wants."

Dervishi's mocking tone reads as scathing as it does because his ear for the music field's aesthetic discourse proved so good. Composers' reframing of song as an expert domain, explicable only in their own elevated language, had empowered them during the 1960s and 1970s. Professional composers wielded expertise, their own sometimes opaque "theoretical-phyliosophical" languages, whether discursive or musical, with a savvy that ultimately insulated them from the tumult of national politics. But younger members of the field increasingly perceived the aesthetic discourses Dervishi so expertly sends up as constraining. By the mid-1980s, the creative space composers had forged during the turbulent 1960s and 1970s began to feel limiting for these younger musicians.

STAGNATION AND CRITIQUE

For professionalized musicians, perceptions of constraint emerged bit by bit, folded into the cultural field by the very nature of planning and the checks and balances it had built into the domestic production and consumption of new works. In order to gain access to the cultural economy's means of distribution, its broadcasts, publications, and so on, a person first had to have been considered experienced or affirmed, *me përvojë* or *i/e afirmuar*, by more established colleagues sitting on the field-specific artistic commissions that evaluated original works. But to have become affirmed, young intellectuals had to have demonstrated professionalism. And they did this by rehearsing the discourses or cultural practices propagated by older, more distinguished members of the field. Moreover, the planned cultural economy held finite resources at its center, whether in terms of printed pages in journals, gallery wall space, or broadcast airtime; it also restricted intellectuals' access to opportunities beyond the state's borders. Not without good reason, some individuals perceived this system as engendering creative stagnation.

In 1981, Edmond Zhulali, by the time of my fieldwork one of Tirana's top popular music producers, received a summons to an administrator's office at the Conservatory. The previous year, he had successfully applied to both trumpet and composition tracks, subsequently beginning the latter program. But after six months, Zhulali was reassigned to the performance track. It was only after reading his socialist-era dossier in the 1990s that he fully realized the byzantine political logic behind the decision, a decision that had severely curtailed his professional opportunities until 1992.

"After graduation, I was named music director of the theater in Peshkopi," Zhulali told me. This assignment to the country's distant periphery was not wholly negative. Peshkopi was "a great school." "I could orchestrate, compose. I did the work of a composer and a director there, and I also played accordion, trumpet, piano. I wrote many songs for children, some light songs, newly composed folk songs, folk song arrangements, music for theater. But sure, the conditions were difficult, in this period after graduation. I wrote a concerto for trumpet, and one for violin. A large amount of production, but as I was far from the center, it was difficult to have works performed in Tirana or on the state media." Without structural reforms to the planned economy, Zhulali's career trajectory would probably have kept him, and his works, at the planned economy's margins.

But even those composers lucky, talented, or connected enough to have won appointments at the center in the 1980s began experiencing the economy as narrow, stifling. Paradoxically, baroque formulations of these musicians' teachers on "innovation," "originality," or "individuality" resulted in the opposite. These critical terms and the music practices that derived from them obligated participants in the music field to reproduce its terms over, and over again. Younger composers began chafing at this imperative, their frustrations exacerbated by the limited number of ensembles, concerts, and opportunities to present material. The founding of a new annual song event, *Kur Vjen Pranvera*, better known as the Spring Concert, eased these constraints temporarily for younger composers oriented toward light music. Founded in 1983 as a lower-profile and less politically charged alternative to the December Festival of Song, the Spring Festival was the brainchild of the Radio-Television's director, Marash Hajati. Named director of television programming during the post–Eleventh Festival shake-up in 1974, Hajati replaced Thanas Nano as general director in the late 1970s. The event seems to have been established in response to the perceived need for more "small," "intimate" light music songs aimed at high school– and university-age listeners. The Spring Festival's songs were performed by a smaller pop ensemble of drum kit, synthesizer, electric bass, and electric guitar. A younger cohort of composers, poets, and singers, including men like Demokrat Shahini, Vladimir Kotani, and Jorgo Papingji, and singers like Parashqevi Simaku, the Libohova sisters, Ermira Babaliu, and Luan Zhegu, dominated these Spring Festivals. In the late 1980s, several of these musicians successfully made the leap to the December Festival.

At the same time, the domestic consumption of popular music also began changing, as young listeners increasingly tuned in to Italian and Yugoslav radio-television broadcasts by the mid-1980s. For many urbanites, *kanoçka*, the improvised homemade antennae that enabled Albanians to secretly access foreign broadcasts in their homes, represent the spirit of late socialism. Crafted from tin cans and wire, *kanoçka* were unfurled at night from apartment windows. *Besnik, born in 1973, remembered watching an Italian broadcast about Elvis Presley via *kanoçka* while still in grammar school. "A typical Albanian family," he and his parents consumed foreign radio and television programs together, though they did not discuss this outside the house. By high school, Besnik listened regularly to the Hit Parade on Italian radio and, together with his friends, had become enamored of American and British rock bands. Not public, this consumption was *intime*, or private. And this is what drew Besnik to rock music. It was something a few very close friends could do together, usually at the lake park behind the University or in a friend's home.

*Sotir, a university student in the 1980s, tried to more reflexively contextualize for me his friends' attraction to foreign groups like the Beatles, Pink Floyd, or Deep Purple. "In our system, we were so isolated that everything foreign was seen as good. There was such a focus on things from outside." This sentiment resonates with the close ethnographic work of Nicola Mai and his collaborators on this period. Drawing on interviews with economic migrants to Italy in the 1990s, Mai has described Italian television as having functioned as a kind of "periscope," offering late socialism's consumers "access to radically different ways of being, having, and behaving."[13] "By turning their desiring gazes away from the official, moralized, naturalized mediascape," Mai and coauthor Richard King claim elsewhere, "Albanian people started disembodying themselves from the regime's authoritarian libinal economy which denied them existence as individual desiring subjects."[14]

But as consumers and young musicians increasingly watched, listened, and desired beyond the borders of the domestic economy, its veterans retrenched. Established composers began publishing articles criticizing younger musicians at the economy's periphery for exhibiting what Çesk Zadeja decried as manifestations of *shabllonizëm*, or mechanical imitation.[15] Vaçe Zela worried in print about young singers who "standardized" songs, meaning they sang in a "shouting," overly declamatory manner, had not professionally developed their individuality, or simply lacked professional vocal training. Festival critics dedicated growing space in their reviews to a cluster of "technical problems" that indicated young musicians' troubling lack of "cultural and professional level": a tendency toward "dilettante communication, without fantasy and with vocal restrictions"; "a spiritless *mezzo voce*" that cannot arrive at a real *forte*; poor intonation; and a lack of "original and soloistic" voices.[16] In late 1987, noted physician Petrit Muka even published a medical analysis of student voices. His findings concurred with calls for a special course to be created to better train young popular singers.[17]

The target of these criticisms were small efforts among younger musicians to create works freed from "schematism," from epico-phyliosophical ideo-emotions, to create songs closer to the audibly modern broadcasts they heard on Italian and Yugoslav broadcasts. If the leaders of the field reacted to these works with indignation, the tenor of their criticisms also betrayed their wistfulness, maybe even bitterness. Consider how Agim Prodani, a pioneer of 1950s song and longtime bandleader in Tirana, diagnosed the younger generation's "weaknesses" in a 1988 interview: "When you sit down at the piano without any thought in mind. When you are supported mechanically in foreign schema. When you think that every day you can write a new song. When you haven't read any books of poetry. When you think that to write a contemporary song, the rhythms of our folk music [offer only] 'archaic and rudimentary' elements. When you hold the impression that meters like 3/4, 3/8, 6/8, and 4/4 have now been 'surpassed' by the times."[18]

INNOVATION'S PROSPECTS

In a very real sense, the times were surpassing older musicians. As the men and women trained in the eastern bloc approached their sixties and seventies by the late 1980s, many retired or assumed reduced working hours. And as icons like Vaçe Zela ceded the stage to younger starlets, nostalgia for their earlier performances boomed among middle-aged fans who began viewing the 1960s as a golden age. At Festivals of Song held after 1985, organizers began inviting older stars to perform their now decades-old hits; the Radio-Television also created a new *Festivali i Interpretuesve*, or the Interpreters' Festival, where young vocalists performed older repertoire. In a field still dominated by demands to ceaselessly "bring something new," and in an economy founded on the imperative to create vanguard art, this nostalgic turn raised insoluble contradictions.

But the criticisms of retired composers and singers were not the sole factor dulling innovation within the music field. The field's reliance on expert theoretical discourse had calcified its structure over time, homogenizing music specialists' critical and musical faculties. Even as calls for reform grew in the related artistic subfields of the visual arts, theater, and literature, music specialists moved to protect the status quo. In part, the nature of musical training and production encouraged equilibrium. Individuals tended to view pedagogue-student relationships in Tirana as foundational to their creative voices. Within popular music, the intensely personal nature of collaboration between singer, composer, and lyricist wove deeply asymmetrical power relations into the field's fabric. And finally, the music field's dependence on state resources—rehearsal spaces and time, instruments that had to be procured from abroad, broadcast technologies, or performance venues—more deeply enmeshed musicians in the planned cultural economy's institutional structures than, for instance, the literary field enmeshed writers.

As a result, many musicians found themselves unprepared for change. The final creative discussions on light music organized before the onset of the *tranzicion*, suggestively subtitled "Song Must Democratize Even Further," demonstrated the gulf separating composers from emerging realities.[19] At the February 1990 meeting, Çesk Zadeja stressed now decades-old complaints about professionalism, "the education of the masses" and "the formation of good musical tastes," and "the problem of national originality." Feim Ibrahimi lectured once again on the importance of "the cultural elevation of creators, orchestrators, and interpreters." At last, Dritëro Agolli, general secretary of the League of Writers and Artists, interjected. Predicting that soon "a family of composers concerned only with song will be created," the writer welcomed the time when individuals would "create songs in a voluntary manner, for pleasure, or in a spontaneous manner." But then Agolli went further, scolding composers that "like it or not," rock music influenced popular music, and light song creators must realize an equilibrium among its "national, Balkan, and European" elements.

"Our song has formed a tradition," he said. "The national sound certainly derives from this tradition. Yet it is not only folklore that gives the Albanian sound. This song tradition that we have formed also gives an Albanian sound. This tradition, together with the people's spiritual culture, gives a still fuller Albanian sound. Yet even with all of these achievements, composers must continuously seek more. To seek as the painters who are rejuvenating painting seek. Composers have been a bit clumsy in exploring the great breadth of discoveries now spreading across all fields of our life, in the economic and cultural fields, in the field of painting, poetry, the novel, the film."

With the People waning as an object for aesthetic uplift, how could these "clumsy" composers gain their footing in the changing cultural economy? And if Agolli's prediction proved correct, that "a family of composers" oriented entirely toward light music would soon emerge, what would this mean for the music field? Composers found themselves soon obligated to answer these questions, with new signifiers like Democracy, Freedom, and Europe waxing as objects of media policy, and as a loose cohort of non-professionalized popular musicians began to monopolize the Festival of Song. But these changes could occur only after a series of major political events.

Musical Signs of Transition

In December 1989, the fall of the Berlin Wall presented viewers worldwide with a powerful image of a global order in transformation. In Tirana, the state media cautiously curated this image for domestic consumption, waiting three days to report any substantive details.[20] But two weeks later, its broadcast of the Twenty-eighth Festival of Song offered an audible statement of sorts on these changes by two of Albania's leading intellectuals, "Toka e Diellit" (Land of the Sun), which the official jury consecrated with first prize. Composed by Aleksandër Peçi on a lyric by fellow elite, the poet Xhevahir Spahiu, the work caused a stir among younger reform-minded intellectuals.

Spahiu's lyric poetically addressed the political situation in Albania and abroad. "O Albania, give me spring seasons," the trio sings in the refrain, "Like an eagle through the world, soar! soar! Like an eagle, soar! As the word Freedom gives birth to a new world / It enlightens this one." The text can certainly be read as commentary on the mounting changes then beginning to envelop the eastern bloc. But replete with visions of spring, eagles, stars, oceans, and so on, the lyric drew largely from the stylized corpus of symbolic and allegorical imagery found in post-1974 popular music. Similarly, Peçi's musical setting commingled the audible traces of both newer and older compositional techniques. Named director of the National Ensemble of Folk Songs and Dances in 1985, the composer had been predominantly oriented toward concert music and elevated film scores that imaginatively drew on folklore. His best-known song, for instance, "Shtepia Jonë" (Our Home), performed by Vaçe Zela in the title track to the 1979 film *Në Shtëpinë Tonë* (In Our Home), deconstructed the intervals of northern men's folk songs for the development of its melody.

"Toka e Diellit," however, juxtaposed two jarring features. Peçi's vocalists swooped and extemporized, freely alluding to an African-American gospel style. But his work's main theme, performed on *pipëza*, a small shepherd's folk flute, provided the basis for the melodies they sang. In an interview conducted immediately after the Festival, Peçi called the extemporized style "the form of variations (the basis of folk and cultivated music)."[21] When I met the composer twenty years later, I expected him to tell me that this interview did not relate the full story about the song, that maybe it partially covered for the more potentially subversive, American-inspired musical elements that, to my ear, were so evident. But he wanted to emphasize the Albanian-ness of the work, its national qualities, and we slipped comfortably into what—again, to my ear—had been distinctly socialist discourses on creativity.

To what extent could professionalized intellectuals step outside the aesthetic codes of their respective fields in order to create potent political statements? This composition raises thorny questions about the degree to which "schematism," in the sense presented by Dervishi, had penetrated the music field. Could intellectuals working from within the socialist mode of cultural production craft novel critiques, statements expurgated of the "ready-made figures" of the past? And if not, how were listeners to interpret their statements?

TRANZICION

The final question was fast becoming moot for many Albanians. In March 1990, the town of Kavaja surged with the transition's first popular protests under the motto "Freedom and Democracy," as described in this chapter's introduction. By June, impoverished citizens began forcing their way into Tirana's embassies. When police measures failed to turn them out, the state granted thousands the right to leave. Party officials and several intellectuals criticized the asylum seekers as *alabakë*, Tirana slang for loafers. In a televised statement, Prime Minister Alia summarily dismissed *të ikur*, those who had left, saying, "They are not Albania." Immediate government concessions initially sought to appease restive rural constituencies as well as international actors concerned about mass migrations. In late July, the Party held a congress to dismiss several hardliners, and voted to allow limited retail and to extend plots of individual land for cultivation. In October, Ismail Kadare, a privileged writer, boarded an airplane for Paris. Self-described as "one of the few writers of this half century to have not only provided intellectual nourishment to [his] countrymen, but to have provided it in quantity," Tirana's foremost intellectual sought political asylum once in France. But events quickly proved premature Kadare's assertion to *Le Monde* that "the promises of democracy are dead."[22] In December, massive demonstrations prompted the government to recognize the opposition Democratic Party. New waves of refugees left for Greece and Italy, as between March 1991 and October 1992 an estimated 300,000 citizens, nearly 10 percent of Albania's population, migrated.[23]

Simultaneous with these massive political and social dislocations, the Radio-Television began broadcasting musical signs of transition. Between spring 1990 and February 1992, the performance and broadcast of light music songs circulated potential symbolic materials for a nonsocialist cultural program, albeit one imagined by a particular cohort of intellectuals in Tirana. To recoup how this cohort began to imagine a nonsocialist program in song, here my tone shifts to focus on three exemplary works on freedom, democracy, and slavery.[24] Contextualized against rapidly shifting political events, the musical and lyrical content of these works and the circumstances of their production demonstrate the political potentials, but also the practical ambiguities, for light music artists to voice transition from state-socialism.

Freedom, March 1990
In the weeks following the Kavaja protests, chants of *Liri-Demokraci* spread to other towns, effectively eliding Freedom and Democracy in affective terms. As these keywords became indelibly linked to a nascent opposition over 1990, they began to appear—and to be scrutinized—on Radio-Television broadcasts. At the March 1990 Spring Festival, Zhuljana Jorganxhiu composed a text "Ne, Bijtë e Lirisë" (We, Freedom's Children), the first of several lyrics she wrote between 1990 and 1992 invoking tropes of "freedom" and "democracy." Framed by Romeo and Juliet's universal story of tragic love, the lyric begins from the innocuous cliché that "love conquers all." The bridge, however, dispensed with allegory to insist that the peaceful Youth universally will demand its rights in the face of violence: "With two fingers raised / Youth everywhere has beautiful eyes / But someone seeks to blind them." The refrain's text then calls three times for "freedom!"—that of the "heart's fire," the "mother tongue," and "dream's wing"— in "a language we can understand": "Libertà, Liberté, Liberty, Freiheit! O Liri!" Jorganxhiu's lyric concluded with an even more general call for peace: "O world, we are freedom's beautiful sons / And so we don't want to see violence and tears throughout the world."

As a long-time employee at the state media, Jorganxhiu had cultivated a sense for submitting lyrics safe from rejection on ideological grounds. This lyric drew on a trope, the "sons of liberty," used previously to describe partisan guerrillas.[25] But it also retained overwhelming ambiguity in referencing no specific events or groups other than the Youth. According to Jorganxhiu, the song's composer, her nephew Gjergj Leka, had sought a text "concerning the struggle of the youth for freedom and democracy throughout the world." But officials, Jorganxhiu has suggested, were wary of an association with domestic protests. "[Critics claimed] Gjergji [Leka] and I had made a 'hymn to Kavaja,' because a revolt had occurred those days in this city, and all this because the text had the words DEMOCRACY and FREEDOM."[26] Yet according to its singer, Frederik Ndoci, audience members understood the song as advocating "freedom" for Kosovar Albanians, then increasingly subordinated by the Serbian state and mobilizing a separatist movement that summer. But the Spring Festival's artistic director, Ndoci has asserted, knowingly scolded, "The time has not yet come to raise fingers for Kosova," which the singer understood as suggesting that the director perceived the lyric's "two fingers"—the middle and forefinger raised after Winston Churchill's famous victory sign—to be masked references to the use of this gesture in Kavaja.[27] If Jorganxhiu had presumed the polysemic keyword *liri* would pass, she was wrong. The Central Committee's Office of Propaganda requested the song be pulled from broadcast. Yet even though Party officials criticized the lyric on ideological grounds, the Radio-Television nevertheless aired Ndoci's performance without changes.

Moreover, despite presenting itself as a call for freedom "in a language we can understand," "Ne, Bijtë" musically and linguistically rendered a polyvocal *liri* existing beyond Albania's borders. With iterations in Italian, French, English, German, and only then Albanian, the refrain located freedom as a seemingly universal condition, albeit one best expressed through Western Europe's primary diplomatic languages. At the same time, the musical language of the song articulated freedom through African-American sonic signifiers, with Ndoci's gospel-inspired phrasings and Leka's orchestration evoking a 1980s black commercial music aesthetic. The pianist played jazzy seventh chords in an introduction and comping patterns over the verse and bridge; Leka orchestrated a shout call-and-response refrain between Ndoci and backup vocalists and included a saxophone solo. In this way "Ne, Bijtë" rendered a multilingual, jubilant shout for freedom in Europe's languages, but voiced through the globally circulating sounds of the United States—and lacking any definable "national" content as defined by the socialist-era field.

Europe, December 1990

In December 1990, student representatives met with Ramiz Alia to protest conditions at the University. One symbolically read aloud their rights according to the Helsinki Accords, an agreement Enver Hoxha had mockingly dismissed in 1975 but which Alia had signed under pressure from the international community in late 1989.[28] The December Movement, as it has come to be called, chanted into existence a new slogan: *E duam Shqipërinë si Gjithë Evropa*, We Want an Albania Like the Rest of Europe. This movement remains a contentious point in postsocialist historiography, a period of "fairytales," according to participant and political scientist Shinasi Rama.[29] Alia initially used Berisha as a go-between in discussions with the students, but Berisha later pushed the students to demand *pluralizëm*—political pluralism, which when granted later placed him in a powerful position at their head.[30]

Just weeks later, the guitar group Tingulli i Zjarrtë (The Fiery Sound) presented the Festival of Song's first rock composition, "Jemi Emri i Vet' Jetës" (We Are the Name of Life Itself) on another text by Jorganxhiu. Fronted by vocalist and songwriter Elton Deda, the high school–age son of longtime Radio-Television Orchestra conductor Ferdinand Deda, and composed of Lyceum and Conservatory students, the group had previously performed light rock–inspired arrangements of classical music on state broadcasts. Organizers also invited other examples of what they now called "instrumental-vocal ensembles" after the Soviet usage, though with the exception of Tingulli i Zjarrtë, these predominantly male, guitar-oriented rock bands performed songs commissioned from established composers.

Tingulli i Zjarrtë's staging represented a radical departure for the Radio-Television. Deda wore his hair long and, dressed in matching blue jeans and jean jacket, tapped a sneaker-shod foot while the rest of the band stood alongside him on stage. During an instrumental break and guitar solo, the electric guitarists and bassist stepped to the front of the stage in arena-rock formation, guitar necks jutting out in studied synchronicity. Presented from the point of view of the Youth, Jorganxhiu's lyric concerned the energetic unity embodied by this ensemble. Throughout, Deda sang in the first-person plural, speaking (through Jorganxhiu's words, of course) for all Youth: "With the daring of our age, our heart speaks: 'We demand those beautiful things, o life!'" The final setting of the refrain following the guitar solo, presented a sing-a-long anthem.

> We! are the name of life itself / We! seek the future today.
> We! like no one else for the Fatherland / We! will bring it to Europe.

Like "Ne, Bijtë," this composition linked rapprochement with "Europe" to the power of the Youth in discursive and musical terms. Using a musical form legible to those young, urban listeners in Tirana oriented toward Western-style rock, this composition seemed to propose the sonic and discursive notions of "Europe" as a potential rallying cry for the collective "we" of students or young people more generally. But at the same time, the collaboration paired the Radio-Television's longstanding editor with the son of one of Tirana's most elite musicians. Even so, individuals today often misremember "rockers" as having been officially persecuted. "I remember this song was on the festival's first night, and they pulled it quick, because it was unacceptable for the festival of that time," one listener mistakenly recalled in 2012. "But I liked this song a lot, and cried when they disqualified it, unfairly, without letting it enter into competition at all."[31] (Actually, it received a prize.)

In actuality, rockers were a diverse group.[32] Some were disaffected young men who had begun congregating in 1989 with their girlfriends and acoustic guitars at Tirana's Grand Lake, a park directly south of the University and Conservatory. These "lake guys" played covers of Italian, British, and American pop, and most were not Conservatory-trained musicians. Some had day jobs, but others formed part of a growing number of alienated young people who chose not to work. Yet others were music students at the University or pupils at the Lyceum. And those with the most up-to-date tastes were the children of elites. It was this last cohort, composed of young musicians who could obtain what my consultants called "beautiful things" like records, blue jeans, and electric guitars available only beyond the state's borders, who received the majority of airtime between 1990 and 1992.

Slavery, August to December 1991

Over the course of 1991, access to life's beautiful things became an increasingly attractive and seemingly realistic proposition to hundreds of thousands of ordinary Albanians. But many soon found the abstract ideals of Freedom and Europe to be illusory. On August 7, 1991, approximately 20,000 people commandeered a boat docked at the southern port of Saranda, ordering its captain to sail for Italy. Italian officials at Bari initially refused to allow the arrivals to disembark, though the ship's lack of water and food soon obligated a change of course. As aid workers relocated passengers to La Vittoria Sports Stadium, refugees in the throes of "a form of mass psychosis," at least from the perspective of a report created by the Council of Europe, resisted.[33] They refused offers of 50,000 lira (then approximately 40 U.S. dollars), clothing, and return passage to Albania. When Italian officials attempted to use military planes and ferries to forcibly repatriate them, violence erupted, and thousands of people barricaded themselves within the stadium.

The winning composition at 1991's Festival of Song, "Jon," presented by composer Ardit Gjebrea in collaboration with lyricist Zhuljana Jorganxhiu, rendered these events in affectively moving terms for urban listeners back in Albania. Positioned between the past and present, Gjebrea's career has exemplified the opportunities and challenges the political transition opened to Tirana's elites. In the 1970s, Gjebrea competed in local children's singing competitions in Shkodra, later relocating to Tirana for advanced studies in composition. After marrying a woman from a politically connected family, Gjebrea held a relatively advantaged position. He received permission to study in Italy in the late 1980s, the first composer to be trained outside Tirana since its break with Moscow in the early 1960s. Those studies granted him not only firsthand experience with contemporary production methods, but also a substantial amount of cultural capital during the increasingly pro-Western transition.

Gjebrea's unique circulations between Albania and Italy formed a poignant, if privileged, parallel to those of the desperate migrants. The text of "Jon," written in collaboration with Jorganxhiu, examined the refugees' experiences in a series of poetic, elevated metaphors. The title itself was a double-reference. *Jon* is the Albanian rendering of the Ionian Sea, but also the given name of Gjebrea's then-newborn son. The first-person lyric plays with this dualism: "You came to me at a desperate time, through pain—Jon! / When the ships like phantasms through a sea of adventures screamed: '*Libertà!*'" Whose pain? Intoned *sotto voce*, in a half-spoken, half-whispered recitative, Gjebrea himself sang these opening lines that mixed personal and social registers of pain. Imagining migrants to cry out for Freedom!—in Italian, of course—Gjebrea softened the potential impact of the onomatopoeic word *klithnin*, translated above as "howled," to a whisper in his dramatic performance. Gjebrea's narrator closed with a warning: "They have gold-plated chains to offer you, but once again you will be a slave." To whom does this warning apply? The newborn—or the refugees?

As a *kantautor*, songwriter, a term borrowed from the Italian *cantautore*, Gjebrea indexed a prime figure of an Italian musical modernity attractive to younger intellectuals: the enlightened (male) vocalist, commenting on society through song. An audible rendering of the refugees' experiences, Gjebrea's composition aestheticized economic desperation, presenting it as a foil to his own personal fears as a father. But the composition also expressed the profound ambivalence of a social stratum that, when crossing Albania's borders, would do so by airplane, not clinging precariously to the sides of a cargo ship. In this way, "Jon" framed a particular moment of transition for an urban audience to whom the change was then a deeply ambiguous proposition. Freedom, whether Albanian *liri* or Italian *libertà*, promised mobility, modernity, and access to Europe. But the opening of Albania—the crossing of both its physical and symbolic borders—might also portend new forms of bondage.

Consider how Gazebo (Paul Mazzolini), an Italian disco one-hit wonder and teen idol in the 1980s who recorded and helped to mix "Jon," has described encountering Gjebrea. "I met him one day in my studio as he came along with an Albanian violinist who came for a session. He asked me if I would arrange a song for him as he wanted to perform at the Tirana song contest. He had no money. But it was so funny, I decided to help him out. Now he is by far the best well known singer and performer in his country. For me it is like if I did another [hit like my early 1980s dance smash] 'I Like Chopin!' "[34] In an economy insulated from outside competition, light songs had in the minds of intellectuals expressed elevated artistic values, they had expressed their creative individuality. Would postsocialist song, even a composition articulating a segment of the intelligentsia's deepest fears about change, aspire only to comparison with a banal, English-language Italo-disco novelty dance hit from 1983?

VOICING A POSTSOCIALIST PROGRAM?

The planned music economy had depended on the strict management of aesthetically and politically correct resources, but also on the prerogative of professionalized musicians to select, cultivate, develop, and raise *vlera*, values, for local listeners. For these listeners, the new symbols, sounds, and images of the transition broadcast at the Festivals of Song between 1989 and 1991 represented a radical departure from the status quo. Emergent ways to audiate *tranzicion*, light song performances suggested overlapping, contested spaces for the potential reimagining of Albania's political-economic order in discursive and musical terms. Though intellectuals had been integrated into a system obligating nothing but the production of ideological statements, none had experience forging original ones based on non-domestic political or aesthetic resources. Tentative moves to render transition in sound between 1989 and 1991 indicate how certain members of the cultural field began strategically linking themselves to two new projects, Democracy and Europe, the projects with which a nonsocialist politics would soon come to be organized.

Yet attempts to propose a symbolic imaginary around which a nonsocialist political program should be organized did not extend automatically from a simple politics of anti-communism. Rather they derived from a source, changes to media policy, that gives rise to new questions. The promotion of rockers like Elton Deda, singers like Ndoci, or composers like Gjergj Leka and Gjebrea seemingly heralded liberalization. But at the same time this change, not unlike its precursor leading up to the Eleventh Festival of Song in the early 1970s, appears to have been part of a wider campaign directed from above. "To combat the obvious disaffection of Albania's youth, a significant social element in a country where in 1989 the average age of the population was twenty-seven," Nicholas Pano writes, "Alia sought to increase recreational facilities and activities for this group and to ease regulations on clothing and hairstyles. . . . He also sanctioned special radio programming (including Western popular music)."[35] Additionally, bureaucrats organized *piknikë* for the Youth, outdoor events featuring live music, food, and games at Tirana's Lake, figuratively and literally seeking to colonize the space of an emerging youth culture.

Listeners today often remember these transitional works as pure expressions of freedom, idealizing these performances as existing outside socialist-era norms of broadcast and cultural production. And yet the shift in policy allowing the broadcast of such works begs comparison to the earlier shift in media policy initiated, and then spectacularly renounced, in the early 1970s. After 1989, the musicians who crafted new musical signs of transition were among the more politically connected individuals in the capital. Family members of elite musicians and politicians or longstanding employees of state organs, these individuals presumably had access to insider knowledge as to which way the wind of change was blowing, or at least the skills to read such clues. This is not to claim that the people promoting new democratic values were cynics, pawns, or worse, but rather to emphasize that the planned music economy set strict limits on who could voice such values for broadcast. The individuals examined in the preceding sections ultimately succeeded in framing themselves as agents of Democracy. Their performances gradually overwhelmed alternative ways of voicing the transition, such as, for instance, composer Spartak Tili's ambivalent meditation, "A Lonely Flower," discussed in this book's opening pages. And when the Democratic Party came to power in 1992, these musicians had set the pro-Western trajectory for future negotiations about what Democracy must sound like.

Democratizing Song, 1992–1995

In March 1992, the Democratic Party received the majority of the popular vote in Albania's first freely contested elections. Sali Berisha became the country's first non-communist leader in over five decades. Addressing the foreign diplomatic corps and press two days later, Berisha flashed two fingers in the victory sign, calling out, "Hello Europe! I hope we find you well!"

Electoral politics leading up to the new Democratic government's accession to power recentered the political field on the problem of Albania's relationship to Democracy, Europe, and the rest of the world.[36] Ramiz Alia, responding to the revolutions taking hold throughout the eastern bloc in 1990, had prematurely declared Albania to be "neither East nor West." But with the advent of pluralism, rapprochement with Europe—like elsewhere in the region—became the leading political project linking abstract ideals like Freedom and Democracy to practical political, economic, and cultural reforms.[37] Even the reconstituted Party of Labor, now named *Partia Socialiste*, the Socialist Party, elevated "Europe" to the center of its revamped nationalist program. "I'm not a Stalinist, I'm not a Maoist, I'm not a Pol Potist," declared its new leader, Fatos Nano, in 1991. "I'm a true Albanian, interested in the integration of Albania in Europe."[38]

Leading up to the 1992 elections, the Socialists campaigned on a platform promising a slow transition from one-party rule heavy on government support. But the Democrats successfully commandeered the idea of rapidly reintegrating into Europe, an appeal that resulted in their overwhelming victory at the March 1992 polls. "Democracy means stable borders," Berisha had told supporters at one stump speech, "but democracy also means the free movement of people. Europe must accept a greater ration of emigration. . . . I will insist on this."[39] As Adrian Brisku has observed, the "projection of Europe as a healing force for all of the country's political and economic ills was, at best, a sign of immaturity on the part of the political class."[40] At worst, this projection signaled political elites' opportunism in registering and then exploiting ordinary people's hunger for transcending the strict borders that had once so closely confined them.

The political promotion of borders-crossing shaped discussion among musicians, artists, and writers about how to liberalize and reform the production of *kulturë*. At the same time, the organization and management of the arts, which had been the driving force behind the planned economy for over four decades, disappeared as a topic for debate. Commentators overnight ceased discussing the problem of administering culture in the terms forged during socialism and instead began arguing over how best to democratize it. The former consolidation regime had heard the leakage of any sounds through its border as contaminants. Immediately, these former contaminants were recast as privileged resources for reintegrating Albania into Europe. Overnight, the cultural field underwent its own remarkable transition, a transition in which younger artists substituted for the state-socialist logic of centralization new techniques that sought to target culture as a site not for expert planning, but for democratization. And song, these individuals proposed, provided a key platform for these reforms, and for examining, reflecting on, and making sense of the consequence of the wider political *tranzicion*.

"LIBERATION FROM THE NARROW NORMS OF THE PAST"

Between 1992 and 1995, a small group of reform-minded intellectuals targeted light music and the Festival of Song as the commonsense object of *çlirim*, that ever-persistent political byword meaning liberation. This liberation was accomplished in diverse ways. At the institutional level, state organs immediately replaced much of their socialist-era personnel. Post-1992 governments staffed the Radio-Television's music office with a number of younger Conservatory graduates, who came to include Alfred Kaçinari, Shpëtim Saraçi, Edmond Zhulali, Adrian Hila, and Selim Ishmaku over the course of the 1990s. These men were oriented toward popular music; several became the architects of the privatized music economy, examined below and in the next chapter. At the same time, new policies were implemented to cleanse airwaves of politically incorrect content and to create broadcast space for new postsocialist works. Employees in the archive performed a "check" of material, listening especially for texts having to do with the Party or Enver Hoxha; my sense from talking with fans from this period, however, is that almost all socialist-era songs were replaced by postsocialist ones or foreign pop and rock songs.

At a public discussion organized in January 1995 by the League of Writers and Artists following the Thirty-third Festival of Song, or Fest '94, musicians discussed the wider stakes of popular music.[41] The roundtable, titled "Albanian Song: Pluralism of Styles and Its Diplomatic Passport," drew freely on current political buzzwords, including *pluralizëm*, *pasaporta*, and *tranzicion*, concerning integration into Europe. Select composers and musicologists responded to three prompts.

1. Song, this "little daughter" of music, has the great ability to bring together thousands and hundreds of thousands of passionate listeners. . . . Yet is it not in danger of simply turning into a consumer product, divested from true art?
2. Though song's creative process may seem simple, it is perhaps among the most difficult, because the duration of its emotion experience is only three minutes. Does this fact not encourage "shortcut-taking"—that is, amateurism, the old sickness of song . . .?
3. In many ways, Albanian song is in the "vanguard" of the arts in terms of its demands, achievements, and new directions. As this century concludes, what can be preserved from its long tradition while (at the same time) integrating it into the genres of European song and maintaining its very identity?

"Certainly individuals have thoughts that vary," the compiler summarized, "and oftentimes they contradict each other (a thing that is completely natural), but one consideration united them: that Albanian song is one of the first musical genres to melt the 'iceberg of thought' created through the years, setting a new equilibrium in creative taste that promises outstanding values for the future."

Responses to these prompts demonstrate the primary contours of debate over how—and why—musicians and policy-makers should liberalize the music economy.

"On the road of Albanian reality's radical transformation," proposed Zhani Ciko, "song . . . not only can survive in every situation, but thanks to the care taken by its creators—and especially the younger ones—may reflect the transition sensitively." Ciko, the nephew of composer Nikolla Zoraqi and a precocious violinist as a student in 1960s Tirana, had been named director of the Theater of Opera and Ballet's orchestra in 1970. Collateral damage from the fallout of the Eleventh Festival, he was banished to a district culture house in 1974, where he worked into the 1980s. After 1990, Ciko assumed prominence as a pro–Democratic Party intellectual, and as the artistic director of the Festivals of Song in the early 1990s he oversaw their democratization. But how would song benefit from the postsocialist relaxation of aesthetic constraints?

"It should suffice to look at the typological 'map' of song," Ciko answered. "Not only do we find a reconfiguration of existing [socialist-era] types, . . . but we find uncharted territories being [explored by] the young authors and groups. . . . [We see] the disappearance of the artistic disjuncture between 'experienced' types and innovations."

Ciko viewed song as "reflecting" important realities, realities he understood younger musicians as best suited to express. The musicologist Zana Shutëriqi echoed Ciko's assessments, but pushed further. "What seems most important is the intent to emancipate our song, to move beyond archaic and spent structures in order to contemporize [song] more closely with the tastes of today. . . . The birth of [rock and pop] complexes, the training of singer-songwriters, and several other phenomena that are accompanying the process of freeing our music from the narrow norms of the past will result in the creation of a group of musicians whose profession will be, precisely, light music."

"Albanian song will always be created by professional musicians," she concluded. "This is the only guarantee. Adaptation to new demands imposed by the completely different reality in which we now live must be accepted as something that will bring new experiences in assimilating elements of our tradition. But for this it seems incorrect to take as models for national song some pieces with a folkloric character, with such archaic baggage that they cannot precede the civilizing processes to which contemporary Albanian society aspires."

Taken on the whole, plans for postsocialist song had to do with the problem of its "liberation" from the socialist period and its integration with European styles. The socialist state's *hermetizëm* from the West coupled to a "programmed *tematizëm* from above," another participant stated, had created this problem. Small wonder these critiques captured the imagination of many younger intellectuals, and even some older ones who, as became plain, found themselves unofficially barred from Festivals, recast as the products of *hermetizëm* and the representatives of *tematizëm*. The plans for reform depended on deeply held ideas about progress, "civilizing processes," and the *telos* of Albanian society—the very problems that had animated the work of intellectuals since the 1920s.

If the problem with light music songs could be heard in their stylistic narrowness, the solution would be for musicians to broaden the range of styles and sounds they used. But here commentators encountered a problem. This broadening, commentators stressed, could not simply be dictated by "the State," as this was not how democratic orders treated their artists. Ciko explained as much in 1995: "It may appear as if there is a contradiction between the imperative to push Albanian song into the European mainstream and that to clearly express its identity," he said. "It is a question that first of all should worry creators.... State organs have a role, but never in the repressive sense of applying the brutal norms of the past, norms which too often moved toward the identification of creativity with folkloric trends."

Responsibility for reflecting on and making sense of *tranzicion* and its aftermath instead would devolve onto individual artists. At Festivals of Song, the practical solution was to radically change what organizers called "the physiognomy" of the Festival at once. From their carefully balanced *tematika* to their meticulously choreographed set lists, socialist-era Festivals had broadcast symmetry redolent of stability and order. At the first postsocialist Festival of Song in December 1992, this organic unity disintegrated with organizers' selection of over fifty compositions—far more than the usual twenty-five or so, and with the majority of acts presenting Western-style rock and pop songs. In short, programming itself highlighted stylistic pluralism, as heavy metal, hip-hop, R&B, and even reggae-influenced compositions came to predominate, and selection committees gradually thinned the Festival rosters of musicians who had been active during the socialist period.

In this way, organizers effectively subcontracted the liberalization of the domestic music economy to a pool of participants who formerly existed firmly beyond its strict borders. These groups included rockers, socialist-era dissidents, ethnic Albanians from the former Yugoslavia, and an emergent group, Shutëriqi's professional song specialists, whom I will call *producentë*, or producers. The performances these groups presented at Festivals of Song after 1992 accomplished novel political work, as the democratization of song rendered *tranzicion* audible in terms that ran parallel to, even if not wholly be encapsulated by, the growing political consensus under Berisha's Democrat-led government.

Rockers and the Light of Democracy

Held nine months after the Democrats' March 1992 victory, the Thirty-first Festival of Song awarded first prize to "Pesha e Fatit" (Destiny's Weight), a decidedly Democratic vision of Democracy's growing pains, with its first prize. "Pesha e Fatit" is a remarkable composition, an epic trio composed by longtime Radio-Television director Osman Mula on a text by Alqi Boshnjaku, the young Democrat poet who replaced Jorganxhiu at the music office in 1992. Mula, nephew of elite baritone Avni Mula and a veteran Radio-Television employee, had with Boshnjaku long been associated with the cultural field's more liberal faction. Mula had performed at the Student Song Festivals preceding the Eleventh Festival of Song on saxophone; in 1990, he broke rank with some

Radio-Television colleagues to support the Democratic Party. Boshnjaku had been employed at the Army Estrada, where he also composed song texts. In 1991, he assembled one of Tirana's earliest rock ensembles, becoming one of the music field's first entrepreneurs.

Their intellectualist passion play gave voice to *tranzicion* through three characters: a Narrator, voiced by the Conservatory-trained tenor Viktor Tahiraj; a Mother/Wife figure, by soprano Manjola Nallbani; and a Migrant, by nonprofessional rocker Aleksandër Gjoka, then frontman for a heavy metal group, X. An orchestral swell leads into a plaintive piano accompaniment, as Tahiraj's opening lines allude to the previous two years: "O my spirit, don't succumb to despair / Our dreams are not drowned in this turbulent sea, in this endless misery." Continuing in a wistful, minor mode, the illuminist Narrator addresses the audience with poetic tropes on light and darkness, oblique references to nineteenth-century nationalist poet Naim Frashëri's *Fjalët e Qiririt*, "The Words of the Candle." "Let us make just a bit of light," Tahiraj intones, "however little, in this long darkness." Suddenly, Gjoka's Migrant interjects, growling out the Narrator's musical material, albeit with a choppy, unpoetic text: "Mother, I'm so far, missing you burns! Though I've money I'm poor, 'cuz I'm not near you! . . . I see your eyes in dreams, and I scream like a madman!" The Narrator, Migrant, and Mother-Wife conclude in unison, singing: "Don't stop, fight! Make light like a Naim, and live!"

The complex, interlocking layers of meaning beg analysis from the listener. In my reading, "Destiny's Weight" renders the postsocialist condition audible in a manner congruent with a particular Democratic politics of transition. Mula set the most emotionally charged moments for the rocker Gjoka's Migrant—the pain of economic migration, his fears about his family's future. But Tahiraj's intellectual Narrator explicates and frames this Migrant's experience, invoking the cultured verse of one of the nation-state's guiding "lights," the poet Naim Frashëri. By the end, the Illuminist-Narrator, it seems, has the final say, bringing the Migrant around to "see" *tranzicion* for what it really was. "For the first time," Narrator and Migrant exclaim, trading lines in the coda, "our eyes saw the light."

Despite these appeals to vision, Gjoka's sound, Mula told me, proved key. A nonconformist during late socialism who fronted several of Albania's first rock groups, Gjoka voiced for Mula an emancipated, authentic form of social commentary on the postsocialist condition, which the composer described to me as a "purity" and a "necessity" for 1990s listeners—a "natural break" with socialist aesthetics. Rockers in general played an increasingly prominent role at postsocialist light music events. Rock and metal groups composed between a quarter and a third of participants at Festivals of Song; they were also recruited to perform at state-sponsored beauty contests for "misses" and at mid-1990s rock festivals sponsored by the Ministry of Culture in Tirana. In interviews with me, rockers often claimed little interest in politics. Yet to intellectuals like Mula and

Boshnjaku, these non-professionalized musicians had the capacity to express an almost ineffable quality of *tranzicion*, its very ethos, in ways mere words alone could not. In the figure of the Migrant, Mula and Boshnjaku made this connection between rock, borders-crossing, and Democracy explicit.

Dissidents and the Communist Prison

If intellectuals heard rockers as voicing the freedom of the present, they promoted another group of musicians to express the unfreedom of the past. At postsocialist Spring Festivals and Festivals of Song, a handful of prominent performances retrospectively aestheticized resistance to communism. Throughout the region, postsocialist politics sought to identify and lionize former resisters to the state. But in comparison with other state-socialist countries, socialist Albania had tolerated neither a well-developed underground literature nor a dissident movement. One key problem facing new political elites after 1992, then, was to imaginatively locate sources of resistance to the former political status quo. Their solution to this problem was ingenious. A handful of musicians heavily promoted the notion that communism had driven potential revolt deep within individuals' souls, that individuals had cultivated an internalized sense of revolt hidden from public view. This hidden dissent became inextricably linked to the popular culture of an imagined West, with the Eleventh Festival of Song signifying a defiant act of anti-communist resistance.

Sherif Merdani, the young vocalist imprisoned and subsequently interned following the Eleventh Festival of Song, presented the first such song explicitly about "communism," "Se Kënduam 'Let It Be'" (Because We Sang 'Let It Be'). "Whatever happened to our youth?" Merdani asks, closing with the lines "And in the sun each morning, yes! / I still have 'Let It Be' to sing!" This composition promoted the narrative that Hoxha personally punished vocalists for singing foreign songs, in this case, the Beatles' 1970 ballad "Let It Be." The song has proved remarkably fertile in propagating the notion that many people were imprisoned for this form of musical revolt, often identifying Merdani as an example of a singer punished "for singing Beatles songs." Even some younger composers told me this, always referencing Merdani and the Eleventh Festival. The claim has been continually reinforced by an anecdote Merdani often tells in interviews. In 1979, an earthquake shook northern Albania, resulting in the escape of a number of political prisoners. Guards were surprised to find Merdani still in his cell. Lost in the sounds of Western music he could hear in his head, the singer had not noticed his surroundings. Merdani first told this evocative story to an Italian newspaper after being named cultural attaché to Rome in the 1990s; I heard him tell it on two separate television programs during my fieldwork in 2010.

Françesk Radi, the singer-songwriter whose performance was also denounced after the Eleventh Festival, became a second key source linking anti-communism and rock music. In 1995, he presented "Rock i Burgut" (Prison Rock), with a lyric by staunch anti-communist Agim Doçi, at the Thirty-fourth Festival of Song. In this homage to a 1950s Elvis-style rock-and-roll that, while never popular in Albania, here indexes the spirit of the West, Radi expressed a generic sound that might have sonically challenged the boundaries of the prison-state. Two female backup vocalists and a saxophone quartet wearing red tuxedos and black sunglasses, Albania's national colors, accompanied Radi on stage. Narrated from the perspective of a young prisoner, Doçi's lyric elided rock with rebellion—"It is our revolutionary rock / How little freedom, how many guards!" But as in Merdani's anecdote, rock music also provided listeners a path to an internalized sense of liberation, albeit one audible only to the "prisoner" himself. "Under rock's rhythm I lose myself," Radi sang, "Freedom's there so far away, but also close to me."

In Merdani's voicing truthful testimony, and Radi's metaphor, Western music in each instance was claimed to have functioned to emancipate communism's captives. If Albania's strict borders had barred citizens from the real freedom of the West, the authors propose, rock music provided a domestic means to imaginatively access internal psychological conditions of resistance. And the prominent media role Merdani and Radi played, in addition to their elevation to government posts, also paralleled the increasingly significant political roles former prisoners were assuming. The Democratic Party had campaigned on a platform promising "national reconciliation." But once elected, Berisha abandoned this policy and began promoting a strident anti-communist rhetoric. Berisha's marked shift to the right culminated in a 1995 "Genocide Law" that ostensibly sought to punish former elites for socialist-era crimes, but in effect eliminated the staunchest of his political opponents. As Democrats' actions began evoking unsettling comparisons with their predecessors, the anti-communist line grew more prominent, with Berisha warning that if he ceded power, the terrors of the past would be renewed.[42]

Efforts to identify who had been a communist or a dissident entailed the retrospective definition of positions, actions, and duties that might constitute culpability or dissent. Revision in many cases, however, proved tricky. Berisha himself had been a Party member and District Secretary; the early Democratic Party incorporated a number of former Sigurimi agents into its ranks. And in consolidating their power, the Democrat-led government increasingly relied on the state media as its unofficial organ. In controversial moves reminiscent of the socialist period, employees holding politically correct—after 1992, meaning Democratic and anti-communist—credentials replaced even employees without explicitly "communist" ties, the state legislature blocked licenses for private radio and television stations, and opposition journalists found themselves harassed and, at times, beaten or imprisoned.[43]

Kosovar Albanians and the Nation's Expanding Geography

Festival organizers did not only aestheticize and musically sound out new national borders through the postsocialist genres they programmed. They also began looking beyond Albania's physical borders for new voices. The inclusion of Albanian-speaking artists from the former Yugoslavia and the diaspora signaled a powerful form of political and musical *pluralizëm*. As Zhani Ciko reacted approvingly in 1995, "This year, participation—or the 'geography' of authors—broadened. Besides Albanians from Kosova, Macedonia, from the Arbëreshë of Italy that have been in the past 2–3 festivals as well, we have authors from America, Germany, and so on. The national identity of song, I believe, is being realized through the editions of the festival."[44]

During the socialist period, relations between Albania and Albanian-speaking populations in Yugoslavia were complicated. Officials in Tirana carefully controlled contact between their citizens and Yugoslavia's Albanians, especially in the Autonomous Republic of Kosovo, concerned about exposing them to the markedly higher living standards just over the border. On the other side, growing national sentiments among Kosovar Albanians, which culminated in the 1981 student protests put down by Yugoslavia's federal government, heightened political concerns in the region about the potential for the growth of pan-Albanian sentiments. For Kosovars, Radio-Television Albania had broadcast a powerful means to imaginatively experience membership in an Albanian nation, especially with the suppression their own Albanian-language media in the 1980s. With its professional production values, highly trained folk ensembles, and nationalist content, Radio-Television Albania became affectively intertwined with meaningful Kosovar constructions of national intimacy. Participation in the Festivals after 1992 thus represented, as Kosovar singer Mihrije Braha has described, "a dream . . . just to hold the microphone at the Radio-Television Albania studios."[45]

But while Tirana's intellectuals had been weaving intricate webs of discourses on "national" music during the socialist period, Albanian-speaking intellectuals in the Yugoslav republics and its Western European diaspora had been cultivating a more pragmatic sense of the Nation as a potent political symbol of resistance. Inflected by institutionalized discrimination, the national intimacies cultivated by Albanian-speakers in Kosova seemed too politically overt, unvarnished, for many Tirana elites. One composer, for instance, described Kosovar Albanians to me as being *nacionalist* in a way he found "frightening." With the Yugoslav conflicts of the early 1990s threatening to draw Albanian-speaking areas into open conflict, Kosovar artists increasingly viewed the Festival as a venue for voicing explicit nationalist statements, such "Zemra e Plagosur" (The Wounded Heart), the actor-singer Sejfullah Fejzullahu's raw call for "a free Kosova." Such performances contributed to stereotypes in Tirana portraying northerners in general as unrefined, and driven by their passions.

At the same time, Albanians from outside Albania helped to import non-local genres, especially dance music and hip-hop, through the early 1990s Festivals. In this Kosovar songwriters posed especially stiff competition to members of the Tirana-based field. Having worked under Yugoslavia's relaxed cultural policies, these musicians had firsthand experience performing and writing in Western idioms. They also had the business acumen and capital musicians in postsocialist Tirana lacked. Festival entries submitted by Albanians from the former Yugoslavia often far outstripped Tirana-produced tracks in terms of their contemporary musical markers. Star Kosovar singer Adelina Ismajli's notorious 1996 performance "Zemrën Nuk ta Fal" (I Don't Spare Your Heart), for instance, produced by Macedonia-based producer Wirusi, featured hip-hop-style scratching, sampling, and synth bass; during the live Festival performance, Ismajli performed synchronized steps with breakdancers. Initially wearing a furry purple jacket over her t-shirt, Ismajli at one point leaves the stage only to return in a sheer dress over red lingerie, a stunt that caused much hand-wringing and pearl-clutching in Tirana.

While the inclusion of Kosovar singers enacted new borders at the Festival, as Ciko lauded, it also posed a symbolic threat to local intellectuals. Kosovar Albanians' performances expressed competing visions of the Nation while also challenging challenging domestic musicians' status. Festival juries and organizers, however, attempted to mitigate the potential challenge. Kosovars rarely received top prizes, instead garnering newly created secondary prizes like "Best Look" or "Best New Artist." In a 1997 interview, Ismajli complained that organizers viewed them as "the Kosovars," implying that non-Tirana artists served a purely performative function.[46] And when Albërie Hadërgjonaj received first-place in 1998, with a composition by former *estrada* singer and postsocialist politician Luan Zhegu, Tirana critics accused jury members of "corruption" and cheating. Unnamed sources even claimed the Kosovar singer had lip-synched at this Festival, the first to be performed live since 1989. Of fifteen first-, second-, and third-place compositions awarded prior to Hadërgjonaj's disputed success, four were presented to Tirana-based composers and eleven went to individuals with connections to Radio-Television Albania. The emergence of this small group of employees, self-described producers, had far-reaching effects on production in the postsocialist music economy.

Composer-Producers and Modern Song Production

The most consequential change to the Tirana-based music field has proven to be the emergence of Shutëriqi's "professional song specialists." A peer group of Conservatory-trained musicians seeking to self-consciously modernize popular music, these men were the first in Tirana to adopt new sampling and recording technologies. The professionalized composer had always worked, my consultants stressed, "with pen and paper." That is, a professional work was one created at the piano and notated for arrangement by the Radio-Television's bandleaders. But younger composer-producers now began calling this process "obsolete," and urgently sought training and the equipment to make more modern sounds.

Assigned in 1990 to the Army Ensemble, Alfred Kaçinari told me he used this position to requisition a 16-track Yamaha sequencer. Following what he nostalgically recalled to me as his "first contact with advanced technology," the composer shortly thereafter left for Italy to raise money to purchase the equipment, or *paisjet*, that comprised his own first, rudimentary recording studio. Composer-producers often described the acquisition of *paisjet* in sharp detail. In 1993, Edmond Zhulali purchased his first synthesizer, capable of making and recording rudimentary digital arrangements. Soon feeling he had outgrown this hardware, he, like Kaçinari, left Tirana to raise funds for a "real" studio.

"In December 1995, I went to work two months in Switzerland, to do music," he told me. "Well, Kosovar Albanians there customarily pay tips, and in two months I made a lot of money not from a salary, but from these tips. I raised quite a bit of money, but this was not for me. The music was drinking music, it was *ordiner*"—a term intellectuals use in a derogatory way to mean bland, common, even vulgar—"and I worked for only two months. I just could not take it in psychological terms. But I bought a very good 24-channel mixer, analog, and I bought a hard disk recorder from America, the first in Albania; and an effects processor, which was also very good at that time."

Speaking pragmatically, recording technologies were, as Zhulali put it, an "absolute necessity" during the financially unstable conditions of the transition. "We used to joke, you can have a whole orchestra in your home, you don't need to get musicians together and have rehearsals," he recalled. "No doubt, the level was not that of live musicians, but in the initial conditions of the 1990s, this technology gave us possibilities." But composer-producers also viewed recording technology as a key means to break with "communist" compositional aesthetics. "Socialist realism as a method was zero, it was damaging," Kaçinari told me, "it mis-educated people—it was like telling schoolchildren that one plus one equaled three."

The adoption of new recording technologies enabled Tirana's new cohort of song specialists to begin producing tracks that more or less approximated the contemporary production values of Western pop, R&B, or hip-hop. Songs created by Zhulali, Kaçinari, and their peers foregrounded synthesized production values, as in Radio-Television-employed composer-producer Shpëtim Saraçi's song "Të Sotmen Jeto" (Live for Today). This typical Saraçi production prominently featured a synth-bell melody line, live electric guitar, drum-machine beat, and a synthesized string wash behind the vocals during the verse and refrain. During its live performance at the Thirty-third Festival of Song in 1994, unamplified members of the Radio-Television Orchestra, seated in semi-darkness at the back of the stage, gamely aped along to the recording. The upbeat sheen of Saraçi's production paralleled the forward-looking optimism of the text, penned by Alqi Boshnjaku, who was recently hired at the Radio-Television to replace Zhuljana Jorganxhiu. "Don't be disappointed by the yesterday that's gone," instructed vocalist Mira Konçi in the refrain, "Enjoy today! Seek the future! Live for today!" Considered one of Tirana's most stylish women in the 1990s, Konçi appeared, as always, with makeup, jewelry, and a fashionably contemporary ensemble.

These self-consciously *moderne* productions came to dominate the postsocialist Festivals, winning top prizes and replacing works drawing on socialist-era aesthetics of beauty, lyricality, or grand-ness. More consequentially, the organization of the postsocialist festival itself came to demand these prerecorded productions. In practical terms, the Radio-Television seems to have lost the funding and overall technological capacity to stage a fully live performance during these years. Ciko claimed in an interview that this was due to the overall lack of funding and the destabilized music field. The cash-strapped government expended less for cultural events, while working composers, lyricists, and musicians traveling from throughout Albania and its diasporas were unable to commit to month-long unpaid rehearsals. Prerecording tracks solved these logistical problems. But prerecorded productions also funneled organization into the hands of the small clique of younger specialists able to navigate new recording technologies. Some older composers began criticizing these younger producers for disqualifying their submissions in favor of more markedly modern pieces. Several claimed sabotage. In 1995, Aleksandër Peçi accused organizers of attempting to poach his singer with offers of cash and prizes; he later claimed they purposely distorted his track, in effect making it unlistenable in the hall during its performance. Composer Naim Gjoshi has accused several composer-producers of "selling prizes," promising productions to singers who paid for both the song and their place in the Festival's finale, a charge he believed led him to be blacklisted from Radio-Television events.

COUNTER-REACTIONS: THE "PRESSURE" OF FOREIGN MUSIC

For commentators like Shutëriqi and Ciko, the outsourcing of light song to the new groups described above audibly challenged the "archaism" and "narrow norms" of socialism. Certainly, not all members of the music field agreed with this assessment. Yet in criticizing what dominant commentators lauded as a pluralism of styles and musical borders-crossing, dissenters from the postsocialist status quo faced what turned out to be an insurmountable challenge. Socialist-era discourses on creativity and new postsocialist forms of political speech alike depended on teleological claims about progress. But the former had to do with the legitimacy of the socialist state to successfully target and solve society's problems, and the latter, with integrating back into the West. The language of progress itself thus raised new contradictions. At the roundtable discussed in the opening to this section, Çesk Zadeja noted that song, "more than any other genre of musical art, moves forward with the times."[47]

"But it must also be understood," he continued, "that it conveys many stylistic elements of a historical character that are refurbished according to the emotional and aesthetic demands of the People itself, and so it preserves the most essential features of the nation.... No doubt, these demands are not solved at once, nor can prescriptions be given for them. But we are all of the opinion that, among other things, this stimulates amateur and professional composers to be more deeply immersed in knowing national culture (as well as the contemporary in general)."

In retrospect, this wishful thinking seems remarkably wrongheaded. Who would "refurbish" these older elements? Who would provide models that mediated, as Zadeja suggested, between local tradition and contemporary styles in order to meet the postsocialist demands of the People? Rockers, dissidents, Kosovars, and producers had no interest in doing this. And the one group that might have, older intellectuals, were no longer presenting songs. For this reason, noted musicologist Sandër Çefa, the "scant participation of affirmed and well-known composers" was particularly troubling. "This phenomenon, I think, represents something concerning and complicated that does not only have to do with reasons of desire, ability, or age," he continued. "It has to do with aspects that are sometimes internal to the creator, [but also] with the peculiar direction that the Festival has taken in terms of its content, with the influences and pressure being exerted by foreign music."[48]

Postsocialist Festivals created space for voicing new ideas about the Nation, Freedom, and Democracy. But at the same time, postsocialist politics precluded discussion about more fundamental shifts in the music field that replaced long-standing concerns about the role of song in elevating the cultural level of listeners with worries about song itself as an object for democratization. This seemingly subtle shift in policy presaged major transformations to the planned economy.

Deterritorializing the Music Economy, 1996–1997

Between the late 1940s and the early 1990s, the dual governmental logic of centralization and redistribution structured the production and consumption of music in Albania. Direct policy contributed to the consolidation of Tirana as a center, to its exercise of a kind of centripetal force over culture and the arts. This force continued to work on ordinary Albanians and intellectuals alike after the end of one-party rule in 1991. With artificial strictures on internal migration relaxed, the capital swelled by the time of my fieldwork to over ten times its former size.

"The desire was to come to Tirana, no other town," one migrant told sociologist Julie Vullnetari. "Even if someone was to offer me a house for free in another town, I wouldn't go there. Tirana ticked all the boxes on our checklist. . . . art is made here, other activities, the modern life as we saw it in films or read it in books. So, Tirana was closest to Europe. . . . This opinion was created before the 1990s, before the changes took place and we thought it was the only opportunity, without having to move abroad."[49]

This should not be read as some sort of false consciousness, the result of propaganda. Rather, the spatial logic of state-socialist cultural production had simultaneously contributed to and derived from symbolic-ideological strategies for governing Albania's population, shaping individual consumers' dreams and desires, their senses of belonging and self. Centralization organized the production and consumption of society's symbolic means within the planned cultural economy. But these symbolic means simultaneously provided socialism's subjects with privileged resources for self-fashioning that, in Albania, had existed exclusively within the strict symbolic and physical borders of the state. Party officials' exaggerated reliance on symbolic-ideological strategies of control made them excessively dependent on strictly policing the borders of their domestic economies. The construction of thousands of concrete bunkers to facilitate guerrilla warfare, bunkers that today still scar the countryside's national boundaries and waterfronts, exemplified this concern. According to this analysis, chanting student protesters did not topple the party-state. It began crumbling when citizens first began unfurling homemade antennae to watch films and listen to popular music from the West. And it fell when desperate migrants breached the consolidation regime's borders to access Greece, Italy, or Tirana's handful of foreign embassies—and officials ordered guards to hold their fire.

This context explains why the postsocialist cultural field became so fascinated with borders, with song's "diplomatic passport." But while some reformers valorized the very act of musical borders-crossing, others raised concerns. After all, the formerly strict aesthetic boundaries of the socialist period had given the music field its shape, molding musicians' senses of themselves as creators as well as their sense of duty toward listeners. And professionalized musicians had themselves policed aesthetic borders. Many soon felt the opening of the music field's borders had engendered immutable contradictions between domestically produced art and its new political and economic contexts.

Critique arose from diverse sources, including even the newly enfranchised groups introduced above. In 1997, the young rocker Bojkën Lako called the previous year's Festival of Song "a regression." "Everything that came from outside the borders this year was *më e kultivuar, më e stilizuar*—more cultivated, more stylish. More thoughtful and pure, while our music, here [in Tirana], swirls around in an unlikeable, parochial whirlpool. [The Festival] is an activity for internal consumption."[50]

Here Lako suggests something essential about the shift from a governmental cultural policy concerned with managing culture to one concerned with sounding out the nature and endpoint of *tranzicion*. In rendering Democracy audible and liberating song from its communist bonds, Festivals served a performative function by broadcasting the symbolic contours of a self-consciously postsocialist modernity. Yet as Lako intuits, these performances were predominantly for "internal consumption," directed at the intellectual field in Tirana itself.[51] Stylistic borders-crossing, understood as the musical promotion of *pluralizëm* in Tirana, necessitated the creative deterritorialization of longstanding aesthetic codes in the music field. The borders of the deterritorialized music field at once became permeable, crossed and crisscrossed by non-professionalized young rockers, dissidents, and Kosovar Albanians, groups formerly excluded from its space by strict political or artistic requirements. Here I use the term *deterritorialization* to begin describing the consequences of *pluralizëm* on what had once been both an extremely rigid and hierarchical form of social organization. The socialist period's aesthetics, formerly understood within the field as the expression of an internalized creative individuality, suddenly mattered far less within the domestic economy. Instead, access to centralized broadcast resources came to depend on the ability of musicians to render the sonic *tranzicion* in a manner congruent with Democrats' understanding of Albania: as necessitating a clean break from an abnormal past and integration within the borders of Europe.

The aesthetic deterritorialization of the music field did not immediately transform the state-socialist mode of cultural production's institutional shape. But it did portend the disembedding of the relations of musical production and consumption from the centrally planned cultural economy. And this disembedding ultimately, as described in the following chapter, would enable the economic reorganization of the field. In short, the political process of creative borders-crossing ran in parallel to an emerging economic process, as the curtailment of state support for culture soon began forcing artists to explore alternative resources for creating and disseminating their music.

This economic process had two sources. First, the end of state subsidy fortuitously coincided with the emergence of a prosumer market for recording technologies. Previously, the Radio-Television's recording studio had been the only means by which a popular song could be recorded, and state airwaves or ensembles, the sole means for its distribution. But after 1992, composers newly able to travel abroad began raising funds to import (relatively) affordable equipment for recording, mixing, and distributing sound. Formerly there existed a single center for sound production; now, potentially any space with a sampling keyboard, microphone, and electricity could function as a mini-center. With the advent of affordable digital recording software, these mini-centers began proliferating. Second, the collapse of the artificial borders ringing socialist Albania's domestic market for music consumption forced local producers to compete with the broader Albanian-speaking world. Initially, Tirana put them at a disadvantage. Jane Sugarman, naming the cities in the former Yugoslavia and Western Europe she observed listed on the back of 1990s Albanian-language cassettes, noted the startling absence of Tirana among emerging "musical capitals," competing diaspora centers that superseded what had formerly been the undisputed symbolic anchor of the Albanian-speaking universe.[52]

Yet Tirana, and especially its Festival of Song, nevertheless persisted as a strong center for the production of popular music into the mid-1990s. On the one hand, local Albanians in general lacked the capital necessary to build infrastructure necessary to support a non-state-subsidized music economy. Tirana's handful of modest studios notwithstanding, little capital existed for investment in private radio-television stations, larger studios, or outfits to press and distribute materials. Some 1990s rock groups even welcomed piracy, as homemade tapes traded among friends were a key way their music could be distributed. On the other hand, Tirana persisted as a center because Berisha's government stifled competition at the institutional level. Its legislature did not ratify a legal framework for licensing private radio or television media, leaving Radio-Television Albania as the only real media option in the country, not wholly unlike before. But it was an increasingly hollow center, ill-suited to administering production under what theater professor Arben Imami, a founding Democrat purged by Berisha soon after the 1992 elections, later termed *demokratura: demokracia* plus *diktatura*.[53] But over the course of approximately sixteen months, in local parlance, *trazira e '97-të*, or the unrest of 1997, each of these problems found its solution.

A SOUNDTRACK FOR "ALBARADO"

Speeding down a coastal highway at sunset in his Mercedes convertible, Ardit Gjebrea in his 1995 music video, "Makina e Memorjes," provided a potent image of prosperity. His girlfriends are stunning, Heather Locklear–types, and they sunbathe, ride his expensive white motorboat, even canter bikini-clad on a horse through the waves. Gjebrea forced nearly every sonic marker of Tirana's postsocialist modernity into this heavily synthesized track: the distorted rock riff, the electronic keyboard, the heavy metal guitar solo. Over the top, the track valorized a vision of the good life, albeit one only a handful of Albanians could experience firsthand.

The growing number of productions promoting local lifestyles of the rich and famous coincided with darker clouds: the rise of Ponzi schemes that, between 1995 and 1997, reshaped the country. Between one-sixth and one-half of the population invested money, and in comparison with pyramid schemes elsewhere in the postsocialist region, participation attained an "unparalleled level of penetration into the fiber of everyday life."[54] Smoki Musaraj relates the following sardonic commentary from this period, reported in a newspaper in 1996: "Almost all citizens of Albarado inherited from the terribly red dictatorship an apartment, which the happily blue democracy gave to them as a gift," the journalist wrote. "The value of the red-blue apartment is $25,000. . . . Thanks to a terribly simple alchemic formula, the villager-citizen, within three months, becomes the owner of four times $25,000, in other words of $100,000!"[55]

Unconscionably, Democrats identified themselves with the magical largesse created by the unsustainable returns on these schemes. At the height of their popularity, Berisha's supporters nicknamed him *Sali-Bollëku*, Sali-Abundance.[56] The firms received their veneer of authenticity from the Democrat-led government, as well as advertising time on the state media next to pop visions of the capitalist good life. When the first schemes began failing in late 1996, the Democrats reacted with tragic indecision. As the larger companies collapsed in early 1997, the country plunged into chaos. Thousands of protesters took to the streets, now chanting, *O Sali O Fajdexhi*, O Sali You Usurer, as public order disintegrated.[57] Rioters looted arms depots, anti-government forces erected a parallel administration in southern Albania, and, as the threat of all-out civil war loomed, the Democratic Party at last ceded power to the Socialists in emergency elections held later that year.

The *trazira* indirectly helped to dismantle the remaining vestiges of the planned music economy. In institutional terms, the shift from the Democrats to the Socialists led to the emergence of a deterritorialized network of private media companies. Because Berisha's government had curbed media reform, only two independent radio stations, modest vanity projects funded by migrant earnings in district towns, had been established since 1992. But in 1996 and 1997, some twenty small companies were founded, private outlets that played significant roles investigating political and social problems, including the pyramid schemes themselves. Enveloped by larger problems, the government turned a deaf ear to these enterprises. According to historian Arben Muka, "When Radio Klan," which would grow into one of two leading domestic media empires by the 2000s, "began to broadcast to Tirana, there was little concern about its registration with judicial or tax institutions, simply because the capital and the entire country were still suffering the effects of the violent unrest."[58] Following the ascension to power of the Socialists, rumors even circulated that the government unofficially gave Klan equipment seized from the VEFA Holding Company, one of the largest schemes. And in 1998, the Socialist-led legislature at last ratified a legal framework for private media companies, leading to their exponential growth over the next six years.

But the *trazira* also affected the economy by disembedding capital from physical assets, as cash-poor people sold their homes and apartments to raise money to invest. Newly liquid capital in turn contributed to the emergence of a *biznesmen* class as well as new business practices, as Albanians exchanged Berisha's *demokratura* for what Dritëro Agolli called *shkërdhatokracia*: a prick-ocracy, in which corruption reigned and cash greased the wheels of politics, business, and culture alike.[59] To my intellectual consultants, the average *nouveau riche* was a philistine. A colleague who worked as a waiter in the 1990s remembered "tough guys coming in, and they'd slap down their car keys and cell phones on the table—and no one had these things then—and then make you change the radio dial from Western rock music to pop-folk." The intellectual Fatos Lubonja, in his semi-fictionalized account of this period, relates his autobiographical protaganist's meeting with Vehbi Alimuça, the head of VEFA, in 1997.

" 'Do you fancy some music?' Vehbi said to him. 'Sure,' he had replied, humouring him. Vehbi had rung a bell and immediately a young woman appeared. 'What piece shall she play?' Vehbi asked. The journalist shook his head indecisively. 'Play that thing of Louise's,' Vehbi decided for him, and she had played Beethoven's *Für Elise*."[60]

The transfer of power from the Democrats to the Socialists averted civil war. But the chaos left 2,000 people dead. At the Thirty-sixth Festival of Song, a young sixteen-year-old singer, Elsa Lila, articulated conciliatory sentiments for the consumption of Tirana's elites with her interpretation of "Larg Urrejtje," "Keep Hatred Distant," by composer Valentin Veizi and lyricist Alqi Boshnjaku. Lila, a precocious Lyceum student with a big voice, had also received first prize in the previous year's Festival. And she had been personally touched by the unrest. Her mother had been murdered in March. "Don't give in to hate—keep hatred far from us," she sang in the refrain of the Whitney Houston–inspired power ballad. And then, after the Festival concluded, Lila got on an airplane, crossing over Albania's borders to rejoin her father in Italy.

The Transitional State

Toward the end of my fieldwork, I sat down with a composer who had joined the Democratic Party just after its founding. On graduation from the Conservatory in the mid-1970s he had been assigned to a large district culture house; by the late 1980s, he had climbed the career ladder to Tirana. After becoming a card-carrying Democrat, his postsocialist career had depended on the Democratic Party's fortunes. With the Party in power during the early 1990s, he retained his post in the capital. With the Party out of power, he scrabbled for several years before landing a plum job with a state agency on Berisha's return as prime minister in 2005. He was, as sympathizers and critics alike might say, *një demokrat i flaktë*, a fiery, maybe even over-ardent, Democrat.

"So you participated in the Democratic movement?" I prompted, moving the conversation toward his concrete experiences of *tranzicion*.

"This is something you must understand," he lectured. "*Everyone* took part in the Democratic movement, without exception. It included everyone. Later of course people split into different groups. But without exception, everyone took part. There was only one exception, those people that we call the *bllokmene*, people who lived in the Block and were bound to the communist system."

"And what did you expect from the movement? What changes did you anticipate?"

"What did I expect? I expected that we would be able to live just like our colleagues in the West. That we would be able to write and think in a free way, that we would be able to *dal jashtë nga korniza* of socialist aesthetics—to step outside the boundaries of socialism. To be able to do the same as our colleagues in Europe."[61]

"Were you disappointed? In terms of what happened to light music?"

"Well, what ended up happening was *një vërshim drejt lirisë*, a mad rush toward freedom. This is what I write about in that article I gave you, so we can move on."

We dropped the topic, and I later read through the short essay he had given me. The issue as he framed it—the "mad rush toward freedom"—had to do with post-1992 changes to Albania's economic model that had "standardized," "narrowed," even simply "minimized" popular music, criticisms with which I had by then become used to hearing from men of his generation and which are examined in the next chapter.

As popular music and the Festival of Song came to be targeted as objects for democratization, a critical distinction began to emerge between "freedom as an ideal, as articulated in struggles against particular regimes of power," and freedom as "a mode of organizing and regulation . . . a certain way of administering a population that depends upon the capacities of free individuals."[62] This chapter has sounded out the emergence of this distinction in the transitional state. An abstract ideal of freedom had been a powerful early keyword of *trancizion*, albeit one initially engaged only with some difficulty by musicians. But musicians' efforts to register the emancipation of the postsocialist present became, over time, enmeshed within an emergent political rationality to democratize social and artistic life.

Accounts of eastern bloc transitions have tended to emphasize the power of new sounds in enfranchising musicians and listeners by signaling pluralism, resolving conflicts, even stimulating democratization. Musical symbols in such readings function as anti-hegemonic vehicles for novel forms of identification.[63] But postsocialist ideals could also engender new hegemonies.[64] And in practice, the turn toward promoting *pluralizëm* had major, contradictory effects on the music field. It enfranchised some non-professionalized musicians while disenfranchising many professionalized composers and singers. Cultural policy came to depend on a new political status quo in Tirana, a new normal that effectively cleansed the airwaves of performances suggesting that the endpoint of the transition might lead to anywhere but Europe.[65] Officials and the musicians they supported valorized the very act of circulation itself, whether of musical styles, capital, or even people. To suggest the music economy's borders could be anything but open became impossible in leading postsocialist political and artistic circles.

Political and economic reforms, however, targeted listeners in contradictory ways. Certainly, media consumption opened up new vistas of self-making, "scripts for possible lives," as Arjun Appadurai put it in his seminal work on the topic. But listeners always choose, as Appadurai also cautioned, among a range of preexisting choices.[66] No longer blocked by protectionist media politics, the scripts Radio-Television Albania produced in the name of *pluralizëm* heavily reinforced a dominant political vision for a European, Western, consumerist modernity. Yet even if you were to argue that listeners had previously had no choice in what they could watch and hear on state-socialist media, and that any choice is better than none, the proliferation of opportunities to choose after 1992 raises another question. Can the apparent emancipation of choice be disentangled from capitalism itself? It may not be surprising that market-oriented policy-makers in Tirana almost overnight began addressing the state's newly freed subjects as defined by their capacity to choose, by their new status as consumers. Postsocialism hailed its subjects under the sign of *liri*. Yet this *liri* proved to be the means by which ordinary practices of media consumption could be substituted for the abstract ideal of political agency, a "mad rush toward freedom" that increasingly troubled even the most reform-minded musicians in Tirana.

At the same time, domestically produced media began facing increasingly stiff competition from foreign imports. In the late 1990s, one ethnographer lived with families from Mirdita, a mountainous district where some residents had previously received Radio-Television Albania's fuzzy signal only on clear days. Relocated to the coast after the local economy collapsed, villagers quickly acquired recently imported satellite dishes. Both sexes of all ages, the ethnographer worried, "watched [even adult] programs like robots, occasionally laughing embarrassedly, but never apparently worried by the impressions the films might be making on their offspring. The explanation seems to be that what is on television is 'modern' and hence must be harmless."[67] Strictly sequestered at home, young girls in particular spent hours watching soap operas, turning on the television when they awoke and watching until the electricity failed.[68] I heard similar stories. When I first visited Tirana in 2004, a twenty-five-year-old friend surprised me by reciting verbatim lyrics by Jim Morrison, the lead singer of the American rock band the Doors. With a just-so story typical of the 1990s, he claimed to have learned English by taping rock and metal songs off the radio and then painstakingly transcribing their texts. He did not follow Albanian light music, though he remembered sometimes tuning in to hear the Festival's foreign guest acts—"when they didn't cancel," he laughed—before promptly turning off the television.

To what extent could domestically produced popular culture present postsocialist listeners with viable models for themselves, whether as Democrats, consumers, Westerners, Europeans, or something else? A friend, *Alban, told me a joke that had circulated through his district town's middle school in the 1990s. At the beginning of each school year, the teacher would ask her students what they wanted to be when they grew up. A beginning-of-term tradition held over from the socialist period, this exercise formerly served to introduce students to teachers, and provided pupils an opportunity to demonstrate their pro-forma, bushy-tailed optimism about Socialist Albania's bright future. But what did young people hope to be after 1992?

"What do you want to be when you grow up, Zana?" asked the teacher.

"I want to become a doctor," answered Zana.

"And what do you want to be when you grow up, Agron?" asked the teacher.

"I want to become a lawyer," Agron answered dutifully.

"And Beni, what do you want to be when you grow up?" asked the teacher.

"I want to be a refugee!" declared Beni.

In the mock-serious tone of a teacher, friends would query each another, doubling Alban and his classmates over with laughter. On returning home from abroad, refugjatë seemed so worldly. These economic migrants wore nice clothes, had ready cash, and owned the latest cassettes of Italian and American popular music, all unavailable in Alban's district town. With Albania's material and symbolic borders now opened to competition, what would be the prospects for a domestically produced, national popular song?

5

Promoting Albania

As the end of my fieldwork approached, I had at last become comfortable with the kind of jokey male bonding that my consultants called *llafa*. So I jumped at the invitation a young composer extended to me for drinks with a few older colleagues, and in late April 2010, two composers, an ethnomusicologist, and a folklorist walked into a bar.

"What conclusions have you drawn, how much have you written?" asked *Petrit before our glasses of *raki* had arrived. "Where are you right now in your thinking?"

Taken aback, I began too formally, describing the timeline of my research, my questions, the archives I had consulted. Brusquely, the composer cut me off, uninterested or maybe feeling I had misunderstood his intent. "Concretely, sir, what are your thoughts about so-called Albanian light music? Do you have any conclusions? Have you talked to *anybody*—who? Now: does an Albanian light music exist? Is there even such a thing? What is your conclusion?"

By this point in my research I knew enough to assume that, though unstressed as he spoke, Petrit's question revolved around the adjective "Albanian." But before I could respond, the folklorist, *Agim, joined us. Petrit, a gregarious middle-aged man, had rolled the sleeves of his shirt up and was wearing wrinkled dark pants—he had been working in his small recording studio all day. Agim, an employee at a state agency in Tirana, was the opposite: thin, sharp, professionally dressed, though just a year or so older than Petrit. We exchanged greetings, Petrit summed up the *llafa*, and Agim waved him off, obviously familiar with this old debate.

"In 1988," he began in professorial tones, turning to face me, "I completed a diploma paper titled 'The National in Our Light Music.' In it, I explained how our light music was cultivated, as a tradition, as a national tradition. A tradition that had its roots well before the Second World War, but that was developed and soon became a professional tradition with the First Festival of Song in Tirana."

"O *bo bo* my friend, what national tradition existed, before the war?" Petrit interrupted. "In Shkodra, singing Italian songs? In Korça, Greek, Yugoslav, whatever sorts of borrowed, half-stolen songs—?"

"Shut your mouth! Quiet!" Agim exploded, winking at me. "If you don't know what you are talking about, shut your mouth! Where was the first ever concert of songs? Where—"

"In Shkodra! It—"

"O, *budalla*—moron! Organized in Tirana, then staged in Shkodra—just stay silent if you do not know! O my friend, what did Shkodra have? All the strands of culture were in Tirana. Where was the Theater of Opera and Ballet? The Conservatory? The first Radio Festival of Song? Where—"

"Okay, but Tish Daija, Tonin Harapi, in Shkodra. Çesk Zadeja, born in Shkodra—"

"O *more*! But they worked in Tirana, by way of Moscow! All in Tirana!" said Agim. "This is where the composers were, this is where the beginnings of culture were organized."

"Okay, but this is beside the point," said Petrit. "The question posed to the gentleman was this: Is there such a thing as Albanian light music? And has he, in his research, been able to define this object? For his project, this is the key question: Does an Albanian light music song exist, does it have any value, what are its values? This is where the project begins and ends, on this question."

Among professionalized musicians in Tirana, contemporary discussions about music and values so often turned to these questions of definition. What is Albanian art today, and what is so Albanian about it? Does it even exist? Or did it *ever* exist? To me, these questions pointed to a dual anxiety my consultants held about contemporary popular music. On the one hand, composers and some listeners alike worried about the ongoing influences of commodification and globalization on postsocialist culture. But on the other hand, *kultura* itself, the domain that so many perceived as besieged by outside forces, had, as an object of their expert oversight, largely resulted from state-socialist cultural policies that are today disavowed. And yet socialist-era ideas and ideals remain enmeshed within contemporary definitions of creativity. Back at the *llafa* session, I was not surprised to hear conversation then turn to mourning *niveli i publikut*, the level of the public or audience, and the sad truth that young listeners today "lack culture." This level, my tablemates told me, gives rise to an ugly cycle: contemporary composers and music producers write songs that appeal to an audience's baser instincts; listeners learn to crave this "fast food music"; and so-called fast food music in turn further lowers the cultural level of the art-loving public in general.

"But had the public really been at such a high level?" I asked, using their terms. "Not just in Tirana, but in the deepest villages? Did they really love art the way people today say they did?"

"Absolutely," responded Agim, "And I will tell you why. It was something exciting: there was one radio, one television station. There was no alternative. People did not have the level to understand serious music. Not everyone can understand a symphony, right? But folk music? Light music? Everyone can understand these genres. In December during the Festival, everyone listened. And everybody sang the songs."

"Even in the most remote villages, you think?"

"I don't think, I know! It was beautiful but also understandable for those listeners."

"But then why did this public abandon their good taste after the 1990s?" I asked.

"You must understand, everyone was thirsty for something different. I will explain it like this. In the early 1990s, we had a mania for discos and misses. Not just the Miss Albania pageant, but Miss Tirana, Miss Durrës, Miss Kavaja, Miss Some Podunk Village, misses everywhere, beauty competitions in the smallest, most backward villages. No, really! It was exciting, plus there was anger about what had happened before. I myself had this anger. But then I got my fill. I got my fill of misses and discos, and I moved on."

Over nearly four decades, musicians had refined ever more complex hierarchies of value, jostling for distinction within an economy that, safeguarded from competition beyond Albania's borders, had secured them a monopoly over production in the name of elevating the cultural level of listeners. But as capital penetrates the borders of the contemporary music economy, it transforms the practices and products of these musicians. And in doing this, capital marketizes the aesthetic discourses on which composers' senses of themselves as artists and social beings had for so long depended. In the market economy, musicians do not compete to gain access to centrally administered resources for the recording and broadcast of their works. But neither do they compete for a market of consumers. Instead, composers now contend with one another and non-professionalized competitors for access to a market of postsocialist singers seeking to promote themselves through radio play, music video clips, competition at private media's song contests, and personal appearances. In the new economy, composers find themselves beholden to singers' strategies for self-promotion and often, in my consultants' view, what they denigrated as a taste for creatively bankrupt songs.

The spirit of *promovim*, or promotion, suffuses even the state-organized Festival of Song. In capitalist societies, "promotion," as Andrew Wernick writes, "come[s] to shape not only that culture's symbolic and ideological contents, but also its ethos, texture, and constitution as a whole."[1] This concluding chapter examines how composers engage what I call the promotional state, the matured organizational form resulting from the political and economic changes of the late 1990s.[2] My tone shifts a final time, and I move between the thick description of my notes on the Forty-eighth Festival of Song, which I observed firsthand in December 2009, and interviews, recording studio visits, and analysis of contemporary cultural policy. Because the domestic popular music economy no longer centers on the Festival, I also weave in notes on its new driving force, private song competitions organized by new media conglomerates. In doing this, I explore two key oppositions in the economy: between the state-run Festival and these private festivals, and between professionalized composers, graduates of the state conservatory, and self-employed producers, *producentë*, the non-professionalized owners of private recording studios. Where Conservatory graduates operate their own modest recording studios, like Petrit above, I indicate this in the text by referring to them as composer-producers.

For the professionalized heirs to men like Zadeja, Dizdari, and Krajka, the path privatization has taken since the late 1990s raises vexing questions about popular song, art, and the role of culture in a contemporary democracy. Officials no longer view state agencies as playing any role in subsidizing, managing, or protecting popular music. Stripped of former safeguards, composers today must cultivate new strategies for apprehending and navigating the creation of popular song. And they do this in a context where culture and the arts, as Agim complained, no longer constitute the centerpiece of a governmental project to raise the level of the public. In this context, the Festival of Song provides composers a measure of respite from the transformative effects of capital on the postsocialist music field. The Festival, the sole state-subsidized cultural event to have continued without interruption after the end of state socialism, remains organized, funded, and administered by the Radio-Television; Ministry officials attend its rehearsals and follow its selection process.

But their concern no longer stems from paternalistic impulses to reshape and elevate the body politic. Officials instead care because they perceive the Festival, since 2004 Albania's selection round for the Eurovision Song Contest, as playing an important role in branding and promoting the Nation to viewers worldwide. "In today's world of overstimulated, undereducated, culturally confused youth," Robert A. Saunders sardonically writes, "a country's image seems to be only as good as its last reference in popular culture." Portrayed in Western popular culture as either backward or farcical, Albania has long projected an "unsavory brand."[3] For elites now concerned with managing the country's image for external consumption, the Nation—Brand "Albania"—becomes an object for governmental concern. And in competing for the right to promote an image of the Nation, composers entangle themselves in the broader ethos of promotion that now inflects all production and consumption in the promotional state.

Organizing the Forty-eighth Festival of Song, November 2009

The young woman, *Jona, adjusted her headphones and then with both hands stretched her stylish black dress down over her knees. "*Gati*? Ready?" asked the engineer to my left, before cuing the CD her composer-producer had given him. The dance track began, and she warbled a few off-key notes before saying, in English, "Stop, stop, stop." The engineer adjusted the levels in her headphones and exhaled deeply. "*Gati*?" Jona started over, again off-key. The composer-producer seated to my right stepped out for a cigarette, while the Festival's stage manager, Osman Mula, muted the intercom and began arguing with the artistic director, Selim Ishmaku. Jona waited.

"What do we do if two or three of these singers do not work out? If they are bad? Do we work with them on this?" Mula asked.

"Later, later," Ishmaku shrugged.

"But it is illogical to organize this *verifikimi*, this verification process, but then to allow them to sing when they cannot—she has serious intonation problems!" The two men continued arguing behind the glass window of the control room as Jona finished, smiled and left, and the next singer entered the Radio-Television's recording studio for his *verifikimi*.

The Forty-eighth Festival of Song featured a new wrinkle borrowed from recent iterations of the Sanremo Festival of Italian Song. Organizers would stage two concurrent competitions over four nights. The first night would introduce the primary songs of the competition performed by established singers, referred to by organizers as "the Bigs," who would then reprise their songs on the third night in the form of duets with other established singers. But the second night would feature newcomers, *të rinjtë*, like Jona. The two top singers receiving votes from this night would then go on to compete with the Bigs on the fourth and final evening for the opportunity to represent Albania at Eurovision.

None of the newcomers seemed to understand why they were coming in for *verifikimi*. And at the appointed time they were to meet in the lobby, no organizers had arrived as I stood waiting with the throng of nervous teenagers and university students. Only twenty minutes later were we ushered upstairs, where Ishmaku invited me to sit with him and the co-organizers behind the Radio-Television's large mixing board, a thick pane of glass separating us from the competitors, most of whom placed the headphones on only hesitantly, unsure of themselves in the recording studio. The purpose only became clear to me when a television journalist interrupted to tape a segment for the evening newscast in the control room. The operator took footage of several singers, eyes closed in intense effort, with the wires and cords of the studio equipment framing their faces, to accompany the short interview with Ishmaku. "This process is a way," Ishmaku told the journalist, "for us to be absolutely sure that the singers meet up to indisputable norms and sing in a natural, true way, that the singing is good. The important thing is that the festival goes out beautifully, and that we have beautiful performances." The cameraman then took more stock shots of Ishmaku and the engineer sitting by the equipment and peering seriously through the glass at one of the newcomers.

Verifikimi, and especially its broadcast to viewers at home, served two functions. It answered the concerns of professionals and a small segment of fans who believe that song must be safeguarded from the negative influences of the market economy, *tregu*, which produces the *antivlera*, or anti-values, that handicap true artistic expression. In this way, verification gives the appearance of artistic rigor and discipline to the minority of observers troubled by the incursion of anti-values into light song by policing the participation of singers who use this event to promote their careers. It targets and polices what professionals perceive to be the site where problems arise, the access point where capital penetrates creativity in the contemporary economy: the singer's voice. To what extent verification actually worked as intended to instill professional values, I am not sure. Even Jona's warbling made it on to the televised broadcasts.

But verification also related to concerns about how to best represent the Nation "on Europe's stage." Since 2004, the Festival of Song has been Albania's selection round for the Eurovision Song Contest. An international competition featuring nation-state members of the European Broadcasting Union, Eurovision was first broadcast in 1956. The contest has several rules. Participants must be members of the Broadcasting Union; songs must be three minutes or shorter; lyrics must not to be "political"; prospective countries must demonstrate the ability to host the following year's contest should they win; and crucially, all vocals must be performed live. To most spectators, whether in Tirana or Western Europe, Eurovision provides kitschy entertainment and, in the phrasing of journalist Mike Atkinson, "generally runs at least ten years behind developments in youth-based genres, if not twenty."[4] But to officials in countries at the European Union's legal or symbolic borders, the contest represents a forum for promoting a positive image of their nation's brand to an imagined "Europe."[5]

Contemporary Festivals thus bear a double burden. Each Festival's winning song goes on, in May of the following year, to compete in a self-conscious celebration of the diversity of Europe's nations. In this way, organizers must stage a competition that results in the promotion of an Albanian nation-brand abroad. But each Festival's organization must at the same time give the appearance of protecting values, of creating a local space where professionalized musicians can compete with one another protected from the polluting dangers of the market. From this double burden arises a paradox. The Festival must serve as a platform for the promotion of the Nation. Yet it must simultaneously insulate its songs from a privatized economy whose driving logic is promotion itself.

THE POST-1997 MUSIC ECONOMY

The late 1990s liberalization of media policy that enabled the emergence of a privatized economy has proved a complicated proposition for professionalized composers and composer-producers. New technologies initially made it possible for non-state-employed individuals to break the government's monopoly on the domestic production of symbols. Since then, the licensing of private media companies has held in check any impulses to control production through national policy, making regulation *nga lart*, or from above, nearly impossible.

But to my consultants, the promises of deregulation also introduced new forms of monopoly. The initial smattering of make-do, shoestring-budgeted private radio transmitters of the late 1990s quickly gave rise to a handful of media empires directed by powerful political and cultural brokers by the mid-2000s. In terms of popular music, these companies have continued the festival model of the previous period, albeit in two distinct waves. During the first wave, companies created private song contests much along the lines as the Festival of Song. Two major contests remained at the time of my fieldwork. The multimedia company KLAN, in collaboration with artist-turned-entrepreneur Ardit Gjebrea, began producing *Kënga Magjike*, Magic Song, in 1999; TopMedia created *TopFest* in 2002. During the second wave, private media groups established Pop Idol–inspired competitions for amateur singers, the most prominent of which was *Ethët e së Premtes Mbrëma*, The Friday Night Fevers, broadcast between 2003 and 2008.

Private festivals and singing competitions transfigured the aesthetically deterritorialized music economy of the 1990s in profound ways. These festivals exponentially increased Tirana's capacity for new song productions. The planned economy's capacity for disseminating new songs at the national level had remained relatively fixed from year to year, subject to broadcasters' understandings of the relationship between popular songs and media policy. In the early 1990s, this capacity expanded slightly at the Festival of Song, which began broadcasting ten or so more songs at each edition. But at the same time, the defunding of *estrada* companies and local-level events drastically reduced national capacity to produce light music songs and performances overall. In sharp contrast, the post-1997 privatized economy's capacity for new songs depends only on the calculations of its new *biznesmen* class as to how much content listeners want to hear—and how much these same entrepreneurs can produce. Magic Song and TopFest, the two major festivals active during my fieldwork, alone accounted for almost nine times the thirty-odd compositions broadcast annually by the Festival of Song. At Magic Song, singers present sixty new productions each year, while at TopFest, over two hundred. In addition, established singers commission new works to broadcast as music video clips on private television channels or to include on albums distributed by *shtëpia disk-ografike*, publishing companies owned by media companies. Singing competitions also require productions, usually not new works but rather backing tracks of Italian and American popular songs or older light music classics that accompany young singers.

The rapid expansion of the domestic music economy's capacity for broadcasting songs in turn has given rise to a loose network of privately owned digital recording studios for creating these productions and backing tracks. Contemporary studios range from the cramped to the luxurious, with a typical space composed of two rooms: the larger control room housing a MIDI-equipped keyboard, computer furnished with recording/editing software, and speakers, and the smaller recording room outfitted with a microphone and headphones for playback. Producers make backing tracks using the software to generate loops and arrangements, editing waveforms visually on the computer screen; many tracks are entirely synthesized using the keyboard and samples. In the small isolation chamber, commissioning singers record their parts, which in addition to a guitar or a clarinet (for pop-folk pieces), is often the only live recorded element in a finished work.

By the time of my fieldwork, digital recording technology had drastically lowered barriers to entry for music production. Anyone with a laptop, software, and a decent microphone could potentially set themselves up as producer, unlike during the 1990s, when the cost of then-necessary hardware and sampling keyboards prohibited entry. To make songs, the producer needs some facility with the keyboard, computer skills, and of course the start-up capital to obtain modest equipment. Unlike "pen and paper" composers, however, he does not need to *di nota*, to have notational literacy. He need only *di kompjutër*, know the computer. The category of producer today includes composer-producers active during the 1990s, as well as a growing number of younger composers (see Figure 5.1). But these Conservatory-trained musicians now find themselves in the minority. Non-professionalized producers, young men in Tirana and other large towns, as well as a large and influential group of musicians based in Prishtina, Kosova, created the overwhelming majority of tracks at the time of my fieldwork.

The rise of media conglomerates and the consequent growth of studios has transformed the social texture of popular music-making, inverting the traditional relationship between the singer and the composer/producer and introducing a new economic logic into the practice of making song. The new commission model elevates the role of predominantly female singers in relation to predominantly male producers. Singers commission songs, and their purchasing power

Figure 5.1 The professionalized composer-producer: Klodian Qafoku in his recording studio.

grants them a markedly larger share of creative control than they had in the past. This model depends on an emerging culture of celebrity driven by the growing perception that a career in music might be attained by almost anyone. An acquaintance told me that nearly everyone in his high school class auditioned for the Friday Night Fevers, Albania's first Pop Idol–style contest, when it held auditions in his small hometown. The number of entrepreneurial high school and university students who are willing and able to invest start-up capital in themselves to explore a career has likewise grown. Would-be stars compose a substantial part of the field at private media festivals; their aspirations fuel the festival model's expansion. Professionalized musicians by and large perceive these singers to be governed by economic rather than artistic motives.

In short, the commission model upends the nature of composing or producing. Song-makers become freelancers, their livelihood dependent on their success in appealing to the market of singers. Through collaboration, the new economy interpolates composers and producers into a complex promotional calculus. Freelancing song-producers must in some way promote themselves in order to attract commissions from singers. Commissioning singers in turn use popular music to promote themselves on private media contests and music video channels. And multimedia companies even use these same songs to brand themselves across different platforms. For instance, Top Media organizes TopFest, a singing contest that prominently programs rock and hip-hop, which resonates with the company's self-branding as an edgy, no-nonsense challenger to the political status quo on its newscasts and talk shows.

The socialist period's calculus of individuality, creativity, and values was no less complex. But while composers on the whole came to more or less understand that period as a coherent system, many of my consultants perceived the contemporary situation as characterized by the absence of order. Older men who had been most active in the 1970s and 1980s denigrate the new economic relations as unnatural, perverse, and immoral, as an expression of *degjenërim* or degeneration. They criticize the inversion of singer-composer roles by calling female singers *rrugaçë*, whores, and suggesting that the men pandering to them are impotent or passive, even artistically cuckolded. Less florid critiques by even democratization's most ardent early proponents, such as Zhani Ciko, characterize the current order as inherently disordered, as "chaos." Ciko and others have even suggested the need for greater political oversight for culture, a major turnabout from the 1990s.[6] In framing the new economy as an object for critique in this way, intellectuals recast deregulation as a form of *dis*-regulation in technological, social, and moral terms. But what my consultants perceived as a lack of order, as the incapacity of the state to manage culture, in fact represents a new governmental strategy.

MAKING SONG "IN MARKET ECONOMY CONDITIONS"

The expansion of the economy's broadcast capacity does not necessarily mean postsocialist officials could not regulate content in some way were it a priority. But the decentralized institutional structure of media companies does complicate regulation. The planned economy's institutional logic, centralization, coupled with its practical drives of accumulation and redistribution, facilitated oversight under socialism. In turn, socialist-era officials and musicians alike came to justify this oversight in the name of elevating the cultural level of the population. But most Albanians have not simply disavowed these logics since the 1990s, but have actively recast them as anti-democratic and irrational. And they have done this in the name of normalizing society.[7]

These appeals to normalcy generate policy. In a singular statement addressing the role of the state in subsidizing culture, the musicologist Zana Shutëriqi addressed a 2001 symposium funded by the Soros Foundation and organized by the newly renamed Ministry of Tourism, Culture, Youth, and Sports. "In market economy conditions," Shutëriqi said, "the state's budget politics for culture must prioritize nonprofit institutions and activities such as opera theaters, symphonic orchestras, [and folk music] festivals. . . . The state must gradually cease support for spectacles and light music festivals, [beauty pageants for] misses, and so on, [events] which can and should have private sponsors."[8] In such a reading, "the state" should retain its role in managing certain domains of musical life, here folk and art musics, while ceding to the market the oversight of other domains, namely popular culture. This appeal is to common sense, and it has become instantiated in policy. It depends on the assumption that such a division of management represents the only way a market-based democracy should conduct business.

The Festival of Song remains the sole exception to the proposition that the market, *tregu*, should organize the production and consumption of popular music in a normal society. Its organizers, however, never explicitly articulate why this should be so. Instead they invoke a series of broad appeals to fair play that draw in equal measure from contemporary political language and socialist-era creative speech. An event overseen by *profesionistë*, organizers told me, the Festival is an exercise *në transparencë*, in transparency, a buzzword of the political field. The Forty-eighth Festival's organization, Selim Ishmaku stressed, revolved around employees' good faith efforts to cultivate and safeguard *transparencë*. In September participants submitted compact discs accompanied by a printed text and information sheet listing the composer, singer, and lyricist. The Radio-Television hired a short-term secretary to collate these submissions in order to "create a distance between the organizers and composers." "At private festivals," Ishmaku claimed, "someone just calls the organizer—makes a phone call, knocks on the door." After collating the songs, identifying each by title and number rather than by name, the secretary then distributed them to a commission, which Ishmaku termed "professional critics, people trained at the Academy, some poets." These professionals then evaluated the songs according to a predetermined points system.

Professionalized committees program Festivals of Song that contrast sharply with Tirana's private festivals, where the majority of songs are created by non-professionalized producers oriented exclusively toward hip-hop, rock, or pop music genres. Participants at recent Festivals have overwhelmingly been Conservatory-trained composer-producers, with a handful of 1990s rocker-turned-producers and two or three diaspora- or Kosova-based musicians competing each year. I was not able to determine to what extent the programming committee actively disqualified non-professionals. My sense is that a good number of producers from Tirana and Prishtina simply do not submit entries. These non-professionalized musicians may naturally find the Radio-Television's heavy promotion of professionalism and narrow definition of values off-putting, directed as it is toward denigrating their own forms of creativity. Yet I also I heard rumors about musicians who aspired to present at Radio-Television Festivals but for one reason or another found themselves blackballed from its airwaves.

To its participants, the Festival of Song's organization instills a measure of management over what they perceive to be an unmanaged economy, carving out a small protected corner for presenting national songs *me vlera*, with values. But the "chaos" perceived by my consultants to exist outside the Festival is not actually equivalent to an absence of management. Policy change that redefines certain segments of the cultural economy as necessitating protection, such as classical music and dance and the folk arts, and other segments as the natural domain of the market, such as popular music, film, literature, and television programming, itself has engendered a new form of oversight. The retraction of more "hands-on" tactics, whether exercised through subsidies, policy, institutional frameworks, and so on, does not portend the withdrawal of power, but rather its restructuring.[9] This restructuring has shifted regulation away from both the state apparatus as well as the music field and toward autonomous individuals. In the privatized popular song economy, new responsibilities to manage both "values" as well as the risk of a career devolve onto individual entrepreneurs, as what had once been field-wide questions of professionalism are recast as problems of personal ethics. Professionalized musicians must work out their own solutions to ethical dilemmas as they navigate entrepreneurship and compete for commissions. These negotiations take place in part in and around the preparations for the Festival of Song.

Entrepreneurship and the Forty-eighth Festival of Song, December 2009

Rehearsals followed *verifikimi*, first with the Radio-Television Orchestra and then with the singers. The Festivals are a change of pace from the everyday work most composers do at the Conservatory, state institutions, or their private studios. Musicians talked about "tradition" without my prompting during rehearsal breaks, and several pointed out commemorative plaques at the Radio-Television building honoring the "fathers" of Albanian music, like the late Ferdinand Deda. The Radio-Television had budgeted two weeks of rehearsals with the orchestra and one week with the singers to begin in early December. During this period composer-producers actively worked, albeit to greater and lesser extents, to ensure their presentations received the best hearing that they can at the broadcasts in late December. From my vantage point, unobtrusively seated at the side of the orchestra musicians and then in the hall among the participants, the process appeared unduly chaotic.

At the orchestral rehearsals, Festival organizers prepared the string sections of the Radio-Television Orchestra to perform simple accompaniments to playback tracks produced in the participants' studios. Like the singers, the orchestra must perform "live." Organizers emphasized this as a feature that distinguished the Festival of Song from its private competitors.[10] The orchestral musicians could have easily sight-read the simple parts. Only a quarter of participants had submitted scores, and the Radio-Television staff did not finish copying out parts until fifteen minutes into the first rehearsal. The parts were riddled with errors: missing measures, incorrect meters, wrong key signatures. Some just sounded bad. Synching the live string parts with the recordings also proved to be a logistical nightmare. Several composers had created backing tracks with synthesized string parts that sounded jarring when played back in unison with the orchestra. The mix between the recorded tracks, amplified through the substandard speakers of the rehearsal hall, and the orchestral musicians, increasingly short-tempered, was awful. After moving to the performance venue, the arrival of the singers injected new forms of confusion. The ostensible purpose of these rehearsals was to finalize the mix between vocals, strings, and the prerecorded backing tracks. But certain singers delayed the process by coming late, demanding extra time on stage, or refusing to sing in full voice; other composers kept bringing in new backing tracks, which of course forced the engineers to recalibrate the levels in the live mix again and again.

Composer-producers endeavored to mitigate this disorder in different ways. Less-established younger composer-producers were, in my view, the most conscientious. They were more likely to have submitted string parts on time, and their parts were more likely to be correct. They attended the first orchestra rehearsals, arriving early to confer on the mix or jumping up on the podium to conduct and give notes to the orchestral musicians. These men were punctual, telling me they "respected" the rehearsal schedule. They draped an arm around organizers, made the rounds greeting other composers and singers, climbed over chairs up and into the playback booth to discuss their mix with the sound engineers—even showed up on time for interviews with the foreign researcher. They stood on stage with their singers, listening to the mix themselves, offering advice on pronunciations or interpretations, and giving notes on phrasing (see Figure 5.2). And once on stage, these composers begged and pleaded for more time as organizers—barking "*Nesër, të lutëm, ik!* Tomorrow's another day, move it!"—hustled their singers off stage.

Established composer-producers behaved differently. The most well known did not attend the early rehearsals, and when they did come to the dress rehearsals, refused to recognize the organizers' schedule. One appeared just twice, each time bearing a new compact disc. Another, a powerful, connected man now working at a private media station, came only as the rehearsals were ending one night, insisting his singer run her song three times and keeping the musicians over an hour late to fine-tune the live sound. When the musicians protested, the Radio-Television's general director, Petrit Beci, came onstage and screamed at them. In contrast to the rigid schedule enforced for less established composer-singer duos, time could be stretched and pulled for composers *me namë*, literally

Figure 5.2 Kristi Popa listens to the mix at the Forty-eighth Festival of Song

with names, meaning well known. Their singers received substantially more time on stage, not an unimportant consideration given the recurring problems with the mix in the hall. I saw two big name composers even refuse to sign Radio-Television contracts stipulating their honorariums for participating as well as broadcast rights, which I presumed must have clashed with their post-Festival plans for their songs.

After a particularly heated exchange at one rehearsal, an orchestral musician invited me to the musicians' canteen at the Radio-Television building. Over the previous sessions, he had continually sought to catch my eye, raising an eyebrow or gesturing to make sure I jotted down notes on a composer's misbehavior, an organizer's rudeness, or technical malfunctions. Once seated, he apologized. "It was not like this before," he told me. "We used to have discipline." An older colleague interjected, saying that this new generation of composers behaved differently, *pa kulturë*, without culture, in contrast to the men he worked with in the 1970s and 1980s. A composer my age, too young to feel this nostalgia colored by the forgetfulness of passing time, later made the same criticism. After someone arrived late only to argue with organizers before storming out, I asked him to interpret his colleague's behavior. "He is just *jokorrekt*, improper," he said, "*dhe u soll pa kulturë*, and acts unculturedly."

My consultants often explained misbehavior or incorrectness with the rehearsed fatalism so stereotypically common more broadly in the region: "We are in the Balkans, Niku, what can you expect?" But these different forms of behavior also point to the tactics and strategies composers pursue in making careers for themselves in contemporary Tirana. For established composer-producers, the Festival of Song represents one opportunity among many others available to them in the relatively more lucrative privatized media industry. But for less established composers, participation in the Festival of Song demands an investment of time and social capital in order to make connections, establish a reputation, and develop a career. These men may waive their usual rates to remix songs for colleagues, they work one-on-one with singers, and they know whose hand to shake. They become upset by snubs, real or perceived. After another rehearsal, one composer told me he felt an established producer had acted coolly toward him. He later brought this up again, concerned about what it portended for making future connections in the industry.

Managing Careers and Making Money

For established and less-established professionals alike, the Festival of Song is one element among others in a complex promotional calculus they must manage to maximize their earnings while navigating the effects of capital on their creativity. Until 1992, composers' careers followed a relatively stable trajectory from professional training, to post-graduation placement, to—potentially—a climb up the rungs of the planned economy from its peripheries to its center. One musician described the socialist period to me by moving his hand across a flat plane, then contrasting this by moving his hand up in an erratic, wavy series of loops to describe the present. The high points are higher, he suggested, but the low points are also lower. For composers oriented toward song, the non-state-administered music economy is particularly unstable. The radically desubsidized public sector provides fewer positions to musicians, while the privatized economy can seem disorienting or confusing. Over the course of my trips to Tirana beginning in 2004, I watched as one friend struggled to correctly calibrate the balance between public and private sector careers. As an employee at a state institution, he received relatively little pay but enjoyed stability. When his work as a producer began growing, however, he quickly began earning the equivalent of a month's salary per song production. He kept his state job, perhaps as a hedge against fallow periods, although whenever I stopped by during working hours to greet him he was usually absent, working at his private studio across town.

The privatized economy is risky. A string of bad luck with singers or black-balling by the organizers of a private festival could lead commissions, and your nascent career, to vanish. Aspiring composer-producers consequently view this risk as something to be managed through their approach to the wider promotional economy of song production. Different actors in the promotional economy have, in the exemplary terms of one composer, *interesa*, or economic interests. Singers have an economic interest in *promovim*, or promoting themselves. Because singers' primary sources of income come from personal appearances in the diaspora and live concerts during the summer, they carefully cultivate images intended to draw and maintain a large fan base. Elvana Gjata, a Tirana-based singer, was among the most popular draws at the time of my fieldwork. Her career began as a print model when she was an acting student in Tirana. She and her managers carefully curate her image through social media like Facebook and Instagram, giving fans behind-the-scenes looks at her hair and makeup regimens, her shoes and fashion accessories, and so on. In summer 2015, Gjata even began a social media campaign where fans posted pictures of themselves wearing their hair and makeup in her style with the hashtag #*sielvana*, "like Elvana." For singers like Gjata, songs and their accompanying video clips function as part of a broader promotional strategy focused on building brand awareness and loyalty. When such singers participate in festivals, they do so with at least an eye toward enhancing their personal image.

In contrast, composers and producers pursue distinctly different economic priorities from singers. At the time of my fieldwork, composers or producers received a flat fee ranging from €200 to €1,000 to write a song and text, produce the backing track in their studio, and then record, mix, and master the final production with the commissioning singer.[11] But at this point Albania's lack of copyright protections in practice limits the potential to profit from any one production. Because mechanisms for royalty payments in effect did not work in 2010, composers or producers profited only from the fees they collected for individual productions. To maximize these earnings, they consequently sought either to create more productions over shorter periods of time, to charge singers higher fees per production, or to pursue a combination of both approaches. A composer or producer can charge a higher fee, however, only by promoting himself as a hit-maker with business connections to private media outlets. The father of one aspiring young singer, a high school student in Tirana, told me that he had negotiated fees ranging up to €1,000 per production. He had recently paid the latter fee, he claimed, to a composer-producer with business connections who had guaranteed the song would be placed in the finals of a private festival, and a subsequent music video, in heavy rotation. His daughter aspired to be a pop star; he viewed this investment in her promotion as a necessary first step toward that goal. (The composer-producer, he told me at another meeting, later gouged him for even more.)

Different festivals play different roles in mediating the relationship composers and producers have to singers and their capital. Magic Song on TV KLAN, allows participants to submit multiple entries, and so producers can potentially increase their earnings if several singers approach them for a commission.

Ardit Gjebrea, the festival's host and organizer, also heavily promotes the songs and prominently discusses their producers and lyricists on his weekly television program, which in turn raises the profile of the participants. TopFest on Top Channel also allows multiple submissions. Yet because organizers do not as prominently advertise the producers and lyricists, instead focusing on the singers, one composer told me this was not a venue where one *krijon famë*, creates fame or a reputation. The Festival of Song has the strictest rules governing participation: an individual may submit only one composition, and the Radio-Television itself pays participants nominal honorariums. This predetermined pay scale inhibits the normal way of conducting business, as in theory no money is exchanged between singers and composers; several participants complained the Radio-Television paid them substantially below their market value. But the Festival of Song represents, especially for younger professionalized composers who lack connections to private media companies, the fastest route to establishing a reputation. A good showing and prominent news coverage on nightly newscasts can enhance a young composer's reputation overnight, enabling him to work with more established singers at future Radio-Television Festivals, to attract lesser-known singers for collaborations at private festivals, or to gain invitations to private festivals. The December Festival, one composer told me, gave him "the green light" when he first began producing tracks, exponentially increasing his rates and singers' interest in working with him.

Critics of this wider promotional economy and its effects on creativity link questions of professionalism, national identity, and the absence of state management. Some individuals, one composer said, simply behave immorally when presented with opportunities to accumulate capital by quickly batch-producing what he perceived to be artistically bankrupt tracks for dilettante singers.

"They are more *fitimprures*, profit-seeking, they just stick a melody into the computer, figure out the orchestration, and the result is a very simple product. I have not and do not accept this—this is a major blow to Albanian culture. The influence on listeners' tastes persists. It is not like a construction company that builds an illegal house, which the state destroys and the next day there is nothing there. It takes time for tastes to be fixed. Even my children do not have a clear idea of Albanian folklore, because all day long on television they see singers in Albanian costumes singing who-knows-what—this is incalculable cultural damage."

"But you make money doing these kinds of songs, right?"

"Sure, but only by addressing the low level of listeners. And as I told you, our ability to profit is extremely limited. If you put out an album in the United States and it sells, that is when your success begins. From a hit song and its broadcast, you profit, while we profit only when the singer pays you the $500. Let's say you make $500 for a song in the United States—but then you make $5 million from its broadcasts. Here, the music market does not work. You cannot call it a business, it is just survival."

What he called survival might less dramatically be termed self-management. To profit, composers must cultivate fame or a reputation, which in turn will enable them to demand higher rates or attract more potential collaborators. Yet they are also careful to maintain the appearance of professionalism, to maintain a reputation for artistic integrity by refusing to too baldly address the "low level" of the public. By retaining an image of integrity, these men qualify for state employment in concert music or folk music, which may in turn insulate them against the intrinsic precarity of postsocialist economic forces—the highs and lows, ups and downs of the singers' market. The calculation may seem straightforward. But in practice, not all individuals enjoy the same access to private media broadcasts, and thus the ability to attract commissions from singers who base their decisions on composers' business connections.

CLANS, FESTIVALS, AND THE APPEARANCE OF SUCCESS

"I participate in all the festivals, private and public, but each has its own people," one composer-producer told me after a Festival of Song rehearsal. "It is absolutely this clan mentality." The dominant rhetoric surrounding all of Tirana's festivals concerns their transparency. But any one individual's access to programs depends on what my consultants popularly called klanë, or clans. "Jam shkëputur, I've been blackballed, from the Festival for two years," another composer told me. "It is all controlled by clans, and the reason is poverty: when you do not have any money, you want to accumulate more of it for yourself and the people you work with by accepting their songs over those of others." Most complainants pointed to Ardit Gjebrea's Magic Song festival as notoriously skewed toward a small, tight-knit group of composer-producers, and its 2009 program seemed to lend credence to such assertions. Of the fifty-odd songs broadcast, four individuals produced twenty-five backing tracks and five created twenty-four compositions, or nearly half of the competing selections.

To many observers, this artificial cornering of the market exemplifies the problems inherent in a system that drives all actors—businessmen, producers, and singers—to ceaselessly promote themselves. But many other people believe this korrupsion to be symptomatic of a larger cultural problem. I became used to hearing musicians and listeners lament the clan as simply the natural form of social organization for a backward country. "Listen Niku, you have to realize, Albania had a feudal system up to 1940," one person told me. "There was no bourgeoisie, it was feudal, man! You understand? The system changed all that." The implication here is that while the transition from feudalism to state socialism eradicated a measure of backwardness, the more recent transition to capitalism may have reversed those gains.

But it was the structure of the socialist-era economy itself that facilitated the initial growth of so-called clans. By centralizing production at the Radio-Television, state-socialist cultural policy paradoxically created conditions for the system that many professionalized musicians today see as the scourge of creativity, and which the Festival of Song must guard against. Several factors initially concentrated production at the Radio-Television: the persistence of socialist-era networks and centralization, the defunding of the state's cultural infrastructure, political barriers to private media, and the domestic lack of capital. Then in the years following the *trazira* of 1997, the increased circulation of capital subsequently led to what one journalist called "the unseemly privatization" of light music. And this privatization began at the Festival of Song itself.

"While all Albanian life is smothered by rising corruption," an anonymous editorialist wrote in 2001, "there is no way even a festival can be saved from this thing, especially when at the head of a jury is a person who not a week ago won a political mandate by fixing the vote and cheating. After the organizers took prizes for themselves, they figured they'd leave some for the others: Festival Director, Adrian Hila, first prize; Artistic Director Alfred Kaçinari, best orchestration, festival stage designer, career prize; the Festival orchestra, a special prize; the omnipresent [Jorgo] Papingji (with four texts in the finale night, [so] if not one then the other would take a prize), two or three prizes; the conductor [Edmond] Zhulali, the best composer [award], and so on."[12]

Composer-producer Adrian Hila became a lightning rod for criticisms. After graduating from the Conservatory, Hila secured an editorial position at the Radio-Television, directing the Festival between 1998 and 2001 and winning twice during this period. As artistic director, Hila was publicly criticized for "selling songs": producing commissions for singers whom he also assured prizes or placement in the Festival's final night. Vocalists submitted Hila's compositions under their own name, allowing the composer to profit from multiple commissions. In 1998, the press reported rumors Hila had "sold" a song to a well-known *estrada* star for the then outrageous sum of €800, pressuring jury members to place her in the finals. A bigger scandal arrived the following December. The jury announced that vocalist Rovena Dilo had won with a composition by Alfred Kaçinari. But the following morning, the Radio-Television announced that the votes had been "incorrectly tallied," and Hila with his singer Aurela Gaçe were awarded first prize. A government official and close personal friend of Hila's, several composers told me, intervened on his behalf. A journalist called Hila a *padron*, meaning a Mafia boss, naming him as a member of "the *nomenklatura* of Telebingo," a lottery ticket game show hosted by Hila's colleague Ardit Gjebrea.[13]

To their detractors, this clan did not simply circumvent fair play concerning awards, but also pioneered new strategies for accumulating capital by artificially cornering the emerging market of singers. After the 2001 Festival, the outspoken young composer and arranger Miron Kotani published a harsh editorial that accused Hila of composing eleven of twenty submissions.[14] A journalist, tipped off by a disgruntled competitor, then corroborated these charges after organizers publicized the names of participating singers, but not their composers or lyricists.[15] One well-placed Radio-Television employee active during the 1990s told me there had technically been no rule barring multiple submissions at this point, as no one had ever thought to submit more than one song. This practice allowed certain musicians, their detractors claim, to create reputations seemingly out of thin air. "So-and-so was a nobody, a student hanging out at the Conservatory and puttering around Tirana on his scooter, and then all of a sudden he owns a $100,000 studio?" one person exaggerated to me.

Criticisms, gossip, and half-truths about this system continued to animate a number of conspiracy theories about its ubiquity and powers at the time of my fieldwork. All festivals, one composer told me, promote their procedures for selecting songs and handing out prizes as being *demokratik*, democratic, but in practice their organizers act in a way that is *autokratik*, or autocratic. Ardit Gjebrea, for instance, explains the voting at his Magic Song contest, where participants evaluate for their peers, at length during broadcasts. In 2009, a newspaper even published the full results for all fifty-plus singers in the newspaper. But this is *një fasadë*, a façade, a disgruntled younger composer-producer told me: "It is laughable that singers vote for each other, and even more laughable that organizers make such noise about *transparencë*." In reality one person decides, the composer claimed, distributing money and favors among aspiring composer-producers and producers. As an example, he stated that one well-known producer had his reputation made at a single festival. "In 2007, he won the top three prizes, suddenly becoming the most famous 'composer' in all Albania? But he does not even know how to read music! He is just a good engineer—he knows how to work the computer. We worked together briefly at a private radio in the 1990s; he just moved knobs up and down and pressed buttons—I saw it with my own eyes." The organizers, this critic alleged, really wrote the songs credited to him, which he merely arranged, and all shared in the profits.

There is no way to corroborate these conspiracy theories, which permeated discussions I had with younger composers and composer-producers at the margins of the new promotional economy. And these particular consultants are themselves perhaps not the most reliable sources available on this topic. None are well integrated into these private business networks, and many perceive themselves to be blacklisted or even persecuted by them. Conspiracy theories, I sense, may even occlude more accurate diagnoses of the underlying structural changes at play. Under socialism, the quantity of work you produced did not matter. Claims about values, manifested in particular creative practices, primarily determined the potential range of positions you might occupy within the music field's hierarchy. This hierarchy in turn drove an economy where ideas about values and individuality conditioned your access to the non-capital-based resources at its center. But the promotional economy organizes a very different field. Its resources are decentralized, in the form of economic and social capital available for accumulation through collaboration with commissioning singers. And its opportunities for broadcast are subject to these "clan"-based business networks, an oligopoly-type system that stifles open competition.

The socialist-era model no doubt seemed opaque to some musicians. Particular gatekeepers discerned what kinds of expression should be deemed professional and thus broadcast-worthy; members of the field in good standing perceived particular compositional practices to be the audible expression of internalized expression of these aesthetically, not to mention politically, correct forms of creativity. You knew a good piece when you heard it. But this new system, for the professionalized musicians to whom the extinct prestige economy nevertheless remains a reference point, seems to in principle privilege superficial appearances over audible substance. Relationships with singers, the source for capital, must be cultivated. But these singers in turn carefully cultivate their own images, with songs serving as the soundtrack to music video clips intended to burnish or reinvent their personal brands. The most telling indicator of this shift can be seen in the production credits introducing clips, which list the singer's hair stylist, makeup artist, and sponsors, often clothing stores, travel agencies, or car dealerships—and on occasion omit the music producer and/or lyricist. But composers and producers also must create an image of themselves as being connected, in-demand, and current. The most popular non-professionalized producers sometimes even insert themselves into clips, appearing alongside their singers or in the background working mixers, offering spoken-word interjections or even rapping.[16]

To composers this results in an occult admixture of *promovim*, where the image of success gives rise to the new collaborations whereby singers promote themselves, which may in turn give the appearance of connectedness. Professionalized musicians perceive this alchemy to have arisen because the State has ceded oversight of culture to the market. But they also charge certain networks in the privatized field with ceding their own self-responsibility to maintain order in exchange for unseemly profits. "Without friends you can never get ahead," one singer complained to a journalist in 1999. "It looks like this is our fatal mistake and unforgivable naiveté. You can never express [your musical] values if you aren't playing the underground cards, which are oftentimes more powerful."[17]

At the Festival of Song, organizers publicize safeguards as being in place to correct the problems of the past and to stanch the flow of capital into its program—to allow composers to compete on the merits of their values without fear of someone playing "underground cards." Yet the extent to which these safeguards succeed remains hotly contested. In spring 2014, the journalist Dalina Buzi, reporting gossip around Tirana, tweeted the name of the winning singer of the Fifty-third Festival of Song—a full six months before it occurred, and months before the program had even been announced.[18] And despite the best efforts of organizers to give a veneer of impartiality to the Forty-eighth Festival of Song, the event I observed, several musicians told me in advance they expected Ardit Gjebrea would win.

"Why else would he participate?" one asked me. "If he has agreed to take part"—given his successful private festival, Magic Song, and that he has not participated in over a decade—"then he is competing so he can go to Eurovision. And have you seen the jury? They are all his friends. There is always *korrupsion*, we expect it."

"Do you really think this? That it has been decided?"

"Psychologically, this is what you have to think. You prepare for it, but we will see."

Marketing Albania to Europe

Concerns about *korrupsion* lingered, always near the surface during preparations for the Forty-eighth Festival of Song. But composers also strategized as to how best to musically represent the Nation in a way that the jury, even if the fix were in, might hear as worthy of the top prize. And they approached this task as a legitimate forum for demonstrating their professional skills to the Albanian public. After all, the professionalized field continues to view the Festival to be an institution of social life, the place where many of their teachers and their teachers' mentors had competed with now classic songs. If the market demands "here today, gone tomorrow" ditties, songs at the Festival should—in professionals' minds—stand the test of time. Yet Eurovision, I sensed, complicated these ambitions. During the rehearsals, I stepped out into the hall for a cigarette with a composer to discuss what he considered when composing for recent Festivals of Song. Did he think about how it would be received by listeners? By his colleagues? By the jury? "You have been listening to all these pieces, right?" he replied. "You can hear that we are all thinking about one thing. We are all thinking about Eurovision. That is why each song has, in some way or other, an Albanian tinge."

But composers can interpret this "Albanian tinge" in multiple ways. Most commonly, authors insert a short folk-sounding sample or riff into their introduction, bridge, or short break. Others sometimes more self-consciously reference national source material. One 2009 entrant, rocker Bojkën Lako and his Banda Adriatica, quoted an early-twentieth-century urban folk song, arranging it for pan-Balkan-style brass band. Several entries drew on a general "Mediterranean" world music sound, employing acoustic guitars, simple arrangements, and breathy flute samples, an easy-listening aesthetic most fully realized at the Forty-eighth Festival by Adrian Hila. And a final small group of entrants performed straight-ahead pop or dance pieces with no obviously national musical referents, including Mariza Ikonomi's "La La La," Voltan Prodani's "Ndonjëherë" (Sometimes), and Gjebrea's "Nuk Mundem Pa Ty" (I Won't Make It Without You).

The prevalence of these strategies spur discussions in public forums, some acrimonious, as to whether the Festival can produce appropriately national results. Banda Adriatica's "Love Love Love," for instance, quoted "Për Mue Paska Qenë Kismet," a song popularized during the socialist period by one of the country's most renowned professional folk performers, the Shkodra-born singer Luçie Miloti. But online critics heard in its brass-band arrangement either a "Serbian" or "gypsy" sound that, while increasingly popular in its circulations throughout Europe, did not properly index the Nation.[19] Beneath an online video clip from the Festival, one user called it *gabelçe* and *magjypsisht*, each colloquially meaning "gypsy-like." "Shame! Shame! Shame! on the festival directors for letting this Serbian song into the national Albanian Festival," wrote another. "The directors should at least publicly apologize for allowing it to be sung."[20] If certain songs can be criticized as incorrectly national by being too "Balkan," other songs can be criticized as insufficiently national. To some listeners, the generic "Mediterranean" sound of other entries represented an empty signifier, a bland placeholder that had little to do with the Nation. And the last group of songs, simple pop tunes intended to simply sound "modern" or "European," engender little public debate among nonspecialists, as neither incorrectly nor insufficiently indexical of the Nation. Rather, such entries can be heard as indexing Albania's status as a fully integrated member of the European family.

Composers choose among these strategies. As they choose, they make calculations as to what kinds of sounds they believe will be successful at both the national Festival of Song and then at Eurovision. But their calculations do not occur in a vacuum, nor can they exist outside the structures of the promotional economy.

CREATING "A SONG FOR EUROPE," DECEMBER 2008–MAY 2009

In December 2008, Edmond Zhulali won the Festival of Song with Kejsi Tola, receiving the right to present "Më Merr në Ëndërr," later translated as "Carry Me in Your Dreams" in its English-language version, at the Eurovision Song Contest in Moscow that following May. Its production demonstrates how composers and their singers move among different options in attempting to craft a work not only for domestic broadcast, but also capable of succeeding "on Europe's stage."

By the time of this win, Zhulali had become an extremely well connected musician, a director in the state media as well as a highly successful private producer. As a Radio-Tirana employee, he had overseen the Festival's entrance into the Eurovision era, winning the right to represent Albania during its first appearance in 2004 with the young singer Anjeza Shahini.

Scandal followed Zhulali, as it does all major players in the economy. Zhulali, one singer commented to me, is "one of the handful of composers that guarantee you a chance to succeed." During my fieldwork in 2009, he had received first prize twice and nearly a third time out of six opportunities, beaten out by three-time winner Adrian Hila in 2007 under suspicious circumstances. Five jury members had awarded him maximum votes during the public evaluation—and two, zero. "Seeing such an extremism regarding the points," he had said at the time, "it seems to me not a vote [about the songs] as a vote against." Zhulali resigned in protest from his post at the Radio-Television, further insinuating the votes against had occurred because his singers were Kosovar Albanians, and consequently viewed by some as inappropriate for representing Albania. "This festival had so many mysteries that may only be explained with the passing of time," the journalist stated, "but the one certainty is that the ugly image of this festival will accompany Albanian light song for a while."[21] Others less sympathetic to Zhulali, of course, often pointed out to me the hypocrisy of this talk. He had been competing despite also acting as the Festival's artistic director for several years running, and had himself traded prizes with the previous director, Adrian Hila, each year excepting 2006.

These insinuations and suspicions notwithstanding, Zhulali is also a remarkably earnest man, not only politically connected but also an outspoken proponent of protecting and promoting national values. These qualities merge in his approach to composing for the Festival of Song, and thus for Eurovision. "At Eurovision," he told me, "the songs come from countries trying to give a sense of their national-ness. And there are beautiful models—from Macedonia, Spain, Greece, Ukraine—that when you hear a song, you know that this one is Greek, or that one is Spanish. And I think I do this, too. Because that is the only way you will be noticed there! In that competition, you cannot go and simply say, 'This is the best singer of the festival,' because all the orchestrators, all the singers, all the composers are wonderful. So you are distinguished by your musical motives, by who has that special sound."

Songs like "Më Merr," Zhulali asserted, sound "both modern *and* Albanian"— "you hear it, and it sounds Albanian." "Modern" elements included the track's pulsing dance beat and its text about romantic love by veteran lyricist Agim Doçi. Zhulali also selected high school student Kejsi Tola, at that time prominent as the most recent winner of the Albanian Pop Idol program the Friday Night Fevers, as his singer. To her, the collaboration was a professional coming out. On the Fevers, she performed mainly cover songs; that win substantially raised her profile in the field. My sense is that for Zhulali, Tola represented the right mix between vocal talent, local popularity, and the right image. And as others have suggested, unestablished singers also dominate post-2004 Festivals because they look like a prototypical Eurovision contestant. Young, fresh-faced, attractive, almost all have been women in their late teens or early twenties.

The "Albanian" elements in "Më Merr" included both samples of folk instruments and the development of what Zhulali described as national motives. The composer incorporated two folk instruments from northern Albania, the *zumare*, a four-note hornpipe, set over a drone on the *lahutë*, a one-stringed spike fiddle. A professional folk musician from Lezha, Xhovalin Ndreca, recorded the *zumare* sample live, which the composer then manipulated for the track. Zhulali used a synthesized drone sound to evoke the *lahutë*. In common practice, neither instrument would be performed together. Young shepherds in rural areas traditionally used the solo *zumare* for amusement, to perform songs, dances, and free improvisations.[22] Solo male singers, *rapsodë* or *lahutarë*, used the fiddle to accompany their renditions of epic songs with historical or mythological themes.[23] Though also distributed throughout Slavic-speaking neighboring areas as well, the *lahutë* no doubt evokes in even the average Albanian listener national sentiments. Its image, for instance, often graces the covers of school books on national folklore, and it has functioned as a national symbol in Albanian intellectual thought dating from the 1930s. But in contrast, the *zumare* has not been constructed as authentically Albanian. Rarely presented as a symbolic marker of the nation in staged folklore, local scholars view the *zumare* as a foreign import "borrowed" from Near Eastern musicians and subsequently indigenized.[24]

What Zhulali called "ethnic" instruments, like the *zumare* or *lahutë*, could be easily inserted as you would a guitar solo. But the development and integration of national motives, the composer told me, proved difficult. He wanted to use what he termed the "northern Albanian" or "Phrygian" mode, which he called the most "characteristic" of northern Albanian folklore. "Modern contemporary music" and "foreign genres are all in pure modes—major or minor" with simple harmonies, Zhulali said. So the fitting into a Western pop model of non-diatonic melodic materials that would not traditionally have been harmonized was challenging. And complicating this challenge was the nature of the melodic material itself. "Out in the world," Zhulali explained, "the Phrygian mode sounds very much like a Spanish song, and you can quickly run into problems with your song sounding Spanish." Spanish flamenco music and the "northern Albanian mode" each share in common a prominent augmented second, each derived from a common source in Turkish and Arabic modal practice. What Zhulali euphemistically termed "northern Albanian" would have been called *zyli* by *ahengxhijtë*, nineteenth- and early-twentieth-century professional Romani musicians who performed an urban repertoire in northern Albanian-speaking towns. And this augmented second is the interval Western composers often prominently use to evoke an "Eastern," "oriental," or simply exotic sound.

What to make of this strategizing? I had the sense that Zhulali and many of his peers viewed their works as meaningful ways to experiment with making national songs, and the Festival as a platform for self-expression that, in their day-to-day work, was often subordinated to the wishes of singers. Zhulali and others, for instance, often stressed that the Festival was a welcome respite from hustling for commissions that at times were artistically unsatisfying. "If I want to compose," one person told me, "I have to wait for the singer to approach me— otherwise I have to pay them." The process at the Festival feels more organic or natural to composers, who themselves select singers and rehearse them, not unlike during the socialist period. In the private commission model, singers bring not only their ideas, but also on occasion CDs or MP3s of foreign songs they require composers to follow. Composer-producers find this kind of work stultifying. In formal interviews, all claimed to refuse this kind of commission, though informally, most shrugged it off as part of the game.

But at the same time, the Festival's new significance as the selection round for Eurovision also creates new rules about how to render the Nation audible. Composer-producers must make Albania audible in a manner that will first receive the Festival jury's top prize, and thus the right to move on to the Eurovision Song Contest, and then garner votes of viewers across Europe who text to select the Eurovision winner. "Më Merr" exemplifies this imperative, fitting neatly within the then-popular "trend toward rewarding self-consciously 'ethnic' styles."[25] It followed the strict model that had resulted in top prizes for the Greek singer Helena Paparizou in 2004 and the Ukrainian singer Ruslana in 2005, a model omnipresent at Eurovision contests in the 2000s (see Table 5.1). Remarkably rigid, the formula provided a paint-by-numbers recipe for musical branding by 2008. Within this model, composer-producers space short "ethnic" interludes—brief introductions, breaks using folk instruments, and so on. These folkloric markers index the entry's particular Nation to Western listeners; they also provide the (usually female) artist a brief pause from singing to perform a short choreography.

This model asks participants to folklorize themselves in a way that registers with Eurovision viewers, which in turn impels the selection of sometimes reductive stereotypes. For countries with internationally recognizable sounds and dances, like the Greeks' twangy lyra or bouzouki and Zorba-style steps, the result is catchy folk-kitsch. But the same strategy can also stir debate in the home country. Turkish singer Sertab Erener's 2004 performance paired belly-dancing with an energetic, suggestive eroticism that tapped into deeply held stereotypes

Table 5.1 A "modern and Albanian" winner compared to recent Eurovision models[a]

0'00"	0'00": *Intro outlining the "northern mode"*	0'00"": *Intro with bouzouki sample*	0'00": *Intro with alpenhorn sample*	0'00": Introduction 0'04": Verse
	0'16": Verse 1	0'18": Verse 1	0'31": Verse 1	
	0'30": Verse 2	0'36": Verse 2	0'43": Verse 2	
	0'49": Refrain	0'50": Refrain		
1'00"	1'05": Refrain × 2	1'10":Refrain × 2	1'00": Refrain	1'00": *Short interlude with folk sample*
	1'24": Verse 1	1'27": Verse 3	1'28": Verse 3	
				1'49": Refrain
2'00"	2'00": *Break with zumare sample*	2'02": Refrain × 2	2'08": *Break with folk ululations*	2'15": *Break with lyra sample*
	2'15": Bridge	2'20": *Folk instrument*	2'26": Abridged verse	2'24": Refrain
	2'35": Refrain	2'38": Refrain	2'36": Refrain	
3'00"	Thank you, Europe!	Thank you!	Thank you, Europe!	Thank you, Europe!
	Kejsi Tola, "Carry Me in Your Dreams" (2009, Albania)	Kalomira, "My Secret Combination" (2009, Greece)	Ruslana, "Dances with Wolves" (2005, Ukraine)	Helena Paparizou, "My Number One" (2004, Greece)

[a] Folk elements in italics.

about "the East." For commentators in Istanbul, the performance mischaracterized Turkey as an oversexed and underdeveloped periphery to Europe.[26] But viewers abroad rewarded Erener with first place.

For countries like Albania with no obviously national markers that might immediately resonate with European viewers, the essentializing move to self-folklorize can easily veer toward self-exoticization. As presented in its English-language version to Eurovision, "Carry Me in Your Dreams" excised what Albanian listeners might have heard as the sole national element, the *lahutë*, instead foregrounding the *zumare* with its locally dubious "Eastern" associations. Coupled with the introduction and main melody's emphasis on that prominent augmented second, the aurally unmistakable sonic cliché of the East, the finished product suggested its makers had settled on a strategy of auto-orientalization. To non-Albanian listeners, the overall effect may suggest a Balkan or Near Eastern nation-brand as much as a specifically "Albanian" one.

Domestic rhetoric surrounding the song (and Zhulali's discussion of its genesis with me) emphasized its folkloric elements and the composer's professional development of national resource material. But this talk is produced in large measure for consumption among a small group of professionals in Tirana, a group concerned with who will "go to Eurovision" and with what image they will promote the Nation "to Europe." Once at Eurovision, however, these domestic concerns are forgotten. Media coverage illustrates this shift that occurs between the December Festival and the May Contest. For five months, Albanian media focuses primarily on the composer and sometimes lyricist, interviewing these men, broadcasting footage of them working in the studio or traveling to mix their song, and asking their colleagues to evaluate the work's chances. But after arriving in the host city, this emphasis shifts to the singer. The Contest's promotional apparatus kicks into gear, with hosts and journalists focused on procuring human-interest stories about the singers, their experiences in the host city, their wardrobe, their hairstyles, and so on.

And despite the very public emphasis in Tirana on values, professionalism, and safeguarding song during and after the Festival, songs that do well at the Festival are not ones that are the "best" or most creative, or even ones that domestic listeners might want to hear. Instead, winning Festival songs are ones perceived as having the best chance to place well at Eurovision. My sense is that organizers on the ground cede decision-making to certain powerful culture brokers, whether employees at the Ministry of Culture, upper-level administrators at the Radio-Television, or even the composer-producers themselves, men whom they view as having the authority to "know what Europe wants." But all potential decision-makers, whether jury members, administrators, or musicians, proceed with insufficient knowledge, inaccurate assumptions, or even simply the inability to execute their strategies.

So the Festival can host spectacular misfires. In 2011, organizers placed a stream of updating social media comments next to the live webcast of the Festival of Song on its website. Observing from the United States, I estimated about three-quarters of the predominantly English-language comments came from Eurovision super-fans in Western Europe who follow not only the Eurovision Song Contest itself, but also the selection rounds in participating countries.[27] At my laptop in Massachusetts, I wondered if organizers were following to collect real-time data about this demographic's reactions. After all, similar viewers would be judging whether to vote for one of the program's songs just five months later. Many comments were, to say the least, unkind. "Oh no!" one mocked as a performance began, " 'All aboard, the Mediterranean cruise ship!' " Remarkably, the handful of Albanian commentators tweeting did not defend the songs. Instead, these fans were trying to explain to European viewers that the Festival of Song's program did not accurately represent contemporary popular music in Tirana. Real Albanian music, these commenters posted, the hip-hop, rock, and pop artists that most young people follow, could be found at the private festivals.

THE FORTY-EIGHTH FESTIVAL OF
SONG: FINALE, DECEMBER 27

The finale night of the Forty-eighth Festival opened with its hosts addressing the audience in a newly serious tone. This night, they told us, would have no commentary, only the songs, in order to avoid even the potential for any undue *influencat* to sway the professional jury members seated in the front row. The order of singers had been chosen by draw, also to avoid any influence due to the sequence of performances. The hosts would announce only the names of the singers, songs, and their collaborators. We were to experience the festival as pure musical sound, with only the bare minimum of explanation (and, of course, short breaks for advertisements on the telecast). And with that, a host introduced the first singer.

I had attended each of the previous three nights of the Festival, taking careful notes on how the hosts' scripted remarks framed different singers, what kinds of applause each garnered, and how the composers and lyricists present in the hall reacted. At the finale, I was immediately struck by the composition of the audience. The crowd was much older, and many had dressed up. Most men wore at least jackets and ties. Many women had had their hair professionally done; almost all wore expensive-looking gowns. By this point, I had a sense from observing the previous audiences' reactions and talking with friends as to who seemed to be considered the front-runners for the top prize. Two acts, Bojkën Lako with his Banda Adriatica and Anjeza Shahini, had consistently received callbacks and the most sustained applause, with singer Kamela Islami close behind. But I was also struck by the hosts' seemingly closer attention to certain acts, including Gjebrea's singer Juliana Pasha, especially in inviting them back on stage for curtain calls even as applause in the hall waned. And as audience members settled into their seats, I was also surprised to see the director of the Radio-Television personally walk down to exchange a quick word with the cameraman closest to me, gesturing to Ardit Gjebrea's seat in the bottom section of the hall. During the voting two hours later, it was this cameraman's angle that recorded the composer's reactions once it became apparent he had won.

True to their word, the hosts simply introduced each act. But some acts then seemed to require callbacks. One very well-known performer left to only a smattering of applause, yet the hosts called him back on stage, saying, "Bravo! Bravo." At the same time, the hosts tried to move quickly between acts, which led to several awkward moments. Following Lako's performance, he and the band walked slowly offstage to thundering applause. The host initially walked on stage and began to talk over the clapping to introduce the next singer, but the crowd grew louder and Lako reappeared for a quick bow. Kamela Islami, who performed last, received similar treatment. Unlike the mostly tightly rehearsed performances up to that point, she brought an energy to her singing that the crowd rewarded with the most sustained cheering of the evening. After she left, the hosts came on, directed the professional jury to exit to the closed room where they would make their decision, and introduced the commercial break.

There is no way to know whether the audience in the hall represented the average Albanian fan; my sense is that they not only skewed older and more educated than average listeners, but also tended to be more likely to come from its small creative class. I recognized writers, artists, filmmakers, and politicians. And I came away feeling that this group, like myself and the composers themselves, were also thinking about and evaluating how each performance might possibly represent Albania—that we were all considering performances primarily as as to their success in branding the Nation to European viewers. So the most applauded performances, in my estimation, tended to be either the catchiest Western-style pop songs, such as Anjeza Shahini's dramatic ballad or Kamela Islami's driving dance tune, or the most successful folk-inspired songs, such as Banda Adriatica's brassy rocker. Complicating my perceptions, the most popular Tirana-based singers had contingents of cheering friends and family; I began to ignore the reactions to one singer after realizing that most of the applause came from a block of women who looked just like her.

When the jury returned, the audience had the opportunity to make its preferences known one final time. Each jury member had distributed between 1 and 20 points to each act, which a screen projected on stage tabulating the numbers in real time. The hosts announced each act, requesting that each jury member announce live how many points he or she had awarded. I noted a handful of uncomfortable moments when the audience responded to what they perceived to be suspicious spreads. One ill-conceived and poorly performed song received a low score of 2 and an improbably high score of 15; another, a low score of 1 and a high of 16. Audience members murmured, quietly grousing to the people in their row. Shahini, the sixth act according to that night's running order, was the first front-runner to be announced: "Fourteen." "Eighteen." "Sixteen." "Eighteen." "Nineteen." "Thirteen." "Twenty!" The crowd erupted, applauding a full fifty seconds in the hall. But just two acts later, the winner became clear.

"Juliana Pasha with 'Nuk Mundem Pa Ty,'" announced the hosts, "composer, Ardit Gjebrea and lyrics by Ardit Gjebrea and Pirro Çako. The points, please."

"Twenty." Murmurs.

"Twenty."

"Twenty." More murmurs.

"Twenty." Growing excitement, but mingled with some small noises of disbelief.

"Twenty." Louder, and—

"Twenty." —louder still, with some scattered clapping.

"Thir-teen," pronounced the seventh and final juror, journalist Agron Tufaj, over-articulating each syllable. The hall then exploded in applause. But what were they applauding? Some were applauding the song, clearly now the winner given its near perfect scores. But a healthy amount, it seemed to me, were cheering Tufaj's "thirteen," his refusal to award a flawless string of "twenties."

The announcement of the voting for the remaining twelve acts lacked drama, with all other acts statistically eliminated from contention, but not audience engagement. When the sixth jury member awarded Bojken Lako's group 2 points, in stark contrast to the other voters' spread between 11 and 19 points, the audience jeered him, I believe suspecting that, as another composer later suggested to me, this evidenced collusion. "They must give the appearance of integrity," he told me, "but in reality that one score makes it impossible to win." The outlier knocked Lako's entry down to sixth place, seventeen points below the top three. And when Kamela Islami, announced last, received scores vaulting her into third place, she received applause second only to Shahini, who ultimately came in second.

Pasha's reprise performance ended the night. It felt anticlimactic after all the talking and bloodless reciting of numbers, and the people sitting around me in the hall rose and gathered their belongings to leave while she sang. In the coming weeks, Pasha and Gjebrea appeared on a number of television programs and in glossy magazines. Coverage focused heavily on Gjebrea, emphasizing that the song was being reworked into a version that would meet international standards and stressing the composer's credentials to do this. "[Gjebrea is doing] the recording and mixing in the studios of Europe, the mastering in New York, and [is preparing] a special performance," glowed one exemplary report. "The violin of Olen Cezar"—maybe not coincidentally, I found myself suspecting, the professional jury member who gave Lako 2 points—"and three American singers are accompanying Juliana Pasha on May 25 at the European Festival, Eurovision 2010." The version sent to compete at Eurovision had been translated into English as "It's All About You," and Pasha, coached to approximate an American accent. The original piece, Gjebrea stated in interviews, had even been constructed to be Eurovision-ized: three minutes long, and with a simple melody and syllabic text that he believed could be easily retrofitted for European ears.

The following May, Pasha progressed from the semifinals to the finals in Russia, where she came in a disappointing sixteenth out of the field of thirty-nine. The Festival of Song jury did, however, guess right as to what "Europe" wanted. Fatigued by folksy productions and ballads, Eurovision viewers awarded first prize to Lena Meyer-Landrut of Germany. Lena, who won the right to represent Germany via a Pop Idol–style contest held on public television, won with her bubble-gum sweet song "Satellite," an English-language pop ditty crafted by an American-British songwriting team.

Light Song and the Promotional Economy

In the months following the Forty-eighth Festival of Song, Ardit Gjebrea's composition and Juliana Pasha's face became ubiquitous in the media. But except for a handful of interviews with the singer and a sparsely attended send-off party broadcast by Radio-Television Albania, most of the promotion occurred on Gjebrea's home station, TV KLAN. This led one conspiracy-minded colleague of mine to suspect that the Festival itself was in the process of being hijacked by private broadcasters, at last privatized and brought fully under the control of purely economic interests. This has not turned out to be true. Yet other than Gjebrea's song, I did not hear the other performances from the Festival again, whether on private or public stations. One or two performers released music video clips, but the Radio-Television did not broadcast or promote the songs in any systematic way. In fact, one week after the finale, I found myself in the bowels of the Radio-Television building, visiting the archives about another matter. While I chatted with an archivist, an engineer came in looking for the recordings of the Festival songs. After digging around in a few piles of papers and compact discs, he gave up and left without finding them.

This situation could not be more different from the socialist period. Before 1991, the state broadcaster heavily promoted the newest light songs for months after the Festival. Performances provided fodder for discussion and gossip in schools and offices, and listeners often recalled whistling their favorite songs in the days and weeks following their initial broadcast. But though song had been so integral to projects aiming to elevate the tastes of ordinary listeners, it underwent a marked change during the 1990s, becoming an object for internal consumption by elites aiming to define the meanings of Democracy and Freedom to themselves. Eurovision has at once attenuated and refined this progression toward internal consumption in the 2000s. A mere handful of composers and officials today vie to make songs promoting what the Nation should look and sound like. And this exercise addresses elites themselves, stakeholders in the larger political project to manage Albania's image abroad.

At the level of the music field, the calculations that composers make as to how the synergy between personal creativity and national branding might be accomplished arise within and between multiple, competing kinds of promotion. Winning performances at the Festival of Song must promote the Nation to Europe. But at the same time, the composer-producers penning these songs are also promoting themselves to singers, who in turn then assess potential commissions according to how they will contribute to furthering their own personal brands. These nesting levels of promotion can be tricky for composer-producers to navigate. A few months before the Forty-eighth Festival of Song, I visited the cramped storefront studio of one aspiring composer-producer, *Gjergji, a recent Conservatory graduate. Though he had competed at several previous Festivals, his 2009 entry had not been accepted. He had agreed to a collaboration with an up-and-coming young singer: an attractive, strong-voiced university student who had recently risen to prominence by reaching the semifinals on a privately broadcast singing contest. But then a more established composer approached her and she, weighing the promotional benefits of performing his song against breaking her commitment, had left Gjergji in the lurch just before the submission deadline. He scrambled to find and record another singer; the one he settled on had not been as strong nor the song as well-suited to her voice. Describing why he did not simply give up, he explained his thinking.

"Just having a song is *publiciteti, një reklamë*, publicity or a good advertisement, as long as it is well-done."

"But if it is advertising for the singer *and* you, does this make compensation complicated? Will they pay you to do it, or do you just do it for free to get the exposure?"

"It depends, really. It is kind of a strange market in this way. This is because with names, well-known singers, success is guaranteed. If you have a singer with a big name, you are set. But the singers themselves are disoriented, they are *çorientuar*."

Gjergji's perceptions aligned with others critical of the promotional economy as having "no direction" or "lacking organization." At the same time, I increasingly found myself thinking that professionalized composers like Gjergji may themselves be misdirected, socialized into a nearly moribund value system that leaves them largely unprepared for this "strange market." In an interview published in the run-up to the Fiftieth Festival of Song in 2011, musicologist and Conservatory pedagogue Nestor Kraja sounded bewildered by his students' lack of success at the Festival in particular and within the popular music economy in general.

"The Radio-Television's Festival of Song," he argued, "must target national artistic values."

"I put such a strong emphasis on the coagulation of national values in light music songs because, on the extreme side, today we see that we have authors who have become practitioners, who take ready-made rhythmic formulas from the [outside] world and add a totally simple and ordinary melody on top, and in this way are able to penetrate [a festival] jury's filter. I think that our [Conservatory] students, too, must be involved with light music, because they take some important insights in school that they should be allowed to demonstrate in light music. But the introduction of studios makes it so that some of these students cannot take part at all in the festival's competition. Before the festival was a big deal for all creators, while now the song must be produced, and . . . many young composers who graduate from the Academy of Arts do not have the technical mindset.[28]

Without the "technical mindset" needed to appeal to singers, Kraja asserted, professionalized composers cannot penetrate the economy's new "filters." Effectively barred in this way from participation in the music economy, they lack the platform for expressing values that might reorient the market of singers. Or so the argument goes. But if singers are no longer primarily oriented by composers and their discourses of value and professionalism, that does not mean they are dis- or un-oriented. Instead, these singers are oriented by the tastes of listeners, their fans who follow them on social media, watch their music video clips online, and pay to see their live performances. Yet professionalized composers themselves seem to misapprehend this new capacity of the public, viewing it as a destabilizing influence rather than the driving economic force it has become. Their misapprehension grates on more practical-minded members of the newly enlarged, postsocialist music field. Reacting to the habitual barbs of professionals, one singer posted a public screed, railing against the "ignorance" of these men to their contemporary situation.[29]

"A question for 'the professors' that claim to be making 'art' but who understand nothing at all about it. . . . My question is, when you hear and see [foreign] artists on stage, what do you think besides, 'Wow, these are great?' Do you hear how simple and understandable they are for a public that doesn't read music and cannot analyze music besides knowing very well how to feel and enjoy it? Ah, maybe you 'beloved professors' say, 'Well, outside the [Albanian] state there exists another public'—'THIS public here is ignorant'—'It does not understand us.' No, darlings, no. We are the People, while you are a music elite. But 'you were mistakenly born here, you shouldn't be here because you are of a high caliber and here they don't understand your art.' Blah, blah, blah. . . . The more unintelligible your 'works' are, that much more you believe you are making art. But in fact it is the opposite. Bye."

THE POLITICS OF THE ENTREPRENEURIAL SPIRIT

It might be hard to muster much sympathy for the professionalized men who for decades controlled production of a domain they called culture and the arts.[30] But their situation reveals the sinuous nature of government as it unfolds over time, cutting across and remaking social groups through concrete practices like promotion. The imperative of *promovim*, the will to promotion that permeates creative work, has depended on major structural changes to the contemporary cultural economy. At the institutional level, the deregulation and subsequent oligarchization of media production have had two consequences. This process has created and elevated the roles of new actors, especially *biznesmen*, non-professionalized producers, and singers, while at the same time drastically curtailing the space in which intellectuals—in the sense used throughout the preceding chapters—might pursue what they feel to be meaningful creative work. But at the interpersonal level, bodies of knowledge and practice about the "best" or most "professional" way to make "art" have seemingly persisted, albeit against long odds. Yet composers now invoke professionalism to brand themselves as distinct from non-professionals.

In this way the very discourses professionals use to criticize the new economic status quo simultaneously bind them to it as self-promoting, entrepreneurial subjects. The creators who most harshly criticize the promotional economy, for sure, voice their displeasure from its margins or its outside. But not all professionalized musicians opt out. Some roll up their sleeves and work. These composer-producers become enmeshed within emergent logics of promotion, especially by competing for the right to represent the Nation to Europe. During my fieldwork, I often found myself wondering at the energy spent, the vitriol streaming out from my consultants in discussing the contemporary situation for music-making. This was in part due to the nature of my circle as it developed over time, which heavily comprised older men, Conservatory-based musicians, and lesser-known composer-producers. During the socialist period, these people made up the bulk of the popular music-making field. Today, they comprise a working minority suborned to the new status quo. And to work today, you simply have to promote yourself. The ethos of *promovim* infects—a verb used here advisedly—all levels of creativity, from collaboration, to individual musical decisions, to the system of festivals, to even national policy. "The capitalism virus," one melodramatic friend put it in a mock-serious whisper, "has touched all of us!"

Self-promotion makes professionalized musicians into entrepreneurs, and as these musicians become entrepreneurs, they cede the socialist-era duties of the public intellectual to comment on society or craft its values. Questions of intellectual knowledge—How should we live? Who should we be?—increasingly find answers in the market. Under socialism, these questions were bound up with wider considerations about the political field's legitimacy, its unassailable claim to be best suited to identify and answer society's cultural needs. But humanists and social scientists actually crafted the answers in the form of symphonies, folk troupes, novels, poetry, histories, sociological texts, films, and of course light music songs. And the objects of these answers were not only the People or the Masses, imaginary domains targeted in official speech for cultivation, elevation, or reform, but the actual people who watched, read, laughed, listened, and grew up with these works. Under capitalism today, professionalized musicians seem ill-suited to even consider such questions. In practical terms, the entrepreneurial composer thinks about making connections, gaining commissions, establishing a reputation, all of which militate against telling consumers how they should live rather than apprehending and fulfilling their desires about how they want to live.

But an ethos of *promovim* suffuses the very texture of government itself. Governance at the national level depends on the appearance of Western-ness and European-ness, and cultural politics in turn reflects this by transforming into a politics of branding. The 1990s name change from the Ministry of Culture to the Ministry of Tourism, Culture, Youth, and Sports suggests as much. (Its change back since the end of my fieldwork may suggest another shift not covered here.) The imbrication of *kultura* with branding points to the wider ramifications of the prominence of appearances. And this in turn suggests new political consequences. "What happens to notions of national sovereignty, citizenship, and democratic governance under a regime of branding?" asks Nadia Kaneva. "In other words, what are the consequences of re-imagining the nation as brand?"[31] At the Festival of Song, branding seems to have undercut the potential for light music songs to connect their creators with listeners. The Nation expressed in these works seems hollower, crafted for consumption by "Europe" rather than domestic listeners. And this might be explained by the rise of the image above all else. The image of Albania "on Europe's stage," the image of *transparencë* during the Festival's organization, the image of professionalism all gain new significance, while composers compete to present an image of themselves as connected, as best suited to present the Nation to Europe. This is not to imply that sound had somehow been a more essentially authentic sense for nation-building or a more honest medium for creative expression. But rather this shows how the image of the Nation has been elevated as a governmental object for concern.

This is a problem when the image obscures lived realities. One critique prominent at the time of my fieldwork had to do with concerns that elected officials were successively hollowing out the State, promoting the appearance of democracy over its institutions and practices. Sali Berisha committed Albanian troops to the U.S.-led War on Terror, for instance, making Albania one of only four countries to join George W. Bush's "coalition of the willing" during the active combat phase of Operation Enduring Freedom. An opposition newspaper routinely mocked him as DigiSal because of his propensity for appearing in public surrounded by iPads, laptops, and other forms of "advanced" technology. To critics, tone-deaf attempts to show that Albania is a key partner to global superpowers in the West, or that its leaders are technologically advanced, represent a hokey façade designed to obscure persistent poverty, crumbling infrastructure, and endemic corruption.

At the Festival of Song, competitors had once imagined their light music compositions as addressing an Albanian population, at various times conceived to be the Youth, the Masses, or the People. Contemporary productions, however, have to do with representing the Nation to a new audience: Europe. From these calculations about how best to address Europe emerge an entire host of concerns that find little resonance with local listeners. This is not to say that local listeners do not care about Albania's image abroad. Many care deeply, as their Nation's brand influences the foreign policies that shape opportunities for travel, study, and work beyond Albania's borders. Others care because of their sense of pride for their country. And yet this pride itself had in large part been shaped by state-socialist cultural policy, policy that heavily promoted identification with the Nation. In contrast, younger people are today being targeted by a host of new factors, and especially including domestically produced music and television that closely approximate foreign models. But how do older Albanians, the target of the subjectivity forming means disseminated under socialism, react?

One middle-aged woman, a waitress at the restaurant next to my apartment, often talked about socialist-era light music with me while we waited for our food. That a foreign researcher might consider this music and its artists worth introducing to an English-language readership made her proud, but also a bit incredulous. That the older artists were, in her mind, being forgotten in Tirana was disappointing. She described to me, crisply, the problem of the past two decades from her particular vantage point.

Në Shqipëri ka hyrë bota, dhe u zhduk Shqipëria.

"The world entered Albania, and Albania disappeared."

"There Is No State"

After six decades, light music song as a domain for state oversight has once again begun slipping into inaudibility. The officials who might "protect" it today no longer can hear *këngë kombëtare*, national songs, as objects needing management or cultivation. The very notion of management has been itself recast as abnormal, as contrary to the open and transparent practice (at least in theory) of democracy. Professionalized musicians themselves helped to make this view commonsense during the 1990s. And today it seems difficult to imagine an alternative in postsocialist Tirana, even while "the socialist past remains a prime reference point for many people in their own personal histories and memories as they struggle to make sense of the present."[32]

"During socialism," the composer Agim Krajka was telling me, "there was the Ensemble of Folk Songs and Dances, the National Theater, the Radio, the Academy, the Theater of Opera and Ballet. The State sent educated people to the villages, and in each village there were culture houses staffed by people who had degrees in singing, accordion, piano, composition." The composer had been rehearsing for me the notion that, if political will existed, culture and the arts could be better organized today.

"So why doesn't this happen today? Is there no will, no money—*s'ka dëshirë? S'ka lekë?*"

"There's no State—*s'ka shtet!* The State does not invest in culture. And private media invests in things like rap or rock. Will this be our passport to Europe? Why not make our own, autochthonous folk music our passport?"

A few months later, the singer Bashkim Alibali identified *një komplot*, a conspiracy, in the lack of management, a form of creative destruction unleashed against subjectivity itself. "I call it—and I have said this publicly in interviews— I see what I call *agresioni* toward Albanian music and Albanian identity. It is an attempt to strip away identity, to leave nothing, to destroy values. The people who attempt to do this—"

"So it is purposeful?"

"Of course, I would say it is certainly purposeful. When you have private television stations that air foreign music, exploit the state Radio-Television without any check, how can it be anything but that? When songs are taken, rearranged, deformed, degenerated, this is an attack on identity and national values. The archives are sold at ridiculous prices, artists are not compensated, these cultural monuments are in turn deformed. Then these microbes disperse, they infect."

"But who is at fault here?"

"The system is at fault. The State is at fault. Bashkim Alibali is not at fault. So-and-so is not at fault. The State is at fault."

"But what should the State do?"

"Simple! The state licenses television and radio stations. It can pull their license for this *agresioni*, for these anti-national attacks. How can it *not* do this, if the Nation is being attacked? It has a duty to protect values from attack."

What does it mean to argue that the State refuses to protect the Nation? Or even to claim "there is no State?" In one sense, these musicians are correct. Something they might recognize today as "the State" does seem, held against the measuring stick of the past, to have disappeared. (Though bemoaning the absence of the State in a postsocialist context like Albania pushes irony to its breaking point.)

Yet these critics might also be, in Foucault's phrasing, "overvaluing of the problem of the state."[33] In understanding the State solely as an instrument of power rather than an effect, an ahistorical object rather than "a dynamic and contingent form of societal power relations," such critiques ascribe to the State too much authority.[34] The very form their critique takes fails to "mak[e] visible a singularity at places where there is a temptation to invoke a historical constant, an immediate anthropological trait, or an obviousness which imposes itself uniformly on all."[35] What they bemoan as the disappearance of the State, this chapter has suggested, might better be understood as itself an emerging governmental strategy. At the level of policy, this strategy leaves symbolic production to the market. The market in turn shifts new entrepreneurial responsibilities onto musicians, duties they must domesticate within more broadly circulating ideas about the social value and meaning of art. And this shift, it seems, is in turn transforming what it means to be a musician or listener, what it means to make and consume song today.

Epilogue

Hearing Like a State

The preceding chapters examined how politics, economics, and the daily creative practice of intellectuals in Tirana intersect, tracing not only the disjunctures, but also the continuities between nominally distinct orders as musicians, listeners, and the music they make and consume have become audible objects for government over time. My narrative emphasized how state-socialist projects instrumentalized presocialist nationalist concerns with backwardness, as well as how postsocialist politics and emerging market mechanisms today fragment and transfigure once coherent social domains. And I have stressed government's positive, constitutive effects in rendering conditions of possibility by which light music songs could be created and broadcast, as well as the conditions whereby listeners and musicians alike could be made subject to government. This epilogue concludes by considering the wider stakes of such an approach. I begin from the cultural field's mourning of the passing of Vaçe Zela, an event I followed online in early 2014.

"'Albania's Golden Voice,' 'the Blessed Icon of Albanian Song,' 'the Giantess of the Albanian State,'" reported one exemplary news story, "these are but a few of the epithets given the Albanian singer Vaçe Zela, who following a lengthy sickness passed away the morning of February 6, 2014, at the age of seventy-five in a hospital in Basel, Switzerland, where she had been living."[1] Zela's death from lung cancer initiated a sustained period of mourning in Tirana. She had not performed on stage since 1992 and, given her failing health and residence abroad, had for some time been distant from the public's ear. Yet her star had not dimmed during this period but burned brighter. The Ministry of Culture declared 2009 "the year of Vaçe Zela" to honor her seventieth birthday. Televised spectacles and tributes promoted her songs to a new generation. Adulatory biographies and liner notes called her "the unique one," *papërsëritshmja*, expounding on the "magic" of her songs, which a Ministry-produced multi-disc retrospective termed "models of a valuable heritage in the music field, as well as a manifestation of the Albanian school of interpretation."[2] On her passing, the government recognized the singer with what amounted to a state funeral. Mourners came to the Theater of Opera and Ballet to pay their last respects as her casket lay, ensconced in lilies and illuminated by a single spotlight, on its stage.

Musicologists, singers, composers, and politicians alike eulogized her in baroque public statements. Most used her first name, speaking intimately. "A member of our family," one said, "has left us."[3] Some praised her musicianship and work ethic, her timbre, intonation, and style. Others emphasized her championing of a specifically national, deeply Albanian song. "During these days I have felt something special," the composer Aleksandër Lalo stated after her funeral, "a national feeling that cannot be denied." And several people even dared link "our Vaçe," albeit gingerly, to politics, as having represented "an oasis of freedom in the desert" of the socialist period. "Nobody educated us better than you with [your song] 'E Dua Vendin Tim' (I Love My Country)," rhapsodized Osman Mula. More pointedly: "We lived in an Albania that groaned and languished, where the singer was imprisoned when he sang and where the poet was sent to the firing squad for his work," claimed Sherif Merdani. "Yet God did not kill our hope, but sent a voice to ease our pain and give us hope."

Prime Minister Edi Rama, a painter and the son of the socialist-era Sculptor of the People Kristaq Rama, delivered an address in which he reminisced about watching Zela during Radio-Television broadcasts of the socialist-era Festival of Song. "I would watch the festival, and it was always the same old thing every time until Vaçe Zela came on stage—with her flowing hair outside the stated norms, a smile that filled the entire screen . . . she electrified the air in our [home]. She was a voice that would have electrified the sky of the entire world had she lived during another time, but in our locked sky she could do nothing else but burn as a star. And she left her voice locked inside the black-and-white television set. . . . Vaçe Zela has not died but has left this world completely. . . . On behalf of all those who share with me these experiences, I want to say, I am thankful that you existed when our existence was frozen stiff."[4]

Remembrances remarkably and nearly uniformly insisted on simplifying Zela to the essence of sound, as një zë, simply "a voice." Hers became an ideal voice in the retelling, an unadulterated sonic force that could be feted by postsocialist commentators. As pure sound, this voice had provided nourishment and eased the psychic distress of having lived in "frozen Albania." It existed outside a politics that her eulogizers represented as essentially repressive. It existed fundamentally outside, almost, even reality itself. The journalist Edison Ypi wrote, in an essay titled "Voce Zela," literally "Voice Zela" using the Italian word, that "Voce Zela was, is, and will forever be, something else entirely. A breath, a quality, an atmosphere, ether, that in its materiality can link with nothing direct, vulgar, mediocre."[5]

But real people are not ether. They do have a materiality and, in a *polemikë* immediately and nearly unanimously rejected by the Tirana commentariat as itself reprehensibly "direct, vulgar, and mediocre," the journalist Fatos Lubonja pointed this out about Zela. Lubonja, son of the former director of Radio-Television Albania Todi Lubonja, had himself been sentenced—twice—to prison camps under state socialism. Since the 1990s, he has emerged as a publisher, provocateur, and outspoken critic of Tirana's political establishment in its successive guises.

"Once upon a time," Lubonja began, "even I loved Vaçe. But I must say this feeling belongs to the period when a person still trusts grown-ups, and so I believed that our songs were the most beautiful in the world, that I was living 'in the beautiful fatherland, where a new life was blossoming,' when I still knew no other world beyond the Albanian one, [no] books besides those written by socialist realist authors, no other language, and no other songs of the singers of the world."[6] But once he and his friends discovered these other worlds, he claimed, they paid Vaçe and her state-subsidized ilk no more attention. Vaçe "sought to teach us about boundless love for the homeland, comrade Enver, the Party, revolution, socialism." Her songs "served as military defense against the attacks of the musical revolution of rock, pop, and so on that the world came to know from the 1960s to the 1990s." The hysteria over her death pointed to "an epidemic of conformism, hypocrisy, and a large-scale handicap." And most chillingly, Lubonja wrote, Zela's passing was now providing cover for the expression of a morally and politically debilitating nostalgia. It demonstrated that mourners had internalized the "enverist fairy-tales" that socialism had not been so bad. But totalitarianism, Lubonja wrote, citing Solzhenitsyn's famous formulation, had been "the great lie": "And these songs were an expression of the deceptive content [of communist ideology]."

The positive eulogies no doubt stemmed in part from several late- and postsocialist trends identified in this book's final chapters, including the emergence of the 1960s as a golden age, the anti-communist narrative reframing socialist-era song as a site for internalized dissent, or the rise of those contemporary pop stars to whom intellectuals nostalgically contrast more "cultured" singers like Zela as a critical foil. Lubonja invoked a rather standard mass culture critique, a stance commonly found not in contemporary Tirana, but among mid-twentieth-century scholars in the West.[7] Light song was propaganda, he argued, and it had apparently brainwashed Albanians, as attested to by their outpouring of grief. Each side's statements seemingly shared little ideological space. But under the surface, each side rested on common epistemological ground. Both perspectives depended on a particular construction of creative agency, approaching musicians as existing either fully outside or wholly within the broader field of power. The eulogies appealed to a subjectivity that takes its form in the contravening or refusing of politics. Lubonja's criticism appealed to a subjectivity that either emerges from the universal light of political truth, a broader position popularized by thinkers like Havel or Solzhenitsyn, or must remain shrouded by the debilitating darkness of propagandistic lies. These oversimplifications each propose that the individual subject precedes politics. Such subjects either react to or are acted upon by the political-economic orders in which they find themselves making or enjoying song.

The debate over Zela's legacy ended quickly, with Lubonja overwhelmed by dissenting op-eds, tweets, and posts on social media. This in itself conveys something about the nature of history-making and remembrance in the postsocialist cultural field, albeit something that lies beyond the scope of these concluding pages. For my purposes here, the *polemikë* suggests how the problem of researching popular culture in so-called illiberal societies emerges at the point where epistemology and methodology intersect. How do people living in non-liberal state orders know what they know about creativity and art? By what methods can researchers examine this? And more broadly, by the light of what knowledge do scholars themselves formulate research agendas to examine the lives and creative work of their consultants in these societies?

In a sense these questions are simply the taken-for-granted, bread-and-butter concerns of the contemporary humanities and humanistic social sciences, especially following their turn to questions of power, representation, and writing. But the legacy of the Cold War complicates the direct examination of these questions in state-socialist, postsocialist, or even simply non-capitalist societies. Jonathyne Briggs has recently summarized this legacy as it applies to popular music: "In terms of the East, youth culture is understood as purely political, but only along the axis of ideology, with rock and roll, the music of youth culture, often romanticized as a pure expression of youth angst against a soulless, totalitarian Communist system."[8] Some specialists on the region may quibble with Briggs's use of the present tense. Yet this summation accurately characterizes more widely circulating ideas about the nature of music and resistance in general, and in Eastern Europe in particular.

But the situation on the ground, as ethnographers know, always remains decidedly murkier. If Zela's reception in Tirana has proved contradictory—her songs at once sources of propaganda and pleasure, and her creative output able to be understood as simultaneously inside and outside something Albanians today recognize as the State—this itself demonstrates a key feature of modern political-economic orders. Modern societies, Foucault wrote in his later work, are "truly demonic."[9] With this, he meant that modern regimes do not comprise discrete systems of power, but always diabolical admixtures: complex, layered orders of overlapping techniques and technologies for defining, overseeing, and directing human life. An analytics of government in turn urges us, William

Walters writes, "to view the present as multiply constituted, polytemporal . . . and not just the expression of a singular logic or the resultant of a linear process."[10] A careful analysis of the hybrid combinations making up what we come to call "society," however, should not merely elucidate complexity for complexity's sake. Government depends on a particular "politics to combination," Walters continues. "It is the combination of quite different arts of government that can make the state so dangerous."[11]

The practice of history and ethnography may aspire to lay bare these politics. Foucault aimed to diagnose liberal orders in the West, but I have proceeded from the assumption that the precept remains suited to non-liberal orders as well. We might ask: What features have characterized the politics of combination in post–World War II societies in Eastern Europe? How did projects to oversee cultural life fit into this politics? And given the diversity of this region, can insights about Albania prompt broader areas of inquiry? My approach suggested how government in state-socialist Albania fluidly combined what, following Katherine Verdery, I called symbolic-ideological and coercive strategies. Its post-1992 trajectory has been characterized by the rapid dwindling of these strategies' significance. The politics of the former period gave rise to a powerful bloc of professionalized musicians and the expansion of new audible domains for state action. The politics of the latter heralded this group's decline, rendering some formerly audible domains silent and leading to the rise of the visual. This approach broadly resonates with one of Alexei Yurchak's proposals for the Soviet Union. The relationship between cultural production and state control, Yurchak writes, "needed to be revisited throughout Soviet history, suggesting the enduring tension at socialism's core."[12] If we accept this proposition, then the politics animating the non-liberal combination and recombination of governmental techniques in Eastern Europe might be expressed as a politics in which the relationship between positive and negative strategies for shaping human life *nga lart*, from above, had to be perpetually balanced, with the ascension of the one resulting in the fall of the other and vice-versa. The transition from state-socialist forms of political and economic organization did not resolve this core tension, but has instead substituted new tensions between creativity and capital, and among memories of the past, experiences of the present, and plans for the future.

If these tensions are characteristic of the region, the inevitable failures of efforts to resolve them are not. Would-be governors never resolve the tensions at the core of their projects to administer society. They never achieve equilibrium, at least not for any lasting period of time. Government, even in its most determined guises, reveals itself always to be a habitually failing enterprise at each turn. And so while James C. Scott, arguing that modern societies seek to conduct their subjects through mechanisms of vision, titled his foundational work *Seeing Like a State*, his subtitle, *How Certain Schemes to Improve the Human*

Condition Have Failed, emphasized government's inevitably unsuccessful out-comes in practice.[13] So "habitually failing" may be the wrong phrasing, implying as it does that governmental schemes might be perfected, that control can ever be made absolute. Total control is merely the fantasy of the powerful. Miller and Rose's phrasing, "congenitally failing," more accurately characterizes govern-ment in practice.[14] That is to say, the dynamic give-and-take of different actors' positions-taking that give rise to mutations in government over time is an inher-ent property of government in its modern forms, as are blind spots, social spaces illegible to oversight or reform.

Given these assumptions about how modern orders work, what might be gained by renewed engagement with questions of "the State" in music studies? By cultivating new metaphors of sound, audibility, and audition? By asking what it means to "hear like a state?" First, audibility trains our ears on the positive, rather than negative, functioning of power. Liberal traditions of thought valo-rize the ability to "have a voice," to "make oneself heard," even to "speak truth to power." As a corollary, to be silenced is to be stripped of your agency, your power. Recasting audibility as a process impels us to recognize that the mere act of "having a voice" may not in itself be a universal condition for all subjects at any point in time, that it cannot arise outside the structures of political and eco-nomic life. Nor can silence be assumed to constitute mere absence, an absence that diagnoses the sites where power has been brought to bear on its abject subjects. Rather, modern societies are made up of overlapping, sometimes con-flicting strategies that render certain aspects of social life audible and inaudible. These domains change and mutate over time and within particular economies of symbolic production.

Second, a focus on audibility raises new potential questions about political authority, legitimacy, and management. As a non-discursive, inherently polyse-mic representational form, sound is prone to evading administration, provoking debate as to its meaning or meanings, and stimulating political action to bring these meanings under control or to harness their affective potentials. Musical sound may convey, evoke, refer to, stand for, or represent multiple ideas, feelings, or symbols all at once.[15] Recognition of this property demands the critical histo-ricization of the dangerousness of sound and, by extension, musicians, especially in state orders that are relatively more dependent on symbols for their legiti-macy. By harnessing the power of sound, authorities tap into a powerful state resource. But to tap this resource, non-musician authorities need to delegate at least a measure of their control to sound experts. This elevates the role of such specialists, rendering them at once useful and dangerous, and newly subject to recruitment, control, subsidization, training, and so on. And it brings the objects of their work, listeners, into new political relations of intimacy with each other and music specialists.

Finally, an emphasis on audition and audiation urges researchers of music to revisit how we approach listeners and musicians. Sound-consuming and -making under complex orders become enmeshed in political, moral, and aesthetic languages; they depend on technologies, institutions, and infrastructure; and they give rise to creative, economic, and governmental practices. To refocus research on these languages, infrastructures, and practices may allow individual researchers to disconnect their work from the particularities of historical or geographic contexts, making it possible to think through big-picture comparisons in new ways. For instance, music-making in planned economies depended on logics, practices, and institutions—centralization, formalized criticism, unions—that are found, albeit to radically differing degrees, in market economies as well. An approach to political-economic orders dependent on ideal types would have us less productively train our attention toward explaining how "authoritarian states" are characterized by "strict control," or how "benign states" are "generally content to let the music industry go about its daily business uninterrupted and to reap the taxes that industry success brings."[16] Typologies stress difference, and an emphasis on difference can obscure connections. We would do well to adopt approaches that expand rather than limit the horizons our own individual research agendas create for us.

But in adopting these tactics music scholars must also account for the wider economies of knowledge production that structure our research and writing about modern political regimes of all stripes. Invoking anthropologist Saba Mahmood, ethnomusicologists David McDonald and Jeffers Engelhardt have each recently suggested similar propositions. In his ethnography of the musical poetics of political action among Palestinian musicians, for instance, McDonald argues that "the very notion of resistance itself forecloses potentially important discoveries on the dynamics of power given that it often imposes a discursive legacy of progressive and emancipatory politics difficult to see around."[17] Maybe difficult to hear around, too. And in an examination of musical practice in Estonian Orthodoxy, Engelhardt similarly raises the need for a "post-secular ethnomusicology that goes beyond liberal/illiberal binaries in approaching conservative religious modernities."[18] In that spirit, this book has aimed to engage musicians on their own terms and through their own voices, voices that I have argued may be misheard if they are approached through the kinds of liberal categories or narratives that themselves have been and continue to be a product of the Cold War division of the world into free and unfree, liberal and illiberal spheres.[19]

Such categories and narratives present epistemological stumbling blocks that should be engaged through the conceptual schema we adopt, the methodologies we use, and even the writing style we employ. And these stumbling blocks, no doubt, can sometimes trip up the people we work with, too. At one point in my research, a Tirana-born scholar who had emigrated to Great Britain after 1992 criticized my project, questioning the desire of anyone in the English-speaking world to read or care about light music musicians. "They have read this story before," he told me. "It is the story of Stalin's Russia." What he meant was that the story of light music could be told, or perhaps *should only* be told, as the story of musicians challenging the State, and the State in turn repressing these musicians.

Yet researchers and the objects of their research exist within a more complex set of political and economic conditions, conditions that simultaneously make scholarly work possible, but also constrain it. The exposition of these conditions presents their chroniclers with a responsibility that might form the core of a post–Cold War musicology. This responsibility is to apprehending and communicating the inherently contradictory nature of making and enjoying music under modern orders in general, and noncapitalist orders in particular. I found that the people I worked with in Tirana were doing this on their own. Mirela, the middle-aged woman introduced reminiscing about her student days in this book's third chapter, expanded on her motivations for making sense of the past in another conversation with me. We had been talking about what people today call *një këngë e politicizuar*, a politicized song, "Rrugë e Kuqe" (The Red Road) by Pjetër Gaci. I asked her if as a high school student she had really listened to songs like these, operatic mini-arias filled with stilted political slogans. "*Ne hanim atë që na afronin në atë kohë*, she replied, "we ate what they offered during that period."

Her teenage children today cannot seem to understand her previous life, and she does not understand their lives, either. "We are separated, *jemi ndarë*," she told me. That is her motivation for making notes about her memories today. She hoped her children would read them "at least once" in order to understand how different things were for her generation. She wanted them to understand *si liroheshim dhe si pëngoheshim*, "how we were freed and how we were limited." When we met, she had folders filled with scraps of paper, which she arranged and rearranged, editing, organizing, deleting, supplementing, and revising. She had begun making notes twelve years before, just after her children were born; she had yet to share these jottings with them.

"Every time has its own taboos, every time has its own limits," another musician told me, expressing a similar sentiment. "And at times before, these could be quite narrow. Major socialist-era events, for instance, had to include a song 'about the New Life.' Okay, so at the end of one song would be one line about how the Party made this new life possible. *Gjithmonë brenda kësaj kornize*— always within that framework. But it is also true that art and artists were valued. And this is why: Because we created the works. There was never a time without something to do. Right after the Festival, or any event with music, came the invitation to take part in the next one."

Research Materials

Between August 2009 and July 2010, I conducted archival and ethnographic research in Tirana, Albania. Initially, I focused the majority of my research time consulting archival sources and constructing a network of contacts for interviews. At the National State Archives (*Arkivi Qëndror i Shtetit*), I consulted two primary groups of materials filed by the Committee of Arts [and Culture] (*Komiteti i Arteve*; CAC) and Radio-Television Albania (*Radio-Televizioni Shqiptare*; RTSH). The former group comprised a wealth of materials related to the organization of ensembles, arts training programs, folklore collection, and district culture houses between 1944 and the mid-1960s. The latter group comprised materials related to the organization of radio-television programs, broadcast schedules, and personnel at Radio-Television Albania, as well as the minutes from meetings held to organize Festivals of Song between 1962 and the early 1980s. These sources are identified in citations according to dossier number, year, and filing institution (e.g., D21/1975 RTSH, or D[ossier] Number/Year Institution).

As I completed work at the State Archives in Fall 2009, I began researching in the Radio-Television's sound archives. There, I was able to listen to the original recordings of Festival of Song programs broadcast between 1962 and the late 1970s. This experience proved invaluable. While many recordings of classic songs have been remastered and commercially released over the past twenty years, few compositions containing what my consultants termed *politicizëm*, or politicisms, meaning obviously political content, had been made available by 2010. My listening sessions enabled me to situate better-known socialist-era songs within broader Festival trends and media policies. This situation is changing, with fans increasingly uploading content to YouTube and other sites. All the compositions and artists mentioned in the body of this book can now be easily found through quick online searches.

The understanding I gained of quotidian, behind-the-scenes administration confirmed my initial sense that cultural policy had been primarily formulated through debate, negotiation, and consensus among musicians, rather than through the edicts of political elites. This understanding of musicians' agency proved key as I began shifting my research more toward ethnographic interviews. By June 2010, I had conducted forty-four interviews with composers, vocalists, instrumentalists, studio producers, cultural bureaucrats, and light music fans. In most cases, I met with individuals at least twice to introduce myself and my project, and to conduct formal, recorded interviews. My perspectives further benefited from extended, informal meetings with a handful of intellectuals with whom I developed a closer relationship over several months. This interviewing came to focus on a cluster of related issues, including the interrelationships between musicians and non-musicians, codes of artistic conduct, and the effects of political policy statements on creative practices, which did not necessarily focus on questions of "politics," censorship, or repression.

Two other research activities influenced my interviewing. First, in November and December 2009 I observed preparations for the Forty-eighth Festival of Song with the permission of the late Selim Ishmaku, then Artistic Director. This access during two weeks of orchestra rehearsals at the Radio building and five days of dress rehearsals at the Palace of Culture enabled me to meet informally with contemporary popular music producers and to gain an informal, unguarded look at the interactions between Radio-Television organizers, composers, vocalists, and state employees. These observations strongly influenced my later interviews with studio producers, as well as my understanding of postsocialist networks of patronage and influence. Second, I broadly surveyed socialist-era and postsocialist print sources. At the national library, I consulted two primary sources: *Drita* (The Light), an arts weekly and the creative intelligentsia's primary outlet for reviews, articles, and editorials between 1962 and the late 1990s; and *Nëntori* (November), a monthly academic journal with lengthy study articles on the arts published between 1955 and the late 1980s. I also selectively consulted *Estrada*, a socialist-era journal aimed at practical issues facing district variety ensembles, *Radioprogram*, a popular magazine on Radio Albania's programming for general readers, *Zëri i Popullit* (The Voice of the People), Tirana's main daily, and *Zëri i Rinisë* (The Voice of the Youth), a newspaper for students. Though the National Library lacked many print sources from the 1990s and early 2000s, I benefited from the collection of composer Miron Kotani, who allowed me access to his personal archive of press clippings on the Festival between the mid-1990s and early 2000s. Finally, as part of my daily routine I also surveyed the contemporary press.

On my return to the United States, I began elaborating for myself a more critical understanding about integrating archival and published materials produced during the socialist period with ethnographic and published materials created over the past two decades. In Albania, the "truthful" representation of the past continues to be a terrain for contemporary political conflict, while the past two decades have powerfully shaped and reshaped individuals' perspectives on "communism." Many feel they have stories to tell and, with only two exceptions, each referenced in the preceding chapters, individuals I approached were willing, even eager, to meet with me to discuss the socialist period. I found that older intellectuals' experiences of capitalism deeply inflected their views of the past. I met several former culture house directors who, though well-respected and financially secure during the 1970s and 1980s, found themselves near-destitute, unemployed, or even the subject of derision from younger musicians by the time of my fieldwork. Though these men admitted "certain excesses" or "mistakes" had been allowed to occur before 1991, they sometimes expressed an uncritical nostalgia for the past and stinging critiques of the present. In contrast, individuals too young to have experienced the socialist period especially often repeated detailed stories about the "terrors" of communism that have been promoted through contemporary journalistic exposés. This is not to discount the horrors of the secret police and the state-socialist regime, but rather to simply register the effects that contemporary journalists have on memories of the past today.

By endeavoring to represent my consults as accurately as possible, I have felt obligated to recognize and register the contemporary political stakes for individuals seeking, in various ways, to make sense of their lives using the means they have available today. This has entailed cultivating an empathetic ear attuned to how my consultants' contemporary social positions inflect their retrospective assessments of the past. At times, I have even found it useful to understand certain individuals as speaking from a nonsocialist, if not sometimes actively antisocialist, position, a post–Cold War way of recognizing the world that contains and builds on a broader history of techniques and procedures for representing "Albania" and "Communism" and "Democracy." And of course, I am writing from a nonsocialist position as well. My imperfect solution to this question of positions has been to adopt as plain-spoken and accessible a style as I am able to muster, and to situate speakers, including myself, through dialogue where possible. To better communicate the immediacy of exchanges, I have also tried to keep the expected scholarly apparatus in check, using endnotes only when absolutely necessary and listing the dates of interviews here below rather than in the body of the text where they might interrupt the flow of the narrative.

Interviews

Skifter Këlliçi, June 30, 2009
Eno Koço, September 13, 2009
Agim Krajka, September 22, 2009
Haxhi Rama, September 24, 2009
Sadik Bejko, October 5, 2009
Zana Shutëriqi, October 21, 2009
Flamur Shehu, October 26, 2009
Selim Ishmaku, October 30, 2009
Shqipe Zani, November 17, 2009
Françesk Radi, November 19, 2009
Shpëtim Kushta, January 5, 2010
Limos Dizdari, January 7, 2010, and May 21, 2010
Zhani Ciko, January 9, 2010
Arben Duka, January 14, 2010
Alfons Balliçi, January 17 and 22, 2010
Kozma Dushi, January 25, 2010
Ema Qazimi, January 26, 2010
Çimi Leka, January 28, 2010
Edmond Zhulali, February 5, 2010, and June 18, 2010
Osman Mula, February 16, 2010
Miron Kotani, February 17, 2010
Alfred Kaçinari, February 22, 2010, and June 3, 2010
Aleksandër Lalo, February 25, 2010
Redon Makashi, March 2, 2010
Kejsi Tola, March 4, 2010
Haig Zacharian, March 8, 2010
Endri Sina, March 10, 2010
Aleksandër Gjoka, March 15, 2010
Spartak Tili, March 15, 2010
Skënder Selimi, March 17, 2010
Hamideja Stringa, March 22, 2010
Jorgo Papingji, April 20, 2010
Saimir Braho, April 21, 2010
Aleksandër Peçi, April 22 and 29, 2010
Bashkim Alibali, April 28, 2010
Qemal Kërtusha, May 10, 2010
Agron Xhunga, May 12, 2010
Gazmend Mullahi, May 16, 2010

Diana Ziu, May 19, 2010
Alban Karabashi, May 26, 2010
Sabrie Nushi, June 9, 2010
Klodian Qafoku, June 12, 2010
Rovena Dilo, June 15, 2010
Idar Bistri, June 16, 2010
Vitmar Basha, June 22, 2010

Notes

Introduction

1. On the interviews and fieldwork that form the core of my research materials, see the Appendix. Interview dates are listed there, while interviewees' names appear in the text. In rare cases, I have assigned pseudonyms, noted with an asterisk where they first appear (e.g., *Sani).

2. On state-subsidized popular music during the socialist period, see Stites, *Russian Popular Culture*; MacFadyen, *Red Stars* and *Songs for Fat People*; and Vuletic, "Yugoslav Communism and the Power of Popular Music."

3. Exemplary ethnographic works on music that inform my understanding here include White, *Rumba Rules*; Moehn, *Contemporary Carioca*; Silverman, *Romani Routes*; and Pine, *Art of Making Do*.

4. Gramsci, *Prison Notebooks*. On the Eastern European context in particular, see the exemplary works Adams, *Spectacular State*, and Gill, *Symbols and Legitimacy in Soviet Politics*. Verdery, "Theorizing Socialism," has especially influenced my perspective in this book.

5. These metaphors can be found in Hobbes, *Leviathan*; Weber, *Protestant Work Ethic*; and Haraszti, *Velvet Prison*. Gorbachev's characterization is quoted in Mau and Starodubrovskaya, *Challenge of Revolution*, 181; for Havel's statement, see his 1990 New Year's Day speech, reproduced at http://www.vhlf.org/havel-quotes/1990-new-years-speech.

6. Levin, *Hegemony of Vision*, 2.

7. See de Certeau, *Practice of Everyday Life*, xxi; Shteyngart, *Super Sad True Love Story*; Tolkien, *Fellowship of the Ring*.

8. Thompson, *Soundscape of Modernity*, 124.

9. See Gellner, *Nations and Nationalism*. My discussion here draws also from Tester, *Two Sovereigns*, 52–4.

10. See Bauman, *Legislators and Interpreters*, 52.

11. See especially Foucault, *History of Sexuality*. My approach to governmentality draws especially on Gordon, "Afterword"; Burchell et al., *Foucault Effect*; Rose, "Identity, Genealogy, History"; and Dean, *Governmentality*.

12. Verdery, "Theorizing Socialism," 17.

13. Torpey, *Intellectuals, Socialism, and Dissent*, 3.

14. For an exemplary approach that foregrounds language, see for instance Yurchak, *Everything Was Forever*, on the USSR, as well as Baranovitch, *China's New Voices*, on China.

15. For an approach focusing on a non-linguistic domain, classical ballet, see Ezrahi, *Swans of the Kremlin*.

16. Konrád and Szelényi, *Intellectuals on the Road to Class Power*, 30.

17. There exists a long critical tradition in which systems act to regiment or control individuals, and these agents act to evade, escape, resist, or transcend the political-economic systems in which they find themselves. For a foundational essay in this vein, see Adorno, "Fetish Character in Music." First World–authored works on music-making in the Second World, such as Olkhovsky, *Music Under the Soviets*, often assumed this perspective during the twentieth century, with the Cold War forestalling challenges to this framework. For my perspective on this final point, see Tochka, "Pussy Riot." This tendency has been especially pronounced in popular and academic accounts of popular culture in Eastern Europe. In works on non-state-subsidized music in particular, ready metaphors about the potentials for musicians to have "rocked" the socialist state, as in for instance Ryback, *Rock Around the Bloc*, or Ramet, ed., *Rockin' the State*, or for the fall of the socialist state and the adoption of local capitalisms to have enabled the emergence of new voices expressing more authentic forms of identity, have served as touchstones. Pekacz, "Did Rock Smash the Wall?," has critiqued such perspectives for simplifying the political and economic contexts of socialist states and ascribing too much agency to rock musicians. See also Tochka, "Voicing Freedom," 298; Briggs, "East of Teenaged Eden"; and cf. Hofman, "Questioning Socialist Folklorization." Recent scholars, referenced throughout the following chapters, have pursued significantly more nuanced approaches to popular culture in socialist and postsocialist societies. These works include Szemere, *Up from the Underground*; Yurchak, *Everything Was Forever*; Taylor, *Let's Twist Again*; Zhuk, *Rock and Roll in the Rocket City*; the contributors to Risch, ed., *Youth and Rock in the Soviet Bloc*; and Grabarchuk, *Soundtrack of Stagnation*.
18. Aretxaga, "Maddening States," 399.
19. Hansen and Stepputat, *States of Imagination*, 5. Following Foucault like Aretxaga above, the authors emphasize in their approach concern for "the conditions of possibilities of politics: how certain disciplinary forms, certain styles of knowledge and governmentalities made specific policies plausible, specific forms of rationality thinkable, and forms of political discourse possible and intelligible." Ibid., 4.
20. Interview with Carlos Varela, *New York Times*, December 29, 2009, p. A4.
21. Yurchak, *Everything Was Forever*, 6.
22. For exemplary analyses of these gray economies or "scenes," see Steinholt, *Rock in the Reservation*; Zhuk, *Rock and Roll in the Rocket City*; and Silverman, *Romani Routes*, Chapter 7.
23. In addition to several popular biographies of singers and composers, a straightforward overview of light music and the Festival of Song can be found in Slatina, *Festivali i Këngës*.
24. Bercovici, *Incredible Balkans*, and Fraser, *Pictures from the Balkans*, 256. On broader constructions of Southeastern and Eastern Europe in the Western imagination, see Wolff, *Inventing Eastern Europe*, as well as Todorova, *Imagining the Balkans*.
25. Quoted in Vickers, *Albanians*, 171.
26. *The New York Times*, for instance, ran a front-page story in November 2003 describing a criminal who allegedly bartered his toddler for a television set. Scholarly interest on Albania's "sworn virgins," women who take on male roles for social and financial reasons, blood feuds, and political corruption has also grown. In citing these topics, I do not mean to question their legitimacy per se, but rather to note that the most widely circulating knowledge produced about Albania today, whether framed as popular, academic, or journalistic, traffics in prurient, outrageous, or seemingly premodern "traditions" that handcuff contemporary Albanians to a barbaric past.
27. Rose et al., "Governmentality," 100.
28. Dean, *Governmentality*, 18.
29. Rose et al., "Governmentality," 87.
30. Donzelot, "Poverty of Political Culture," 77.
31. Dean, *Governmentality*, 18.

32. In the body of the text, I capitalize these terms to indicate when speakers are referring to each as a domain for reform, improvement, or oversight.

33. Cf., however, DeNora, "Music as a Technology of the Self," and Guilbault, *Governing Sound*.

34. Gordon, "Afterword," 245.

35. Verdery, "Theorizing Socialism," 427ff.

36. Ibid., 427.

37. Yugoslavia, for instance, might be said to have tended toward the normative and remunerative, through cultural policies promoting "brotherhood and unity" and experiments with market socialism. In contrast, states like Albania and Romania tended to mix normative and coercive strategies. Moreover, normative strategies of government were, in the sense described above and as explored in more detail throughout the book, not wholly divorced from those developed in the liberal West. Indeed, Foucault's account of the rise of government as "the conduct of conduct" can be understood as a way to explain the transition between resource-intensive, individualizing modes of coercion so characteristic of premodern orders, an understanding that suggests potential points of contact between liberal and non-liberal regimes of governance.

38. Verdery, *National Ideology Under Socialism*, 88.

39. In conceptualizing the space of musicians as a field of production, I am following the work of Pierre Bourdieu. I approach musicians' space as structured by both practices and practical knowledges that, nested within a hierarchical series of economic, political, and educational fields, provide agents a dynamic sphere for interaction and competition. See especially Bourdieu, *Field of Cultural Production*, as well as *Outline of a Theory of Practice* and *Distinction*. On the compatibility of Bourdieu's field theory with a governmentality approach, see Brook, "Governing Cultural Fields," which early on informed my thinking.

40. Williams, *Marxism and Literature*.

41. Dean, *Governmentality*, 32.

42. See Rose, "Identity, Genealogy, History"; cf. Tochka, " 'To Enlighten and Beautify.' "

43. Miller and Rose, "Governing Economic Life," 10.

44. Ortner, "Theory in Anthropology," 157.

45. Gordon, "Afterword," 250.

46. See Walters, *Governmentality*, 17–19.

47. Veyne, "Foucault Revolutionizes History," 155.

48. Bahro, *Alternative in Eastern Europe*.

49. I have changed identifying details in order to respect his wishes. We met several times after this meeting at concerts, always cordially, and I do not have the sense that reproducing this meeting here violates his refusal. On the contrary, I believe relating this conversation presents to an English-language readership ideas he would have wanted communicated. And the reality that I, a novice academic, rather than he, a major participant in the history that this book relates, have the opportunity to relate this certainly speaks to the larger point at hand.

50. Foucault, "Two Lectures," 102.

51. Frolova-Walker, "The Glib, the Bland, and the Corny," 403.

52. Zemtsovsky, "Musicological Memoirs on Marxism," 186.

53. Clifford, "Introduction: Partial Truths."

Chapter 1

1. This description derives from D16/1949 CAC.

2. Lenin, "What Is to Be Done?"

3. See Gordon, "Afterword," 250.

4. Walters, *Governmentality*, 40–1.

5. See D1/n.d. CAC, 2.

6. See Austin, *Founding a Balkan State*.

7. In this way, Albania contrasts with other eastern bloc states, where intellectuals could later view Soviet wartime intercessions as occupation. As recent archival evidence increasingly demonstrates, Albania did, however, function in the eyes of Stalin as a de facto province of Yugoslavia. The Yugoslavs' break with the Soviets in 1948 precipitated the Albanians' denunciation of Tito as an aggressor with imperial designs on their territory, a break that in the long run preserved the country's autonomy.

8. See Blumi, "Politics of Culture and Power," 386–8.

9. Nassi, "Founding a Symphony Orchestra." Quotations in these opening paragraphs refer to this source.

10. See Tochka, " 'To Enlighten and Beautify' " and WPA, *Albanian Struggle*.

11. See Tërpini, *Djelmuria Korçare*.

12. This phrasing occurs in a notice published by the progressive newspaper *Koha* on September 11, 1920, p. 1.

13. Mato, *Rrjedhave të Artit Paraprofesionist*, 12ff.

14. See Koço, *Tefta Tashko-Koço* and *Kënga Karakteristike Korçare*.

15. This description comes from a headline in the February 25, 1922, edition of *Koha*.

16. Koço, *Tefta Tashko-Koço*; Kalemi, *Maria Kraja Paluca*.

17. Mato, *Rrjedhave të Artit Paraprofesionist*, 257–8.

18. Geography also militated against comprehensive knowledge. Folklorists today distinguish "two primary dialects" of folk music, homophony found in the north and polyphony, in the south. See Sokoli, *Morfologjia*, 127; cf. Zojzi, "Ndamje Krahinore." Before 1945, significant social and musical differences existed between rural northern communities, organized into extended clan kinship networks, and southern ones, stratified by a feudal order headed by an urban landowning class. Men in the north accompanying themselves on either *lahutë*, the "national" one-stringed spike fiddle, or *çifteli*, a two-stringed plucked chordophone with a drone string, performed epic or heroic repertories (*këngë kreshnikësh* or *këngë trimash*). Northern women's genres were more closely associated with life-cycle events, and included laments, wedding songs, and lullabies. Male and female vocal groups in the south performed polyphonic song genres featuring between two and four voices, and generally divided into three discrete ethnographic regions. See Sokoli, *Morfologjia*; Sugarman, "Nightingale and the Partridge" and *Engendering Song*; Shetuni, *Albanian Traditional Song*; and Pistrick, *Performing Nostalgia*.

19. The two most significant works employing rural music practices as source material include *The Albanian Bee*, a volume of song texts created by nationalist Thimi Mitko as a means for "the awakening and uniting of the Albanian people" in 1878, and *The Lahuta of Malësia*, a lengthy poem modeled after orally transmitted epic song created by Franciscan priest Gjergj Fishta in the 1900s. See Sugarman, "Imagining the Homeland," 423; Fishta, *Highland Lute*.

20. WPA, *Albanian Struggle*, 145; see also Koço, *Kënga Karakteristike Korçare*.

21. Vedad Kokona, quoted in Koço, *Tefta Tashko-Koço*, 145.

22. See Austin, *Founding a Balkan State*.

23. Elias, *Civilizing Process*.

24. Nassi, "Founding a Symphony Orchestra."

25. Liri Belishova, quoted in Fevziu, *Jeta Ime*, 282.

26. Jorgjia Truja, as related by her daughter to interviewer Monda Shima, "Fiqirete Shehu Ishte e Vetmja që Dinte të Këndonte" [Fiqirete Shehu was the only one that knew how to sing]. *Shekulli*, March 8, 2013. http://shekulli.com.al/web/p.php? id=18224&kat=104.

27. Claudin-Urondo, *Lenin and the Cultural Revolution*, 27–9 and 69.

28. For exemplary analyses of this phenomenon, see Khalid, "Backwardness and the Quest for Civilization"; Han, *Chinese Discourses on the Peasant*; and Kotsonis, *Making Peasants Backward*.

29. Narskij, "Intellectuals as Missionaries," 338.

30. Kassof, "Administered Society," 558.

31. See Skendi, *Albania*, 284.

32. On the culture house, which Albania imported directly from Soviet practice, see the UNESCO handbook *Cultural Policy in the Union of Soviet Socialist Republics*, edited by Zvorykin et al.

33. Skendi, *Albania*, 129–30.

34. In 1950, bureaucrats learned that 147,983 people attended "artistic performances," for instance, or that 69,543 took part in "cultural evenings." See D41/1951 CAC.

35. Verdery, "Theorizing Socialism," 421–422, informs my thinking in this section, as does Fehér et al., *Dictatorship over Needs* and Kornai, *Socialist System*.

36. See Fehér et al., *Dictatorship over Needs*.

37. See Konrád and Szelényi, *Intellectuals on the Road to Class Power*.

38. D1/1950 CAC.

39. D17/1947 CAC.

40. The material in this paragraph derives from Abdullah Grimci's memoirs, especially Grimci, *Muzikanti*, 121–7.

41. The material in this paragraph derives from Dashnor Kaloçi, "Jeta Tragjike e Muzikologut të Famshëm Ramadan Sokoli: Historia e Panjohur e Profesorit dhe Etnomuzikologut" [The tragic life of the famous musicologist Ramadan Sokoli]. *Shqip*, March 18–19, pp. 18–19. See also Sokoli, *Përtej 16 Shekujve*.

42. Following a failed revolt in September 1946, several members of the Sokoli family were imprisoned. Sokoli's father died in 1957. An older brother did not survive twenty-seven years of prison alternating with internment, while a younger brother had a life sentence commuted only in 1990. Sokoli himself received a five-year sentence, and while in prison met the musicians whose repertoires would form the basis of his later musicological works.

43. Personal connections could alter the consequences of an "anti-popular stance." Soviet-trained writer Llazar Siliqi, for example, a childhood friend from Shkodra, helped arrange positions for Sokoli.

44. Agolli in Fevziu, *Jeta Ime*, 269.

45. D35/1948.

46. East German musicologists planned one expedition in 1957 (see Stockman et al., *Albanische Volksmusik*; cf. Pistrick 2011), as did Romanians in 1959. Until the late 1960s, Albania had no central institution charged exclusively with folk music research.

47. Hajati, *Tish Daija*, 56ff.

48. Grimci 1999, Kalemi 2003:51–4.

49. D18/1951 CAC: 20.

50. D1/1949 CAC: 1–2.

51. D3/1949 CAC: 3.

52. Muka, *70 Radio Shqip*, 16.

53. Strakosha, "Probleme të Propagandimit," 3.

54. Këlliçi, *Historia e Radio-Televizionit Shqiptar*, 38.

55. A typical daily ten-hour program broadcast April 25, 1951, for example, was divided into morning, afternoon, and evening emissions. The morning program broadcast music, morning physical exercises, and the reading of the lead article from the daily newspaper *Voice of the People*. The afternoon included programs for children, discussions, concert music, and news. The evening program broadcast folk and concert music, some dance music, live and prerecorded interviews, and a nightly link to Moscow for its Albanian-language news program.

56. The internment of specialists perceived to have been sympathetic to Italian propagandists caused an acute shortage of qualified personnel, as new hires had to learn on the job with visiting technicians or else were sent abroad for "specialization." Këlliçi, *Historia*, catalogs in staggering detail the ongoing concerns with employees' "professional level" during this period.

57. Këlliçi, *Historia*, 63 and 67.

58. Grimci, *Muzikanti*, 124.
59. Ibid., 125.
60. See the description in *Radioprogram*, August 12, 1951, p. 4.
61. In 1951, the Radio received 141 magnetic tapes for recording, and the following year, one hundred reels. Këlliçi, *Historia*, 72–3.
62. Ibid., 71.
63. This is not to impugn the creativity of individuals who came out of these schools, but to note that they were trained in ways that prioritized their ability to "fit" into predefined roles at culture houses or as members of performing ensembles. See Lazri, *Liceu Artistik*. Musicologist Sokol Shupo has leveled similar, albeit more polemical, critiques in recent years. See his letter to the editor in *Shekulli*, September 21, 2004, p. 19.
64. In ethnomusicology, the most detailed accounts of this process, Rice, *May It Fill Your Soul*, and Buchanan, *Performing Democracy*, both examine Bulgaria. See also Silverman, "Reconstructing Folklore." For the Central Asian Republics, see Levin, "Making Marxist-Leninist Music," and Adams, "Music and Entertainment in Post-Soviet Kazakhstan," Chapter 2. For the early Soviet Union, see especially Olson, *Performing Russia*.
65. See Mëhilli, "Defying De-Stalinization."
66. D36/1950 CAC.
67. Jowitt, *New World Disorder*, 221ff.
68. Zoraqi, *Nikolla Zoraqi*, 164.
69. Ibid.
70. Kalemi, *Tonin Harapi*, 49.
71. Ibid., 50.
72. Zoraqi, *Nikolla Zoraqi*, 196ff.
73. Ibid.
74. See Dritëro Agolli in Fevziu, *Jeta Ime*, 267.
75. Hajati, *Prenkë Jakova*, 48–9.
76. Ibid., 49.
77. In 1948, Radio Tirana employed an "orchestra" of twenty musicians, some of whom later became original elements in the Radio's concert music ensemble; a *saze* ensemble; a "characteristic group," composed of northern Albanian performers (including the future star folk singer Luçie Miloti); a "Shkodran group"; and an "amateur group," composed of Korçar musicians. Këlliçi, *Historia*, 62. The final two ensembles probably performed urban songs or popular music.
78. Cultural organizations established sports teams, theater troupes, and choral ensembles for "students" (*studentë*) and "young men" (*djelmuria*, lit. "[male] youths") that, following the example of the Soviet Union, were later consolidated into a government-administered youth movement. During the Bolshevik revolution, "the youth" had emerged as an important social category in the Soviet Union. The Komsomol (Union of Communist Youth) was incorporated into the structure of the Russian party, but in its early years also functioned as "a site of agreement, negotiation, and resistance between and within generations about what a communist should be and how best to make one." Gorsuch, *Youth in Revolutionary Russia*, 42.
79. Kalemi, *Prenkë Jakova*, 50.
80. *Këngë për Masat* 1, 1.
81. The state recognized two kinds of theatrical companies, each based on presocialist and wartime theater clubs or societies. Ten large, urban theater companies, such as the national Teatri Popullor in Tirana, staged traditional plays, while fifteen smaller "variety," or estrada, companies performed diverse programs with songs, acrobatics, and skits.
82. After 1917, the Soviet state institutionalized and "elevated" a variety of pre-Bolshevik circus acts and "fair-booth" activities popular since the nineteenth century. MacFadyen, *Songs for Fat People*, relates the Soviet incarnation, which was largely standardized in the 1950s, to pre-revolutionary "cafe culture" and bourgeois, salon aesthetic tastes. Though similar in some respects to pre-Soviet Russia, 1930s Albanian theater had been not a form of

mass entertainment, but part of an intellectualized project to create a "civilized" Albanian culture.

83. During the 1950s, many Czech and Russian tourists began vacationing in Durrës and, as young men increasingly went abroad for school, many married fellow students who then came back with them to Tirana and other large cities. Skendi, *Albania*, 24.

84. Vendim Nr. 20324, August 1956.

85. Vendim Nr. 20238, June 1957.

86. The first group included Hysen Pelinku, Koço Uçi, Llazar Morcka, Kostandin Trako, Gaqo Avrazi, and Vath Çangu; high-level administrators included Baki Kongoli and Abdullah Grimci, and district culture house directors included Muharrem Xhediku and Leonard Deda.

87. In *Muzikë Vallzimi*, 26.

88. Shapllo, "Mbi Muzikën e Lehtë e të Vallzimit."

89. Tompkins, "Against 'Pop-Song Poison,'" 47–8.

90. Mëhilli, "Defying De-Stalinization."

91. Agolli, *Vaçe Zela*, 22.

92. Ibid., 22–3.

93. The phrasing "nerve center" and the inspiration for the next paragraphs come from my interview with poet and intellectual Sadik Bejko, who took me on a virtual walking tour of the Tirana of his student days.

Chapter 2

1. This description derives from the Festival's review in *Drita*, December 23, 1962, as well as Çangu and Grimci, "Nga Historiku i Traditës së Re: 'Festivali i Parë i Këngës në Radio'" [From the history of the new tradition: 'The first Festival of Song on the radio']. *Drita*, April 20, 1986, p. 12.

2. Cf. Hofman, *Staging Socialist Femininity*, 38–45, on what she calls "the ambiguity" of music policy in the context of Yugoslavia. In *Struggle for Control*, Herrala presents an exceptionally detailed analysis of the negotiation of Soviet opera policy in the 1930s. For cases elsewhere, see also Calico, "Trial, the Condemnation, and the Cover-up"; Silverberg, "Between Dissonance and Dissidence"; and Tompkins, *Composing the Party Line*.

3. Bourdieu, *Field of Cultural Production*, 36.

4. Christina Ezrahi has also found this to be true of Soviet ballet. "Like classical music," she writes (and music in general, I would add), "the nonrepresentational nature of classical dance makes it an allegorical or symbolic artistic medium whose meaning is not concrete and is difficult to verbalize." *Swans of the Kremlin*, 31.

5. Miller and Rose, "Governing Economic Life," 3.

6. Flori Slatina, interview with Llazar Morcka, "Më tepër Këngë të Bukura për Rininë" [More beautiful songs for the youth]. *Gazeta 55*, November 11, 2000, p.11.

7. See Bennett et al., *Accounting for Tastes*.

8. Rice, *May It Fill Your Soul*, 250.

9. Baranovitch, *China's New Voices*, 214.

10. Cf. Wong, "Geming Gequ."

11. See Pano, *People's Republic of Albania*, 139–54.

12. Beqja, *Gjurmë Jetë*.

13. See Arapi, *Kujtohem Që Jam*. Chief among these was *Drita*, the arts weekly I surveyed as part of my research.

14. See Keen, *Useful Enemies*.

15. Quoted in Verdery, *What Was Socialism*, 24.

16. Quoted in *Drita*, December 30, 1962, p. 4.

17. See Baki Kongoli, "Festivali i Këngës në Radio dhe Disa Mendime mbi Muzikën e Lehtë Tonë" [The festival of song on the radio and some thoughts about our light music]. *Drita*, January 13, 1962, pp. 1–2.

18. Ibid.
19. Ibid., 2.
20. Ibid.
21. Ibid., 1.
22. Trim Gjata, "Shënime për Këngët e Festivalit në Radio" [Notes on the songs of the radio festival]. *Drita,* March 31 and April 7, 1963.
23. Çesk Zadeja, "Nga Problemet e Muzikës Sonë" [On the issues facing our music]. *Drita,* May 12, 1963, pp. 2–4.
24. Ibid., 3–4.
25. Ibid., 3.
26. Quoted in *Drita,* June 16, 1963, p. 1.
27. Ibid.
28. Quoted in *Drita,* May 26, 1963, p. 3.
29. Albert Paparisto, "Plenum mbi Problemet e Muzikës e Lehtë: Referatë" [Plenum on the issues of light music: A report]. *Drita,* July 7, 1963, p. 2.
30. D5/1963 RTSH.
31. Ibid.
32. Këlliçi, "Vaçe Zela, Besnik Taraneshi, Nikoleta Shoshi dhe Unë në Festivalin e Dytë të Këngës në Radio" [Vaçe Zela, Besnik Taraneshi, Nikoleta Shoshi, and I at the Second Festival of Song on the Radio]. *Metropol,* April 25, 2012, p. 13.
33. Ilir Zhilla, "Dosje: Tre Këngë të Mbetura Përgjysëm: Me Këngëtarët Besnik Taraneshi, Justina Aliaj, dhe Sherif Merdani" [Dossier: With the singers Besnik Taraneshi, Justina Aliaj, and Sherif Merdani]. *Drita,* August 18, 1991, pp. 6–7.
34. Ibid.
35. Këlliçi, "Vaçe Zela, Besnik Taraneshi, Nikoleta Shoshi dhe Unë."
36. This and the following paragraph draw on D5/1963 RTSH, undated notes from a January meeting at the Music Editorial Office at the Radio.
37. Çesk Zadeja, "Kanga Jonë Duhet të jetë Shqiptare" [Our song must be Albanian]. *Drita,* February 9, 1964, p. 1.
38. Ibid., 2.
39. Gjoni Athanasi, "Mendime mbi Interpretuesit e Këngëve në Festivalin e Radios" [Thoughts about the interpreters of songs at the radio festival]. *Drita,* February 16, 1964, p. 4.
40. Zadeja, "Kanga Jonë."
41. Athanasi, "Mendime." Emphasis supplied.
42. Giddens, *Constitution of Society,* 341.
43. In the following pages, I have reimagined and adapted their discussion according to the incomplete, handwritten minutes from several meetings included at the end of D8/1964 RTSH.
44. I borrow "patristic texts" from Katerina Clark's seminal work, *Soviet Novel.*
45. Tompkins, "Against 'Pop-Song Poison,'" 50.
46. Prifti, *Socialist Albania Since 1944,* 179–182.
47. See Mëhilli, "Mao and the Albanians."
48. Quoted in ibid., 171 and 168–9.
49. Alia, "Raport i Byrosë Politike."
50. Ibid., 315.
51. Ibid., 320–3.
52. Ibid., 316.
53. Cf. Buchanan, *Performing Democracy,* 40–1.
54. D3/1968 RTSH.
55. Gjelina, "Festivali i VII," 16. I confirmed the author's notions with the composer.
56. Ibid., 20–1.
57. For a similar example, see the interview on "Albanian Waves." Accessed July 13, 2012. www.youtube.com/watch?v=LqGVbB30dHY. Today, a highly developed discourse exists about

"politicized" songs, often proposed by self-styled "love song" composers. Krajka views his songs as not "politicized" (*i/e politicizuar*); on this point we would disagree, as I see such pieces as themselves required by the politically correct *tematika*.

58. Gjelina, "Festivali i VII," 17.

59. Bourdieu, *Field of Cultural Production.*

60. From Hysen Filja, "Kënga e bukur kërkon tekst poetik" [The beautiful song needs a poetic text]. *Drita*, September 8, 1968, p. 2.

61. Ibid.

62. D8/1965 RTSH.

63. See especially Taylor, *Let's Twist Again*; Tsipursky, "Having Fun in the Thaw"; and the contributors to Risch, ed., *Youth and Rock in the Soviet Block.*

64. See Gorsuch and Koenker, *Socialist Sixties.*

65. Quoted in "Festivali i 9-të Këngës në Radio-Televizion" [9th Festival of Song on the Radio-Television]. *Nëntori* 2 (1971): 294.

66. Quoted in "Diskutimi i Festivalit të Këngës në Radio-Televizion" [Discussion on the Festival of Song on the Radio-Television]. *Nëntori* 3 (1971): 229.

67. In contrast, the key "problem" of domestic popular music for officials and musicians elsewhere in the eastern bloc had to with its position vis-à-vis Western popular music. On this key point, see especially Tompkins, "Against 'Pop-Song Poison'" and Vuletic, "Making of a Yugoslav National Music Industry."

68. Shapllo, "Mbi Muzikën e Lehtë e të Vallzimit," 191.

69. Timothy Rice, using more deterministic language than I do here, writes that the Bulgarian state "produced" and "developed new musical workers perfectly matched to its goals," who crucially (in my reading here) over time "embraced the new aesthetics unquestioningly. . . . While they quibbled over the effectiveness of particular arrangements," he continues, "they rarely challenged the need for them." *May It Fill Your Soul*, 227.

70. Cf. Dumit, *Picturing Personhood.*

71. See Carr, "Enactments of Expertise," 19.

72. Quoted in *Drita*, July 7, 1963, p. 4.

73. Cf. Tomoff, *Creative Union.*

74. Gross, *Revolution from Abroad.*

75. See the anonymously authored essay "Në Ndihmen e Kompozitorëve Amatore" [In aid of amateur composers]. *Radioprogram*, March 1967, p. 17.

76. D1/1969 RTSH.

77. Kornai, *Socialist System*, 365–6.

78. Konrád and Szelényi, *Intellectuals on the Road to Class Power*, 30.

Chapter 3

1. For one summary, see Lehmann, "When Everything Was Forever."

2. Miller and Rose, "Governing Economic Life," 9.

3. Even more critically, Radio-Television officials had formerly viewed the singer-songwriter as a politically suspect imitation of American music. A later exception to the rule against singer-songwriters often mentioned is *estrada* star Luan Zhegu. But while Zhegu composed songs during the 1980s, he never performed these songs live. To do so, he told me, might have seemed "too European," phrasing Radi echoed in our interview.

4. See Risch, "Introduction."

5. D3/1965 RTSH.

6. Ibid.

7. Strakosha, "Mbi Disa Probleme," 8.

8. The quotations and analysis in this paragraph derive from my interviews with Shpëtim Kushta, Limos Dizdari, Aleksandër Lalo, and Aleksandër Peçi.

9. Interview by Pierre-Pandeli Simsia, October 6, 2010. http://www.albdreams.net/ishte-kantautori-i-mirenjohur-zija-saraci-dhe-bashkeshortja-e-tij-valentina/.
10. Cf. Appadurai, *Modernity at Large*.
11. *Vjetari Statistikor*, 65.
12. Ibid., 68–9.
13. Logoreci, *Albanians*, 178–9.
14. See Nano, *Hinterland i Kuq*, 58. Cf. Liechty, *Suitably Modern*.
15. Lubonja in Fevziu, *Jeta Ime*, 334.
16. Gleb Tsipursky relates the analogous process in 1950s Soviet Union, before Western-oriented "hipsters," *stiliagi*, became a target for policy under Khrushchev: "[U]nder Stalin, the *stiliagi* style's main participants, children of elites, remained under the protection of their parents. Furthermore, the small number of 'Westernized' youth likely did not inspire worries in the Stalinist leadership, whose concerns lay with the postwar rebuilding of the Soviet Union, the geopolitics of the Cold War, and the struggle for succession." See Tsipursky, "Coercion and Consumption," 58 and 59–63.
17. Ibid., 69.
18. Ibid.
19. On the Lipsi, see Larkey, "Contested Spaces," 52; on Vocal Instrumental Ensembles, see Survilla, "'Ordinary Words,'" 193; Steinholt, *Rock in the Reservation*, 22–5; and Wickström, *Otna Otkroi!*, 119–120. Cf. Rice, *May It Fill Your Soul*, 258–60.
20. Këlliçi, *Historia*, 146.
21. Exchange reproduced in Fatos Veliu, "Enver Hoxha: Thanas Nano nuk i Kupton Shijet e Rinisë për Këngë Moderne" [Enver Hoxha: Thanas Nano doesn't understand the youth's tastes for modern songs]. *Panorama*, December 26, 2005, pp. 16–7.
22. Ibid., emphasis supplied.
23. In the late 1950s, bureaucrats had to redefine the purview of the cultural economy to include popular song within its borders, in the process rendering song administrable under national policy. In the 1970s, music intellectuals and Party officials worked in tandem to widen preexisting symbolic borders in order to include resources that would allow domestically produced content to compete with foreign content. These two moves happened nearly simultaneously in other parts of Eastern Europe, but in Albania, historical and political circumstances separated them, enabling each to be more fully analyzed in isolation from the other.
24. Hoxha, *Mbi Letërsinë dhe Artin*, 329.
25. Ibid.
26. Ibid., 382.
27. Here, my interpretation of this event departs from most local ones. Today commentators often refer to the Eleventh Festival as *një kurth*, a trap, to first draw out and then banish pro-Western elements from the body politic. Consultants often gave me this explanation, which parallels fictional representations as well. See Skifter Këlliçi's 2002 novel, *Festivali Njëmbëdhjetë* (The Eleventh Festival) and author Ismail Kadare's allegorical short story, "Komisioni i Festës" (The Celebration's Commission) (1978).
28. See Verdery, "Theorizing Socialism." The persistently felt need among officials to assert and reassert the subordinate position of the intellectual also suggests the ongoing perception in Albania that these individuals were potentially dangerous.
29. See Mero, *Ëndrra dhe Zhgënjime*, 115–6.
30. Hoxha, "Writers and Artists," 3.
31. Joy Aschenbach, "Europe's Obstinate Albania: Living in a World of Its Own." *National Geographic News Service*, December 1980.
32. Simons, *Constitutions of the Communist World*, 4.
33. Ibid., 7.
34. Sigurimi was analogous to the Securitate in Romania, Stasi in East Germany, or the NKVD in the USSR.

35. Information in this paragraph derives from Kastriot Dervishi, director of the archives of the Ministry of the Interior. Interview by Admirina Peçi, "Ndjesa e Gabuar e Kongolit" [Kongoli's mistaken apology]. *Gazeta Shqiptare*, June 14, 2011. http://www.shqiperia.com/lajme/lajm/nr/11199/ndjesa-e-gabuar-e-kongolit---si-i-fshehu-gjurmet-agjentja-qe-e-njollosi.

36. According to Dervishi, these institutions also included the Albanian Telegraphic Service, the national Kinostudio, the Theater of Opera and Ballet, the People's Theater, the League of Writers and Artists, the state publishing houses, the Gallery of Figurative Arts, the State Estrada, and the Circus.

37. Verdery, *Secrets and Truths*, 26.

38. Agolli interviewed in Fevziu, *Jeta Ime*, 275–6.

39. Ibid. Some intellectuals dispute this account, assigning more blame to organs such as the League and individuals with power, such as Agolli, for being "complicit" in some way with "the state." I quote Agolli at length because he was an elite Party member and thus had insider knowledge some of his critics lack; he enjoys a broad reputation today as an accurate and fair-minded person; and elements of this account accord with ones I encountered elsewhere in my research.

40. Afrim Imaj, "Biografia në Gjermanisht si Shkëlqeu dhe u Kryqezua Këngëtarja Alida Hisku" [The biography of how singer Alida Hisku rose and was cut down]. *Panorama*. October 27, 2010. http://albdreams.blogspot.com/2010/10/biografia-ne-gjermanisht-si-shkelqeu.html.

41. Afrim Imaj, "Tmerri i Këngëtareve të Bukura Nga Maniaket e Sigurimit" [Beautiful singers terrorized by the Sigurimi's maniacs]. *Tirana*. October 31, 2010. http://www.fjala.info/arkiv/fjala1/?p=4552.

42. Ibid. Hisku's statements unleashed waves of commentary in the early 2010s about sexual violence and the state under Hoxha. Much of this commentary, including some from well-known composers, has either sought to discredit Hisku or to minimize her case as "an exception." Recent coverage of another socialist-era singer followed a similar pattern. Some level of gendered violence formed part of the cultural economy that I am describing in this book, but its extent, its influence, and its overall effects on symbolic production remain unclear to me. My inability to access materials beyond hearsay in the field and these newspaper debates represents one potential shortcoming of my model. For the broader picture of gender, violence, and Albanian socialism, see the work of historian and ethnographer Shannon Woodcock, especially "Against the Wall" and *Life Is War*. For her English-language response to the debate over Hisku in Albanian media, see "Alida Hisku Spoke the Truth," a translation of an op-ed originally published on *Reporter.al* on November 3, 2011. https://www.academia.edu/17726932/Alida_Hisku_spoke_the_truth_-_and_everybody_knows.

43. Çobani, *Ju Flet Tirana*, 131.

44. Mato, *Imazhe, Kode dhe Kumte*, 254.

45. Ibid., 254–7.

46. My description of the process related in this paragraph derives from several helpful conversations with Spartak Tili, who was employed by the Radio-Television from the mid-1970s to the early 1990s.

47. Albanians use the word "calculations" to describe the conscious, goal-oriented, and explicitly political practices of *quid pro quo* hustling or horse-trading for privileges.

48. See *Drita*, January 6, 1980.

49. Bourdieu, *Logic of Practice*, 67.

50. What I am describing here resonates with what Baranovitch has described as a kind of "symbiosis" between musicians and political power, *China's New Voices*, 191.

51. Çobani, *Ju Flet Tirana*, 144.

52. Ibid., 145.

53. Seriot, "Officialese and Straight Talk," 206; see also 210–11.

54. Compare this situation with Bulgaria's gray economies, which have been extensively documented. See especially Silverman, *Romani Routes*, Chapter 7. On Russia's informal music economies, see especially Zhuk, *Rock and Roll in the Rocket City*.

Chapter 4

1. Beqja, *Për Rininë*.
2. See Klosi and Rama, *Refleksione*.
3. I came across many of these calls in surveying intellectuals' periodicals; for these particular examples from *Drita*, see Lazër Stani from February 10, 1991, p. 3 and Mentar Belegu on January 20, 1991, p. 12.
4. See, for instance, the *Chicago Tribune*'s headline from June 23, 1991.
5. On Tirana's "statue-corpses," see Mustafaj, *Midis Krimëve dhe Mirazheve*, 127ff and 133. Cf. Verdery, *Political Lives of Dead Bodies*.
6. Berisha, "Intelektuali përballë Detyrave të Kohës," *Drita*, May 20, 1990, p. 6. This quote has been lightly edited for readability to supply the reader with first names and some additional identifying information.
7. For the eyewitness accounts of participants, see Abrahams, *Modern Albania*.
8. Burawoy and Verdery, *Uncertain Transition*.
9. Rose, *Powers of Freedom*, 61.
10. Quoted in Abrahams, *Modern Albania*, 35.
11. Ibid., 36–7.
12. Artan Dervishi, "5 Pika për të Shkruar Një Këngë Skematike" [5 points for writing a schematic song], *Drita*, July 6, 1985, p. 13.
13. Mai, " 'Italy Is Beautiful,' " 178–83.
14. King and Mai, *Out of Albania*, 57.
15. *Drita*, January 15, 1989, p. 2.
16. I report these various senses based on my review of critiques published in *Drita* between 1985 and 1990. For these particular quotations, see the roundtable interview by Fatmir Hysi featuring Vaçe Zela, Çesk Zadeja, conductor Mustafa Krantja, critic Anastas Kuremeno, and students Dhimitër Druga and Leftër Liço. *Drita*, 26 January 1988, pp. 2–3 and 13.
17. Muka, "Këngëtarët e Muzikës së Lehtë" [Light music singers], *Drita*, November 8, 1987, pp. 2–3 and 15.
18. Interview by Arben Kallamata. *Drita*, January 24, 1988, p. 5.
19. The material in this and the following paragraphs derives from the short published write-up in *Drita*, February 18, 1990, pp. 3–4.
20. Abrahams, *Modern Albania*, 31.
21. *Drita*, December 31, 1989, p. 3.
22. Quoted in Hadji-Ristic, "Shaking Albania's Torpor," 10.
23. See Vullnetari, *Albania on the Move*.
24. In doing this, I follow the example set by Baranovitch's *China's New Voices*, which analyzes in detail the textual content of Chinese popular music songs in the 1990s.
25. See for instance the film *Bijtë e Lirisë*, as well as the 1978 memoir by author Sterjo Spasse of the same title about Albanian communists in Spain during the 1930s.
26. Interview by Mujë Buçpapaj, "Levizja e Dhjetorit 21 Vjet Më Vonë" [The December movement 21 years later], *Gazeta Nacional*, December 6, 2011. http://gazeta-nacional.com/?p=1405.
27. Quoted in Kapinova, "Frederik Ndoci," 103.
28. On Hoxha's reaction, see Buçpapaj, "Lëvizja e Dhjetorit."
29. Rama, *Përrallat e Tranzicionit*.
30. "Berisha supporters present the doctor as a committed democrat, who wanted more than anyone to change the regime. Critics claim he was serving Alia, who wanted the students

to push change that the party could control. The most likely scenario is Berisha played both cards. As the highly skilled politician he would soon become, he stayed close to both sides, reacting to subtle shifts." Fred C. Abrahams, "Albanian Students Challenged Communism," *Huffington Post*, December 9, 2014. http://www.huffingtonpost.com/fred-abrahams/albanian-students-challan_b_793819.html.

31. YouTube comment posted on January 5, 2012. Cf. Wong, "Cui Jian."

32. My understanding of early rockers is especially indebted to conversations with Aleksandër Gjoka, Redon Makashi, Elinor Butka, and Saimir Braho, as well as to a number of their fans.

33. See the January 27, 1992 report created by the Council of Europe, Document 6555.

34. Gazebo, interviewed by Zeljko Vujkovic, c. 2004. http://www.italo-interviews.com/Gazebo.html.

35. Pano, "Process of Democratization in Albania," 300.

36. From this point on, Democrat or Democratic, capitalized, refers to Berisha's Democratic Party, and Democracy and Europe, to the abstract domains targeted in postsocialist political speech.

37. On "Europe" as a diplomatic concept, see Rey, " 'Europe Is Our Common Home.' " For one recent study on the interlinking of Europe, popular music, and media in the postsocialist context of Bulgaria, see Livni, "Chalga to the Max!"

38. Quoted in Pettifer and Vickers, *Albanian Question*, 64.

39. Ibid.

40. Brisku, *Bittersweet Europe*, 156.

41. The quotations in this section derive from comments made at the roundtable and published in *Drita*, February 26, 1995, pp. 2–3.

42. See Kajsiu, "Down with Politics!"

43. See Fischer, "Albania Since 1989," 428. For a summary and extended analysis, see Tochka, "Voicing Freedom, Sounding Dissent."

44. Zhani Ciko, quoted in Slatina, *Festivali i Këngës*, 68.

45. Mihrije Braha, roundtable interview with Haxhi Dauti, Albërie Hadërgjonaj, Alma Bektashi, and Zhani Ciko. *Historia Nis Këtu*. TVSH, April 2011.

46. Interview in *Spektër*, August 2005, pp. 6–9. More recently, many Kosovar singers have boycotted the Festival of Song, saying they felt like invited guests rather than integral participants.

47. Drita, February 26, 1995, p. 3.

48. Ibid.

49. Quoted in Vullnetari, *Albania on the Move*, 115.

50. Interview by Nazim Rashidi. *Drita*, January 12, 1997, p. 3.

51. Moreover, as Donna Buchanan writes of Bulgaria during this period, stylistic pluralism should also be linked to the emergence of the consumer economy in general, though this point extends past the scope of my discussion here. "[T]he popular music panorama [of the 1990s] exhibited a diversity, multi-faceted origin, and range of quality analogous to that of other consumer goods flooding the markets." *Performing Democracy*, 421.

52. Sugarman, "Mediated Albanian Musics," 140.

53. Quoted in Abrahams, *Modern Albania*, 125.

54. Musaraj, "Tales from Alborado," 85, 105, and f.n. 5.

55. Ibid., 84.

56. Ibid., 101.

57. Quoted in Pettifer and Vickers, *Albanian Question*, 9.

58. Muka, *70 Radio Shqip*, 72.

59. Quoted in Abrahams, *Modern Albania*, 230; cf. Buchanan, *Performing Democracy*, 430.

60. Lubonja, *False Apocalypse*, 118.

61. Cf. Buchanan, *Performing Democracy*, 25.

62. Rose, *Powers of Freedom*, 64.

63. For instance, see the contributions to Slobin, *Retuning Culture*; Rice, *May It Fill Your Soul*; and Tusty and Tusty, *Singing Revolution*.

64. Music scholarship on this point has tended to examine disenfranchisement accomplished under the sign of the nation during the 1990s, and especially the most extreme case being that of the former Yugoslavia. See especially Gordy, *Culture of Power*; Sugarman, "Kosova Calls For Peace"; and Baker, *Sounds of the Borderland*. The question of how disenfranchised groups talk back to capitalism, as for instance in Daphne Berdahl's work on nostalgia, has tended to figure less prominently in music scholars' work.

65. On the longer historical context of this phenomenon, see Sulstarova, *Arratisja Nga Lindja*. Cf. Nixon, "Always Already European."

66. Appadurai, *Modernity at Large*, 3.

67. de Waal, *Albania Today*, 235.

68. Ibid. Cf. Ginsberg et al., *Media Worlds*.

Chapter 5

1. Wernick, *Promotional Culture*, vii.

2. Cloonan, "Pop and the Nation-State," also uses this term, but to theorize a substantially different phenomenon.

3. Saunders, "Brand Interrupted," 63.

4. Mike Atkinson, "Whose Three-Minute Pop Ditty Will Rule The Continent?" *Slate*, May 17, 2006. www.slate.com/articles/news_and_politics/dispatches/features/2006/america_meet_the_eurovision_song_contest/whose_threeminute_pop_ditty_will_rule_the_continent.html.

5. See especially Solomon, "Articulating the Historical Moment" and Mitrovic, "New Face of Serbia."

6. See Tochka, "Composing on Commission," 200.

7. Cf. Fehérváry, *Politics in Color and Concrete*.

8. From Leka et al, *Politika Kulturore*.

9. Lemke, "Foucault, Governmentality, and Critique."

10. The 2010 TopFest competition, however, used a live band and no backing tracks, a format that was announced prior to the 2009 Festival of Song and which caused much concern among participants and organizers with whom I spoke.

11. Some subcontracted out the texts or worked in teams with lyricists. Others write their own texts in order to not only maintain control over the entire production but also, their critics charge, to retain the entire commission fee.

12. Anonymous editorialist in *Gazeta 55*, December 19, 2001, p. 20.

13. Reported in *Gazeta Shqiptare*, November 11, 1999, p. 19.

14. See "Festivali, korrupsion i përmasave të rrezikshme" [The Festival, corruption of dangerous proportions], *Korrieri*, December 18, 2001, p. 23.

15. Interview with Jonida Maliqi, "Nuk e njoh kompozitorin tim" [I don't know my composer], *Albania*, December 18, 2001, p. 9.

16. Revealingly, one composer attempted to do this during the third night of the Forty-eighth Festival of Song, which featured duets. Instead of inviting another singer to duet with his entrant, he rapped and stood on stage, which several other composers criticized to me as being in poor taste or inartistic.

17. Quoted in *Gazeta Shqiptare*, November 11, 1999.

18. Journalist Dalina Buzi made this claim in *Gazeta Express*, May 25, 2015. http://www.gazetaexpress.com/shkurt-e-shqip/pse-deshtoi-ne-menyre-te-shemtuar-elhaida-103215.

19. On the popularity of "Gypsy brass," see Marković, " 'So That We Look More Gypsy.' "

20. The original Albanian-language criticisms can be found in the comments section underneath the Festival performance. https://youtu.be/m2cx0hRhe88.

21. *Gazeta Sot*, January 2, 2008. https://www.shqiperia.com/Edmond-Zhulali-jep-doreheqjen.3409.

22. Sokoli, *Veglat Muzikore*, 54–9.

23. The *lahutë* is the Albanian version of the *gusle*, and has functioned as a symbol of the nation in varied contexts. Cf. Lord, *Singer of Tales*. As imagined by organologist Pirro Miso, the foremost authority on musical instruments during the socialist period, the instrument "has played and plays an important ethical and moral role [in Albania]." Miso, "Roli dhe Funksioni Etnoartistik i Lahutës," 121.

24. Musicologist Ramadan Sokoli devoted several pages addressing the instrument's heritage in his landmark 1966 study of Albanian folklore, *Veglat Muzikore*, uneasily concluding it might be "Hebrew" [*sic*]. Each instrument, of course, is historically derived from Middle or Near Eastern ones.

25. See Solomon, "Articulating the Historical Moment," 142.

26. Ibid.

27. Because Albania's selection round is usually the first among competing nation-states, the most fervent of Western European fans, excited to kick off the season, tune in. More casual fans only watch the contest itself in May.

28. Interview by Julia Vrapi. *Agjensia e Lajmeve SOT*, October 27, 2011. http://sot.com.al/index.php?option=com_content&view=article&id=8699:nestor-kraja-festivali-i-kenges-ne-rtsh-duhet-te-synoje-vlerat-artistike-nacionale&catid=222:kulture-gazeta&Itemid=483.

29. Posted to Aurela Gaçe's public Facebook fan page, July 2015.

30. A non-musician colleague, on learning that I worked with musicians in Eastern Europe, assumed that I must research Gypsies, and then, villagers. "Actually," I replied, "I research the composers and bureaucrats who have been trying to reform those kinds of musicians for the past half-century." "Why would you work with *them*?" she replied, making a face. Music scholars have traditionally not worked with elites, foregoing opportunities for what Laura Nader famously called "studying up." Cf. Berger, "New Directions for Ethnomusicological Research," 316.

31. Kaneva, *Branding Post-Communist Nations*, 11.

32. Berdahl, *Social Life of Postsocialism*, 131. Cf. Krastev, "Democracy Without Alternatives."

33. Foucault, "Governmentality," 103.

34. Lemke, "An Indigestible Meal," 57.

35. Foucault, "Questions of Method," 76.

Epilogue

1. Obituary published February 6, 2014. http://old.zeri.info/artikulli/26361/ndahet-nga-jeta-artistja-e-madhe-vace-zela.

2. This phrasing comes from the 2009 liner notes to *Vaçe Zela: Larg dhe Pranë Njerëzve* [Vaçe Zela: Far and Near Listeners], produced by the Ministry of Tourism, Culture, Youth, and Sports in cooperation with the Radio-Television Albania.

3. Quotes in this paragraph come from Eliona Lata's reporting of Zela's funeral for *Shekulli*. http://www.shekulli.com.al/p.php?id=40126.

4. Ibid. Similarly, Sali Berisha characterized her oeuvre as expressing "the dissidence of Albanian song from that barbaric regime of anti-values," as reported by *Telegrafi* on February 8, 2014. http://www.telegrafi.com/lajme/lamtumire-vace-zela-78-11304.html.

5. Ypi, "Voce Zela." *MAPO*, February 7, 2014. http://mapo.al/2014/02/07/voce-zela/.

6. Fatos Lubonja, "Letër nga Ferri e Enver Hoxhës për Edi Ramën" [Enver Hoxha's letter from hell to Edi Rama]. *Panorama*, February 1, 2014. http://www.panorama.com.al/funerali-per-vace-zelen-fatos-lubonja-leter-nga-ferri-e-enver-hoxhes-per-edi-ramen/.

7. Only rarely have I heard this kind of critique invoked by my colleagues or consultants, and then, exclusively applied to the postsocialist music industry.

8. Briggs, "East of (Teenaged) Eden," 267.

9. Foucault, "Omnes et Singulatim."
10. Walters, *Governmentality*, 40.
11. Ibid.
12. Yurchak, *Everything Was Forever*, 13. Emphasis supplied.
13. Scott, *Seeing Like a State*.
14. Miller and Rose, "Governing Economic Life," 10.
15. See "Signs of Imagination," on the inherent quality of music that Thomas Turino theorizes as a kind of "semantic snowballing effect."
16. Cloonan, "Pop and the Nation-State," 203–4.
17. McDonald, *My Voice Is My Weapon*, 27.
18. Engelhardt, *Singing the Right Way*, 222.
19. My thinking on the wider effects of the emergence of a Cold War order on scholarship is deeply indebted to Pletsch, "The Three Worlds." See also Tochka, "Pussy Riot."

References

Abrahams, Fred C. *Modern Albania: From Dictatorship to Democracy in Europe.* New York: NYU Press, 2015.

Adams, Laura. *The Spectacular State: Culture and National Identity in Uzbekistan.* Durham, NC: Duke University Press, 2010.

Adams, Margarethe. "Music and Entertainment in Post-Soviet Kazakhstan: Ideology and Legacy." PhD diss., University of Illinois, 2012.

Adorno, Theodor W. "On the Fetish Character in Music and the Regression of Listening." In *The Culture Industry: Selected Essays on Mass Culture,* edited by J. M. Bernstein, 29–61. New York: Routledge, 2001 [1938].

Agolli, Nexhat. *Vaçe Zela: Magjia e Këngës Shqiptare, Monografi.* Lezha: Lisitan, 2001.

Alia, Ramiz. "Raporti i Byrosë Politike të Komitetit Qendror të PPSH-së 'Mbi Rritjen e Rolit të Letërsisë dhe Arteve për Edukimin Komunist të Masave.'" In *PPSH Dokumenta Kryesore IV,* 559–601. Tirana: Instituti i Studimeve Marksiste-Leniniste, 1970 [1965].

Appadurai, Arjun. *Modernity at Large: Cultural Dimensions of Globalization.* Minneapolis: University of Minnesota Press, 1996.

Arapi, Fatos. *Kujtohem Që Jam.* Tirana: n.p., 1997.

Aretxaga, Begoña. "Maddening States." *Annual Review of Anthropology* 32, no. 1 (2003): 393–410.

Austin, Robert Clegg. *Founding a Balkan State: Albania's Experiment with Democracy, 1920–1925.* Toronto: University of Toronto Press, 2012.

Bahro, Rudolph. *The Alternative in Eastern Europe.* London: Verso, 1978.

Baker, Catherine. *Sounds of the Borderland: Popular Music, War and Nationalism in Croatia Since 1991.* London: Ashgate, 2010.

Baranovitch, Nimrod. *China's New Voices: Popular Music, Ethnicity, Gender, and Politics, 1978–1997.* Berkeley: University of California Press, 2004.

Bauman, Zygmunt. *Legislators and Interpreters: On Modernity, Post-modernity and Intellectuals.* Oxford: Polity Press, 1987.

Bennett, Tony, Michael Emmison, and John Frow. *Accounting for Tastes: Australian Everyday Cultures.* Melbourne: Cambridge University Press, 1999.

Beqja, Hamit. *Për Rininë dhe me Rininë.* Tirana: 8 Nëntori, 1991.

Beqja, Hamit. *Gjurmë Jetë: Shënime Autobiografike.* Tirana: Uegen, 2004.

Bercovici, Konrad. *The Incredible Balkans.* New York: Loring & Mussey, 1932.

Berdahl, Daphne. *On the Social Life of Postsocialism: Memory, Consumption, Germany.* Bloomington: Indiana University Press, 2010.

Berger, Harris M. "New Directions for Ethnomusicological Research into the Politics of Music and Culture: Issues, Projects, and Programs." *Ethnomusicology* 58, no. 2 (2014): 315–20.

Blumi, Isa. "The Politics of Culture and Power: The Roots of Hoxha's Postwar State." *East European Quarterly* 31, no. 3 (1997): 379–98.

Bourdieu, Pierre. *Outline of a Theory of Practice.* Cambridge: Cambridge University Press, 1977.

Bourdieu, Pierre. *Distinction: a Social Critique of the Judgment of Taste.* Cambridge, MA: Harvard University Press, 1984.

Bourdieu, Pierre. *The Logic of Practice.* Stanford, CA: Stanford University Press, 1990.

Bourdieu, Pierre. *The Field of Cultural Production: Essays on Art and Literature.* New York: Columbia University Press, 1993.

Bourdieu, Pierre. *Practical Reason: On the Theory of Action.* Stanford, CA: Stanford University Press, 1998.

Briggs, Jonathyne. "East of (Teenaged) Eden, or Is Eastern Youth Culture So Different from the West?" In *Youth and Rock in the Soviet Bloc: Youth Cultures, Music, and the State in Russia and Eastern Europe*, edited by William J. Risch, 267–84. Lanham, MD: Lexington Books, 2014.

Brisku, Adrian. *Bittersweet Europe: Albanian and Georgian Discourses on Europe, 1878–2008.* New York: Berghahn Books, 2013.

Brook, Scott. "Governing Cultural Fields: Governmentality Studies and Pierre Bourdieu." Paper Presented at 'Culture and Citizenship' Conference CRESC, St. Hughes College, University of Oxford, 2008.

Buchanan, Donna. *Performing Democracy: Bulgarian Music and Musicians in Transition.* Chicago: University of Chicago Press, 2006.

Burawoy, Michael, and Katherine Verdery, eds. *Uncertain Transition: Ethnographies of Change in the Postsocialist World.* New York: Rowman & Littlefield Press, 1999.

Burchell, Graham, Colin Gordon, and Peter Miller, eds. *The Foucault Effect: Studies in Governmentality.* Chicago: University of Chicago Press, 1991.

Calico, Joy H. "The Trial, the Condemnation, the Cover-Up: Behind the Scenes of Brecht/Dessau's *Lucullus* Opera(s)." *Cambridge Opera Journal* 14, no. 3 (2002): 313–42.

Carr, E. Summerson. "Enactments of Expertise." *Annual Review of Anthropology* 39 (2010): 17–32.

Clark, Katerina. *The Soviet Novel: History as Ritual.* Bloomington: Indiana University Press, 2000.

Claudin-Urondo, Carmen. *Lenin and the Cultural Revolution.* Translated by Brian Pearce. Sussex: The Harvester Press, 1977.

Clifford, James. "Introduction: Partial Truths." In *Writing Culture: The Poetics and Politics of Ethnography*, edited by James Clifford and George E. Marcus, 1–26. Berkeley: University of California Press, 1986.

Cloonan, Martin. "Pop and the Nation-State: Towards a Theorisation." *Popular Music* 18, no. 2 (1999): 193–207.

Çobani, Agron. *Ju Flet Tirana . . .: Kujtime, Histori, Personazhe.* Tirana: Toena, 2010.

de Certeau, Michel. *The Practice of Everyday Life.* Berkeley: University of California Press, 1984.

de Waal, Clarissa. *Albania Today: A Portrait of Post-Communist Turbulence.* London: I. B. Tauris, 2005.

Dean, Mitchell. *Governmentality: Power and Rule in Modern Society.* London: Sage Publications, 2010.

Denora, Tia. "Music as a Technology of the Self." *Poetics* 27, no. 1 (1999): 31–56.

Donzelot, Jacques. "The Poverty of Political Culture." *Ideology and Consciousness* 5 (1979): 71–86.

Drejtoria e Statistikës. *Vjetari Statistikori i RPSH.* Tirana: Drejtoria e Statistikës, 1965.

Dumit, Joseph. *Picturing Personhood: Brain Scans and Biomedical Identity.* Princeton, NJ: Princeton University Press, 2004.

Elias, Norbert. *The Civilizing Process: The History of Manners, Vol. 1.* New York: Pantheon Press, 1978.

Engelhardt, Jeffers. *Singing the Right Way: Orthodox Christians and Secular Enchantment in Estonia.* New York: Oxford University Press, 2014.

Ezrahi, Christina. *Swans of the Kremlin: Ballet and Power in Soviet Russia.* Pittsburgh, PA: University of Pittsburgh Press, 2012.

Fehér, Ferenc, Agnes Heller, and György Markus. *Dictatorship over Needs: An Analysis of Soviet Societies*. New York: Blackwell, 1983.

Fehérváry, Krisztina. *Politics in Color and Concrete: Socialist Materialities and the Middle Class in Hungary*. Bloomington: Indiana University Press, 2013.

Fevziu, Blendi. *Jeta Ime . . . Interviste Me Blendi Fevziu*. Tirana: UET Press, 2010.

Fischer, Bernd J. "Albania Since 1989: The Hoxhaist Legacy." In *Central and Southeast European Politics Since 1989*, edited by Sabrina P. Ramet, 421–43. Cambridge: Cambridge University Press, 2010.

Fishta, Gjergj. *The Highland Lute (Lahuta e Malcís): The Albanian National Epic*. Translated by Robert Elsie. London: I. B. Tauris, 2005.

Foucault, Michel. *The History of Sexuality, Vol. 1*. Translated By Robert Hurley. New York: Random House, 1978.

Foucault, Michel. "Two Lectures." In *Knowledge/Power: Selected Interviews and Other Writings, 1972–1977*, edited by Colin Gordon, 78–108. London: The Harvester Press, 1980.

Foucault, Michel. "Governmentality." In *The Foucault Effect: Studies in Governmentality*, edited by Colin Gordon, Graham Burchell, and Peter Miller, 87–104. Chicago: University of Chicago Press, 1991.

Foucault, Michel. "Questions of Method." In *The Foucault Effect: Studies in Governmentality*, edited by Colin Gordon, Graham Burchell, and Peter Miller, 73–86. Chicago: University of Chicago Press, 1991.

Foucault, Michel. "*Omnes et Singulatim*: Toward a Critique of Political Reason." In *The Essential Foucault*, edited by Paul Rabinow and Nikolas Rose, 180–202. New York: The New Press, 2004.

Foucault, Michel. "The Subject and Power." In *The Essential Foucault*, edited by Paul Rabinow and Nikolas Rose, 126–44. New York: The New Press, 2004.

Fraser, John Foster. *Pictures from the Balkans*. London: Cassell and Company, 1912.

Frolova-Walker, Marina. "The Glib, the Bland, and the Corny: An Aesthetic of Socialist Realism." In *Music and Dictatorship in Europe and Latin America*, edited by Roberto Illiano and Massimiliano Sala, 403–423. Turnhout: Brepols, 2009.

Gellner, Ernest. *Nations and Nationalism*. Ithaca, NY: Cornell University Press, 1983.

Giddens, Anthony. *The Constitution of Society: Outline of the Theory of Structuration*. Berkeley: University of California Press, 1984.

Gill, Graeme. *Symbols and Legitimacy in Soviet Politics*. Cambridge: Cambridge University Press, 2011.

Ginsburg, Faye, Lila Abu-Lughod, and Brian Larkin, eds. *Media Worlds: Anthropology on New Terrain*. Berkeley: University of California Press, 2002.

Gjelina, Kujtim. "Festivali i VII I Këngës në Radio." Thesis, Instituti i Lartë të Arteve (Tirana), 1969.

Gordon, Colin. "Afterword." In *Knowledge/Power: Selected Interviews and Other Writings, 1972–1977*, edited by Colin Gordon, 229–60. London: The Harvester Press, 1980.

Gordy, Eric D. *Culture of Power in Serbia: Nationalism and the Destruction of Alternatives*. University Park: The Pennsylvania State Press, 2010.

Gorsuch, Anne E. *Youth in Revolutionary Russia: Enthusiasts, Bohemians, Delinquents*. Bloomington: Indiana University Press, 2000.

Gorsuch, Anne E., and Diane P. Koenker, eds. *The Socialist Sixties: Crossing Borders in the Second World*. Bloomington: Indiana University Press, 2013.

Grabarchuk, Alexandra. "The Soundtrack of Stagnation: Paradoxes Within Soviet Rock and Pop of the 1970s." PhD diss., University of California at Los Angeles, 2015.

Gramsci, Antonio. *Selections from The Prison Notebooks*. Translated by Quintin Hoare and Geoffrey Nowell Smith. New York: International Publishers, 1971.

Grimci, Abdullah. *Muzikanti: Fragmente Nga Jeta dhe Veprimtaria e Tij, Biografi Letrare*. Tirana: n.p., 1999.

Gross, Jan T. *Revolution from Abroad: The Soviet Conquest of Poland's Western Ukraine and Western Belorussia*. Princeton, NJ: Princeton University Press, 1988.

Guilbault, Jocelyne. *Governing Sound: The Cultural Politics of Trinidad's Carnival Musics*. Chicago: University of Chicago Press, 2007.

Hadji-Ristic, Petar. "Shaking Albania's Torpor." *Index on Censorship* 20, no. 1(1991): 10–11.

Hajati, Marash. *Tish Daija, i Veçanti*. Tirana: Erik Botime, 2006.

Han, Xiarong. *Chinese Discourses on the Peasant, 1900–1949*. Binghamton, NY: SUNY Press, 2005.

Hansen, Thomas Blom, and Finn Stepputat. *States of Imagination: Ethnographic Explorations of the Postcolonial State*. Durham, NC: Duke University Press, 2001.

Haraszti, Miklos. *The Velvet Prison: Artists Under State Socialism*. London: I. B. Tauris, 1988.

Herrala, Meri Elisabet. *The Struggle for Control of Soviet Music from 1932 to 1948: Socialist Realism vs. Western Formalism*. Lewiston, NY: Edwin Mellen Press, 2012.

Hobbes, Thomas. *Leviathan: Or the Matter, Forme and Power of a Commonwealth, Ecclesiasticall and Civil*. Edited by Ian Shapiro. New Haven, CT: Yale University Press, 2010.

Hofman, Ana. *Staging Socialist Femininity: Gender Politics and Folklore Performance in Serbia*. Leiden: Brill Publishers, 2010.

Hofman, Ana. "Questioning Socialist Folklorization: The Beltinci Folklore Festival in the Slovenian Borderland of Prekmurje." In *Audiovisual Media and Identity Issues in Southeastern Europe*, edited by Eckehard Pistrick, Nicola Scaldaferri, and Gretel Schwörer, 238–57. Cambridge: Cambridge Scholars Publishing, 2011.

Hoxha, Enver. *Raport Mbi Veprimtarinë e KQ të PPSH-Së: Kongres V të PPSH-së*. Tirana: Naim Frashëri, 1966.

Hoxha, Enver. "Writers and Artists Are Aids in the Communist Education of Our Men and Women." In *Enver Hoxha Volume IV: February 1966–July 1975*, 888–934. Tirana: The Institute of Marxist-Leninist Studies at the CC of the PLA, 1986 [1974].

Hoxha, Enver. *Mbi Letërsinë dhe Artin, Nëntor 1942–Nëntor 1976*. Tirana: 8 Nëntori, 1977.

Jowitt, Kenneth. *New World Disorder: The Leninist Extinction*. Berkeley: University of California Press, 1992.

Kajsiu, Blendi. "Down with Politics! The Crisis of Representation in Post-Communist Albania." *East European Politics & Societies* 24, no. 2 (2010): 229–53.

Kalemi, Spiro. *Maria Kraja Paluca*. Tirana: Omsca, 2001.

Kalemi, Spiro. *Tonin Harapi*. Tirana: Enti Botuese "Gjergj Fishta," 2003.

Kalemi, Spiro. *Prenkë Jakova*. Tirana: Enti Botues "Gjergj Fishta," 2006.

Kaneva, Nadia, ed. *Branding Post-Communist Nations: Marketizing National Identities in the "New" Europe*. New York: Routledge, 2011.

Kapinova, Klajd. 2005. "Frederik Ndoci, Superstari Shqiptar." *Albanova Online*.

Kassof, Allen. "The Administered Society: Totalitarianism Without Terror." *World Politics* 16, no. 4 (1964): 558–75.

Keen, David. *Useful Enemies: When Waging Wars Is More Important Than Winning Them*. New Haven, CT: Yale University Press, 2012.

Këlliçi, Skifter. *Festivali i Njëmbëdhjetë: Roman*. Tirana: Toena, 2002.

Këlliçi, Skifter. *Historia e Radio-Televizionit Shqiptar (1938–1990)*. Tirana: Botim TPE, 2003.

Këngë për Masat 1. Tirana: Këshilli Qendror të Bashkimeve Profesjonale të Shqipërisë, 1957.

Khalid, Adeeb. "Backwardness and the Quest for Civilization: Early Soviet Central Asia in Comparative Perspective." *Slavic Review* 65, no. 2 (2006): 231–51.

King, Russell, and Nicola Mai. *Out of Albania: From Crisis Migration to Social Inclusion in Italy*. New York: Berghahn Books, 2008.

Klosi, Ardian, and Edi Rama. *Refleksione*. Tirana: Albania, 1991.

Koço, Eno. *Tefta Tashko-Koço dhe Koha e Saj*. Tirana: Dituria, 2000.

Koço, Eno. *Kënga Karakteristike Korçare*. Tirana: Toena, 2002.

Konrád, George, and Ivan Szelényi. *The Intellectuals on the Road to Class Power: A Sociological Study of the Role of the Intelligentsia in Socialism*. Translated by Andrew Arato and Richard E. Allen. New York: Harcourt, Brace and Jovanovich, 1979.

Kornai, Janos. *The Socialist System: The Political Economy of Communism*. Princeton, NJ: Princeton University Press, 1992.

Kotsonis, Yanni. *Making Peasants Backward: Agricultural Cooperatives and the Agrarian Question in Russia, 1861–1914*. New York: St. Martin's Press, 1999.

Krastev, Ivan. "The Balkans: Democracy Without Choices." *Journal of Democracy* 13, no. 3 (2000): 39–53.

Larkey, Edward. "Contested Spaces: GDR Rock Between Western Influence and Party Control." In *A Sound Legacy? Music and Politics in East Germany*, edited by Edward Larkey, 42–58. Harry & Helen Gray Humanities Program Series 8, 2010.

Lazri, Gjovalin. *Liceu Artistik "J. Misja" në Vitet 1946–1991*. Tirana: Flesh, 2009.

Lehmann, Maike. "When Everything Was Forever: An Introduction." *Slavic Review* 74, no. 1 (2015): 1–8.

Leka, Arian, Erion Kristo, and Shaban Sinani. *Politika Kulturore në Shqipëri: Tiranë 29–30 Prill 2001*. Tirana: Naim Frashëri, 2001.

Lemke, Thomas. "Foucault, Governmentality, and Critique." *Rethinking Marxism* 14, no. 3 (2002): 49–64.

Lemke, Thomas. "An Indigestible Meal? Foucault, Governmentality and State Theory." *Distinktion: Scandinavian Journal of Social Theory* 8, no. 2 (2007): 43–64.

Lenin, Vladimir. "What Is to Be Done? Burning Questions for Our Movement." In *The Lenin Anthology*, edited by Robert C. Tucker, 12–114. New York: Norton, 1975 [1902].

Levin, David Michael, ed. *Modernity and the Hegemony of Vision*. Berkeley: University of California Press, 1993.

Levin, Theodore. "Making Marxist-Leninist Music in Uzbekistan." In *Music and Marx: Ideas, Practice, Politics*, edited by Regula Qureshi, 190–203. New York: Routledge, 2002.

Liechty, Mark. *Suitably Modern: Making Middle-Class Culture in a New Consumer Society*. Princeton, NJ: Princeton University Press, 2003.

Livni, Eran. "Chalga to the Max! Musical Speech and Speech About Music on the Road Between Bulgaria and Modern Europe." PhD diss., Indiana University, 2014.

Lord, Albert B. *The Singer of Tales*. Cambridge, MA: Harvard University Press, 2000 [1960].

Lubonja, Fatos. *The False Apocalypse: From Stalinism to Capitalism*. Translated by John Hodgson. London: Istros Books, 2014.

MacFadyen, David. *Red Stars: Personality and the Soviet Popular Song, 1955–1991*. Quebec City: McGill-Queens University Press, 2001.

MacFadyen, David. *Songs for Fat People: Affect, Emotion, and Celebrity in the Russian Popular Song, 1900–1955*. Quebec City: McGill-Queens University Press, 2002.

Mai, Nicola. "'Italy Is Beautiful': The Role of Italian Television in Albanian Migration to Italy." In *Media and Migration: Constructions of Mobility and Difference*, edited by Russell King and Nancy Wood, 95–109. New York: Routledge, 2001.

Marković, Alexander. "'So That We Look More Gypsy': Strategic Performances and Ambivalent Discourses of Romani Brass for the World Music Scene." *Ethnomusicology Forum* 24, no. 2 (2015): 260–85.

Mato, Jakup. *Imazhe, Kode dhe Kumte: Procesi Krijues dhe Komunikimi Artistik*. Tirana: Akademia e Shkencave (Qendra e Studimit të Arteve), 2001.

Mato, Jakup. *Rrjedhave të Artit Paraprofesionist*. Tirana: Akademia e Shkencave (Qendra e Studimit të Arteve), 2004.

Mau, Vladimir, and Irina Starodubrovskaya. *The Challenge of Revolution: Contemporary Russia in Historical Perspective*. New York: Oxford University Press, 2001.

McDonald, David A. *My Voice Is My Weapon: Music, Nationalism, and the Poetics of Palestinian Resistance*. Durham, NC: Duke University Press, 2013.

Mëhilli, Elidor. "Defying De-Stalinization: Albania's 1956." *Journal of Cold War Studies* 13, no. 4 (2011): 4–56.

Mëhilli, Elidor. "Mao and the Albanians." In *Mao's Little Red Book: A Global History*, edited by Alexander C. Cook, 165–84. Cambridge: University of Cambridge Press, 2014.

Mero, Agim. *Ëndrra dhe Zhgënjime*. Tirana: Fan Noli, 2008.

Miller, Peter, and Nikolas Rose. "Governing Economic Life." *Economy and Society* 19, no. 1 (1990): 1–31.

Miso, Pirro. "Roli dhe Funksioni Etnoartistik i Lahutës." *Kultura Popullore* 2, no. 1 (1984): 121–34.

Mitrovic, Marijana. "'New Face of Serbia' at the Eurovision Song Contest: International Media Spectacle and National Identity." *European Review of History* 17, no. 2 (2010): 171–85.

Moehn, Frederick. *Contemporary Carioca: Technologies of Mixing in a Contemporary Brazilian Scene.* Durham, NC: Duke University Press, 2012.

Muka, Arben. *70 Radio Shqip në 70 Vitë.* Tirana: ABC Media Center, 2008.

Musaraj, Smoki. "Tales from Albarado: The Materiality of Pyramid Schemes in Postsocialist Albania." *Cultural Anthropology* 26, no. 1 (2011): 84–110.

Mustafaj, Besnik. *Midis Krimeve dhe Mirazheve: Ese.* Tirana: Toena, 2009.

Muzikë Vallzimi nga Autorë të Vëndit, III. Tirana: Ministria e Arësimi dhe Kulturës, 1957.

Nano, Mustafa. *Hinterland i Kuq, Njëzet Vjet Më Pas.* Tirana: UET Press, 2009.

Narskij, Igor. "Intellectuals as Missionaries: The Liberal Opposition in Russia and Their Notion of Culture." *Studies in East European Thought* 62, nos. 3–4 (2010): 331–52.

Nixon, Nicola. "Always Already European: The Figure of Skënderbeg in Contemporary Albanian Nationalism." *National Identities* 12, no. 1 (2010): 1–20.

Olkhovsky, Andrey V. *Music Under The Soviets: The Agony of an Art.* London: Routledge, 1955.

Ortner, Sherry B. "Theory in Anthropology Since the Sixties." *Comparative Studies in Society and History* 26, no. 1 (1984): 126–66.

Pano, Nicholas. *The People's Republic of Albania.* Baltimore, MD: Johns Hopkins University Press, 1968.

Pano, Nicholas. "The Process of Democratization in Albania." In *Politics, Power and the Struggle for Democracy in South-East Europe,* edited by Karen and Bruce Parrott Dawisha, 285–353. Cambridge: Cambridge University Press, 1997.

Pekacz, Jolanta. "Did Rock Smash the Wall? The Role of Rock in Political Transition." *Popular Music* 13, no. 1 (1994): 41–51.

Pettifer, James, and Miranda Vickers. *The Albanian Question: Reshaping the Balkans.* London: I. B. Tauris, 2009.

Pine, Jason. *The Art of Making Do in Naples.* Minneapolis: University of Minnesota Press, 2012.

Pistrick, Eckehard. *Performing Nostalgia: Migration Culture and Creativity in South Albania.* London: Ashgate, 2015.

Pletsch, Carl E. "The Three Worlds, or the Division of Social Scientific Labor, Circa 1950–1975." *Comparative Studies in Society and History* 23, no. 4 (1981): 565–90.

Prifti, Peter. *Socialist Albania Since 1944: Domestic and Foreign Developments.* Cambridge, MA: MIT Press, 1978.

Rama, Shinasi. *Përrallat e Tranzicionit Shqiptar.* Tirana: Princi, 2012.

Ramet, Sabrina Petra, ed. *Rocking the State: Rock Music and Politics in Eastern Europe and Russia.* Boulder, CO: Westview Press, 1994.

Rey, Marie-Pierre. "'Europe Is Our Common Home': A Study of Gorbachev's Diplomatic Concept." *Cold War History* 4, no. 2 (2004): 33–65.

Rice, Timothy. *May It Fill Your Soul: Experiencing Bulgarian Music.* Chicago: University of Chicago Press, 1994.

Risch, William Jay, ed. *Youth and Rock in the Soviet Bloc: Youth Cultures, Music, and the State in Russia and Eastern Europe.* Lanham, MD: Lexington Books, 2014.

Rose, Nikolas. "Identity, Genealogy, History." In *Questions of Cultural Identity,* edited by Stuart Hall and Paul Du Gay, 128–51. London: Sage Publications, 1997.

Rose, Nikolas. *Powers of Freedom: Reframing Political Thought.* Cambridge: Cambridge University Press, 1999.

Rose, Nikolas, Pat O'Malley, and Mariana Valverde. "Governmentality." *Annual Review of Law and Social Science* 2 (2006): 83–104.

Ryback, Timothy W. *Rock Around the Bloc: A History of Rock Music in Eastern Europe and the Soviet Union.* New York: Oxford University Press, 1990.

Saunders, Robert A. "Brand Interrupted." *Branding Post-Communist Nations: Marketizing National Identities in the "New" Europe*, edited by Nadia Kaneva, 49–78. New York: Routledge, 2012.

Scott, James C. *Seeing Like a State: How Certain Schemes to Improve the Human Condition Have Failed*. New Haven, CT: Yale University Press, 1998.

Seriot, Patrick. "Officialese and Straight Talk in Socialist Europe." In *Ideology and System Change in the USSR and East Europe*, edited by Michael Urban, 202–14. New York: St. Martin's Press, 1992.

Shapllo, Dalan. "Mbi Muzikën e Lehtë e të Vallzimit." *Nëntori* 6 (1960): 191–200.

Shetuni, Spiro J. *Albanian Traditional Music: An Introduction*. Jefferson, NC: McFarland, 2011.

Shteyngart, Gary. *Super Sad True Love Story: A Novel*. New York: Random House Publishing, 2010.

Silverberg, Laura. "Between Dissonance and Dissidence: Socialist Modernism in the German Democratic Republic." *Journal of Musicology* 26, no. 1 (2009): 44–84.

Silverman, Carol. "Reconstructing Folklore: Media and Cultural Policy in Eastern Europe." *Communication* 11 (1989): 141–60.

Silverman, Carol. *Romani Routes: Cultural Politics and Balkan Music in Diaspora*. New York: Oxford University Press, 2012.

Simons, William B. *The Constitutions of the Communist World*. Alphen aan den Rijn, The Netherlands: Sijthoff & Noordhoff International Publishers, 1980.

Skendi, Stavro. *Albania*. New York: F. A. Praeger, 1956.

Slatina, Flori. *Festivali i Këngës në RTV: 1962–2003*. Tirana: Mokra, 2004.

Slobin, Mark, ed. *Retuning Culture: Musical Changes in Central and Eastern Europe*. Durham, NC: Duke University Press, 1996.

Sokoli, Ramadan. *Folklori Muzikor Shqiptar: Morfologjia*. Tirana: Institute of Folk Culture, 1965.

Sokoli, Ramadan. *Veglat Muzikore Të Popullit Shqiptar*. Tirana: Institute of Folk Culture, 1966.

Sokoli, Ramadan. *Përtej 16 Shekujve*. Tirana: Koha, 2003.

Solomon, Thomas. "Articulating the Historical Moment: Turkey, Europe, and Eurovision 2003." In *A Song for Europe: Popular Music and Politics in the Eurovision Song Contest*, edited by Ivan Raykoff and Robert Deam Tobin, 135–45. London: Ashgate, 2007.

Steinholt, Yngvar. *Rock in the Reservation: Songs from Leningrad Rock Club 1981–86*. New York: Mass Media Music Scholars' Press, 2005.

Stites, Richard. *Russian Popular Culture: Entertainment and Society Since 1900*. Cambridge: Cambridge University Press, 1992.

Stockmann, Doris, Wilfried Fiedler, and Erich Stockmann. *Albanische Volksmusik*. Berlin: Akademie-Verlag, 1965.

Strakosha, Violeta. "Mbi Disa Probleme të Propagandimit të Muzikës në Radio." Thesis, Instituti i Lartë të Arteve (Tirana), 1969.

Sugarman, Jane C. "The Nightingale and the Partridge: Singing and Gender Among Prespa Albanians." *Ethnomusicology* 33, no. 2 (1989): 191–215.

Sugarman, Jane C. *Engendering Song: Singing and Subjectivity at Prespa Albanian Weddings*. Chicago: University of Chicago Press, 1997.

Sugarman, Jane C. "Imagining the Homeland: Poetry, Songs, and the Discourses of Albanian Nationalism." *Ethnomusicology* 43, no. 3 (1999): 419–58.

Sugarman, Jane C. "Mediated Albanian Musics and the Imagining of Modernity." In *New Countries, Old Sounds? Cultural Identity and Social Changes in Southeastern Europe*, edited by Bruno B. Reuer, 134–54. Munich: Verlag Südostdeutsches Kulturwerk, 1999.

Sugarman, Jane C. "Kosova Calls For Peace: Song, Myth, and War in an Age of Global Media." In *Music and Conflict*, edited by John Morgan O'Connell and Salwa El-Shawan Castelo-Branco, 17–45. Champaign: University of Illinois Press, 2010.

Sulstarova, Enis. *Arratisje Nga Lindja: Orientalizmi Shqiptar Nga Naimi Te Kadareja*. Tirana: Globic Press, 2006.

Survilla, Maria Paula. "'Ordinary Words': Sound, Symbolism, and Meaning in Belarusan-Language Rock Music." In *Global Pop, Local Language*, edited by Harris M. Berger, 187–206. Jackson: University Press of Mississippi, 2003.

Szemere, Anna. *Up from the Underground: The Culture of Rock Music in Postsocialist Hungary.* University Park: The Pennsylvania State University Press, 2001.

Taylor, Karin. *Let's Twist Again: Youth and Leisure in Socialist Bulgaria.* New Brunswick, NJ: Transaction Publishers, 2006.

Tërpini, Fori Spiro. *Djelmuria Korçare që Këndoi 'Dua Më Shumë, Shqipërine': Kujtime.* Korça: Self-Published, 2003.

Tester, Keith. *The Two Sovereigns: Social Contradictions of European Modernity.* New York: Routledge, 2002.

Thompson, Emily Ann. *The Soundscape of Modernity: Architectural Acoustics and the Culture of Listening in America, 1900–1933.* Cambridge, MA: MIT Press, 2004.

Tochka, Nicholas. "Pussy Riot, Freedom of Expression, and Popular Music Studies After the Cold War." *Popular Music* 32, no. 2 (2013): 303–11.

Tochka, Nicholas. "Composing on Commission: Entrepreneurship and the Changing Social Basis of Popular Music Collaboration in Postsocialist Tirana, Albania." *Culture, Theory and Critique* 55, no. 2 (2014): 194–211.

Tochka, Nicholas. "Voicing Freedom, Sounding Dissent: Popular Music, Simulation and Citizenship in Democratizing Albania, 1991–1997." *European Journal of Cultural Studies* 17, no. 3 (2014): 298–315.

Tochka, Nicholas. "To 'Enlighten and Beautify': Western Music and the Modern Project of Personhood in Albania, c. 1906–1924." *Ethnomusicology* 59, no. 3 (2015): 398–420.

Todorova, Maria. *Imagining the Balkans.* New York: Oxford University Press, 1997.

Tolkien, J. R. R. *The Fellowship of the Ring.* New York: Houghton Mifflin Harcourt, 2012 [1954].

Tomoff, Kiril. *Creative Union: The Professional Organization of Soviet Composers, 1939–1953.* Ithaca, NY: Cornell University Press, 2006.

Tompkins, David. *Composing the Party Line: Music and Politics in Early Cold War Poland and East Germany.* West Lafayette, IN: Purdue University Press, 2013.

Tompkins, David. "Against 'Pop-Song Poison' from the West: Early Cold War Attempts to Develop a Socialist Popular Music in Poland and the GDR." In *Youth and Rock in the Soviet Bloc: Youth Cultures, Music, and the State in Russia and Eastern Europe,* edited by William Risch, 43–54. Lanham, MD: Lexington Books, 2014.

Torpey, John. *Intellectuals, Socialism, and Dissent: The East German Opposition and Its Legacy.* Minneapolis: University of Minnesota Press, 1995.

Tsipursky, Gleb. "Having Fun in the Thaw: Youth Initiative Clubs in the Post-Stalin Years." *The Carl Beck Papers in Russian and East European Studies* 2201 (2012): 1–68.

Tsipursky, Gleb. "Coercion and Consumption: The Khrushchev Leadership's Ruling Style in the Campaign Against 'Westernized' Youth, 1954–64." In *Youth and Rock in the Soviet Bloc: Youth Cultures, Music, and the State in Russia and Eastern Europe,* edited by William Risch, 345–98. Lanham, MD: Lexington Books, 2014.

Turino, Thomas. "Signs of Imagination, Identity, and Experience: A Peircian Semiotic Theory for Music." *Ethnomusicology* 43, no. 2 (1999): 221–55.

Tusty, James, and Maureen Castle Tusty, dir. *The Singing Revolution.* Armonk, NY: Abramorama, 2007.

Verdery, Katherine. *National Ideology Under Socialism: Identity and Cultural Politics in Ceaușescu's Romania.* Berkeley: University of California Press, 1991.

Verdery, Katherine. "Theorizing Socialism: A Prologue to the Transition." *American Ethnologist* 18, no. 3 (1991): 419–39.

Verdery, Katherine. *What Was Socialism, and What Comes Next?* New York: Cambridge University Press, 1996.

Verdery, Katherine. *The Political Lives of Dead Bodies: Reburial and Postsocialist Change.* New York: Columbia University Press, 1999.

Verdery, Katherine. *Secrets and Truths: Ethnography in the Archive of Romania's Secret Police.* Budapest: Central European University Press, 2014.

Veyne, Paul. "Foucault Revolutionizes History." In *Foucault and His Interlocutors*, edited by Arnold Ira Davidson, 146–82. Chicago: University of Chicago Press, 1997.

Vickers, Miranda. *The Albanians: A Modern History*. London: I. B. Tauris, 1999.

Vickers, Miranda, and James Pettifer. *Albania: From Anarchy to a Balkan Identity*. New York: NYU Press, 2000.

Vuletic, Dean. "Yugoslav Communism and the Power of Popular Music." PhD diss., Columbia University, 2010.

Vuletic, Dean. "The Making of a Yugoslav Popular Music Industry." *Popular Music History* 6, no. 3 (2012): 269–85.

Vullnetari, Julie. *Albania on the Move: Links Between Internal and International Migration*. Amsterdam: Amsterdam University Press, 2012.

Walters, William. *Governmentality: Critical Encounters*. New York: Routledge, 2012.

Weber, Max. *The Protestant Ethic and the Spirit of Capitalism*. Translated by Talcott Parsons. New York: Routledge, 2001 [1930].

Wernick, Andrew. *Promotional Culture: Advertising, Ideology and Symbolic Expression*. Thousand Oaks, CA: Sage Publications, 1991.

White, Bob. *Rumba Rules: The Politics of Dance Music in Mobutu's Zaire*. Durham, NC: Duke University Press, 2008.

Wickström, David-Emil. *"Okna Otkroi!"—"Open the Windows!" Transcultural Flows and Identity Politics in the St. Petersburg Popular Music Scene*. Stuttgart: Ibidem Verlag, 2011.

Williams, Raymond. *Marxism and Literature*. New York: Oxford University Press, 1977.

Wolff, Larry. *Inventing Eastern Europe: The Map of Civilization on the Mind of the Enlightenment*. Stanford, CA: Stanford University Press, 1996.

Wong, Cynthia P. "Cui Jian, Rock Musician and Reluctant Hero." *ACMR Reports* 9, no. 1 (1996): 21–32.

Wong, Isabel K. F. "Geming Gequ: Songs for the Education of the Masses." In *Popular Chinese Literature and Performing Arts in the People's Republic of China, 1949–1979*, edited by Bonnie S. McDougall, 112–43. Berkeley: University of California Press, 1984.

Woodcock, Shannon. "'Against a Wall': Albania's Women Political Prisoners' Struggle to Be Heard." *Cultural Studies Review* 20, no. 2 (2014): 39–65.

Woodcock, Shannon. *Life Is War: Surviving Dictatorship in Communist Albania*. Bristol, UK: Hammeron Press, 2016.

WPA (Works Progress Administration, Federal Writers' Project). *The Albanian Struggle in the Old World and New*. Boston: AMS Press, 1939.

Yurchak, Alexei. *Everything Was Forever, Until It Was No More: The Last Soviet Generation*. Princeton, NJ: Princeton University Press, 2006.

Zemtsovsky, Izaly. "Musicological Memoirs on Marxism." In *Music and Marx: Ideas, Practice, Politics*, edited by Regula Qureshi, 167–89. New York: Routledge, 2002.

Zhuk, Sergui. *Rock and Roll in the Rocket City: The West, Identity, and Ideology in Soviet Dniepropetrovsk, 1960–1985*. Baltimore, MD: Johns Hopkins University Press, 2010.

Zojzi, Rrok. "Ndamje Krahinore e Popullit Shqiptar." *Etnografia Shqiptare* 1 (1962): 16–62.

Zoraqi, Kastriot. *Nikolla Zoraqi: Jeta dhe Vepra e Tij (Kujtime)*. Tirana: Shoqatës Kulturore "Arumunët e Shqipërisë," 2006.

Zvorykin, A. A., Natalia Ivanovna, and Eugene Rabinovich, eds. *Cultural Policy in the Union of Soviet Socialist Republics*. Paris: UNESCO, 1970.

Index

Page numbers in italics indicate illustrations.

247